THE INTERNATIONAL DESIGN YEARBOOK

EDITOR
BOŘEK ŠÍPEK

GENERAL EDITOR
RICK POYNOR

ASSISTANT EDITOR
JENNIFER HUDSON

ABBEVILLE PRESS · PUBLISHERS
LONDON · PARIS · NEW YORK

ISSN 0883–7155
ISBN 1–55859–428–0

This book was designed and produced by Calmann & King Ltd, London

Based on an original idea by Stuart Durant

Designed by Richard Smith and Lee Bullett at Area, London
Printed in Hong Kong

The publisher and editors would like to thank the designers and manufacturers who submitted work for inclusion in this book; Junko Popham for her help in collecting Japanese contributions, and the following photographers and copyright holders for use of their material: Jay Ahrend 1.57; Zwama Akinori 1.124; Satoshi Asakawa 1.60, 5.2; R. Baader 3.13; M. Vihoria Corradi Backhaus 1.35; Aldo Ballo 1.48, 49, 5.52; Santi Caleca 1.67, 98, 2.22, 5.50; Nick Crowe 2.46; D. Bank 3.7, 9; Demner and Merlicek 5.30; Estudicolor 2.11; Sandy Frank 5.36; Carlo Gianni 1.32; Globus 2.7; T. Goffe 2.17; Léon Gulikers pages 8, 11, 12; 1.59, 3.29, 32–39, 48–51, 5.16; Hans Hansen 1.52, 63, 71, 72, 95, 96, 113, 4.37–43; Olaf Hauschulz 5.27; Poul Ib Henriksen 4.26, 27; Yuki Higuchi 4.16; Gerold Hindt 5.45; K. Ichikawa 5.46; Charles Kemper 5.35; Jvo Kovarik 1.33, 34; Jaroslav Kviz 3.21, 5.47; Athos Lecce 3.14, 15; Peter Lemke 1.39; Jochen Littkemann 3.11; Ryuzo Masunaga 5.55, 57; Andrew McKay 1.119; Ian McKinnell 2.36 (top), 3.56; Teturo Mitani 5.20; Marre Moerel 2.42; David Mohney 1.104; Nacása & Partners 2.44, 45; Holger Neu 5.10; Wim Nienhuis 1.107; Guido Niest 3.4, 5.32; Toshitaka Niwa 3.17; Takayuki Ogawa 1.86, 87, 91; Keiichi Ohtake 5.38; Dag Orsk 5.19; Jiří Platenka 1.30; Walter Prina 3.5; Programma Immagine 5.13; Jaroslav Prokop 1.118, 2.41; Raimondi 1.41; Marino Ramazzotti 1.42; Bernd Reibl 5.23; Takashi Sagisaka 4.22, 23; Hidetoyo Sasaki 5.28; Katsuji Sato 4.19, 20; Rudi Schmutz 4.3–11, 28–34; Schnakenburg & Brahl fotografi 1.38; SFH 2.3; L. T. Shaw 3.30; Michael Sieger 3.6; Richard Skanlan 5.56; J. C. Starkey 1.105; Machtelt Stikvoort 4.35; Studio ACA 5.12; Studio Cappelli 2.6; Studio Kusumi 1.99, 100; Studio Seekamp 1.120, 122; Francesco Tapinassi 3.24; Anthony Theakston 3.1; Leo Torri page 6; 3.57–62; Emilio Tremolada pages 7, 9; 1.5, 106, 2.32, 34; Tom Vack 1.27, 64, 65, (with Fabio Padovese) 88; van Sloun/Ramaekers 1.53; Hiroyuki Watanabe 5.18; Rick Whittey 5.9; Miro Zagnoli 1.31.

CONTENTS

INTRODUCTION

Dinner service,
Albertine
(porcelain),
manufactured by
Driade in 1989.

RIGHT:
Chair, **Leonora**
(cherrywood,
polyurethane,
leather),
manufactured by
Aleph-Driade in
1991.

In previous editions of the *International Design Yearbook*, it has been the tradition for guest editors to set down their impressions of the work they have seen in the form of a foreword, and the results have ranged from the brief and pointed to the discursive and analytical. This year, given the personal style and preference of the guest editor, Bořek Šípek, it was decided that an interview would be the most appropriate way to analyse the work he had sifted through and selected, and to examine the light it casts on current trends in design. Where previous guest editors have sometimes deliberated at great length before consigning a design to the out-tray, or more occasionally the in-tray, Bořek Šípek was at all times focused and decisive, and offered firm opinions on the sequence in which the designs should be displayed – a framework broadly followed by the book. Rick Poynor spoke to Bořek Šípek after the selection meeting, at his studio in Amsterdam. (The illustrations all show designs by Bořek Šípek.)

Do you think that the selection of material you looked at was fairly typical of what is happening now in design?

I think it was very typical and I was a little bit disappointed that there was no sign of a new approach. But if you look at what is happening now in theatre, in fashion and in other areas of culture, everything is becoming simpler in a formal sense. It is more important now to find the substance of the thing.

Why do you think this is? What has caused the change?

Maybe one of the reasons is the recession, but I don't think that's the main reason. In the last ten or fifteen years, style went as far as it could go. It was starting to become exhausting, crazy even. Everything was

possible, so nothing was shocking any more. There was nothing in this selection that shocked me, or even particularly surprised me. I think people have become a little bit tired of the sameness of recent design. In the 1980s, we were in a similar position to the Victorians at the end of the nineteenth century; people were piling ornament on top of ornament for its own sake. In my own work I am trying to be more serious and to use fewer ornaments. I like ornament, but I have always needed a reason to use it. Now I need two, three or more reasons. They might be functional, practical, tactile, aesthetic, symbolic, technological or mythological. A designer has to find new goals, new horizons, and for me the aim now is to achieve the same intensity of effect, the same emotion, but with less detail and fewer materials.

And these are the qualities you were looking for as you made your selection?

Yes. I chose very quickly, because if you look for a long time you find reasons why something is good or bad. What is important to me is the visionary image of an object – a kind of emotion at first sight – and this influenced the way I made my choice.

But you also said at one point in the selection meeting that if you had really followed your true taste, there would only have been twenty things in the book.

Yes, but that doesn't mean anything. My taste is only important to me. As an architect and designer you have to be very tolerant towards everything and everybody. There is no mathematical certainty in art, so all you can do is look for some special connection in a design with the culture and society it represents. Other people can work in ways quite different to your own. I think only very bad architects and designers assume that what they produce is the best.

But I am still left with the sense that the pieces you were most inclined to pick were by people whose work has the same emotional flourish as your own – people such as your colleague at Alterego, David Palterer. There is a clear kinship between your work and his.

Perhaps it is because I know these people personally and I know the way that they work. David Palterer has his own way of doing things and I don't always agree, but this is what I mean when I say that I accept what other designers are doing, if they are going about it in a clear, decisive way.

What do you mean when you talk about the "mythological" qualities of a piece of design?

What this means to me is that you are able to find something which is part of contemporary culture almost without your knowing it, something which embodies or summarizes the essence of life in our society at this point. When I also talk about emotion or eroticism it is because these are qualities that we are in danger of losing in our technological society. When you work with computers, for instance, everything comes from the head, from the brain. Years ago, when someone asked me to define my creative motivation, I stated, "I want a return to the Baroque". I was falsely interpreted, sadly, as proposing to use Baroque as a post-modern source of inspiration, but what I really meant to imply at the time was a release into a freer life style, a chance to shake off the "truth of functionalism" and its technical achievements in favour of individual feelings.

Is that also your objection to high tech – that it comes purely "from the head"?

The Daybreak coffee shop, Amsterdam (1989).

Dora (cherrywood,
polyurethane,
leather),
manufactured by
Aleph-Driade in
1991.

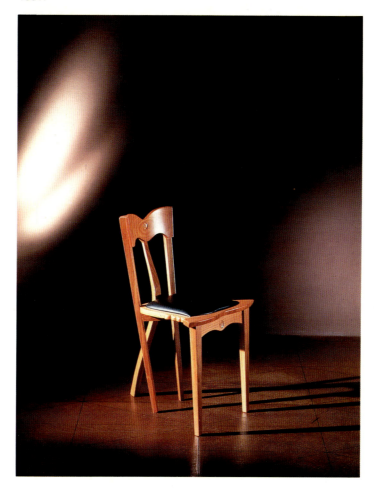

The problem with high tech is that it claims to be functional, but it is not really functional at all. In fact, it is a style which ignores function and disregards human individuality. All it really does is demonstrate a level of technical achievement. A chair with a single tube for a backrest just ends up breaking your back. The only justification for such a coldly formalist style is fashion. For me *comfort* is the most important function of furniture. I believe the apologists of high tech were mistaken, but I can't say that high tech was absolutely wrong. Perhaps we should think of it as a necessary experiment whose day has now passed.

Do you think your own work has managed to escape this trap of fashion? You have been written about in the same magazines and in the same terms as Starck and all the other "star" designers.

I don't think that designing should be an anonymous process, because the designer's personality is an aspect of the mythology of the object. We don't need stars, but we do need identifiable personalities. I did not want to become a star and I was not even looking for success. I just did what interested me and found that people wanted to publish it in magazines. As a result my work became fashionable, but this was never my intention. I will continue to look for new ideas, regardless of fashionable opinion. What I want to do is to make things that people will love. If you stay true to your own vision, you win respect. Look at Sottsass. He is now in his late seventies, but he has maintained his position in the vanguard by his constant progressiveness. Starck, too, remains true to his vision, but this is not static – his style continues to evolve.

When you were sifting through the product designs, you seemed impatient with much of the work. What were you looking for – a more ornamental approach?

Perhaps I am being over critical, but for me too many of these products make us completely stupid. You just push the button of the camera or radio and everything is done for you. In a car radio, preset buttons are a worthwhile development because you should be giving your attention to driving and not to adjusting the radio. But at home you are not faced with the same problem; there is time to look at the radio, to think about it, and touch it. I remember when I was a small child in Prague. I had never been abroad, but I knew all the capital cities of the world because they were printed on the radio and I would read them as I searched for the station I wanted, using my eyes and hand. Perhaps children today experience something comparable with their computers – I don't know – but I have a strong sense that in the rush to streamline

Ota Otanek *(wood, metal, copper), manufactured by Vitra in 1988.*

experience and make the technology do all the work for us, some extra vital dimension has been lost. I think we need a stronger relationship to the instruments we use, and a much greater regard for the importance of the tactile environment, if we are not going to lose the sense of ourselves as physical beings.

You selected a couple of interesting experiments in TV and video monitor design from Sharp, pieces with a very strong "image". Is this the kind of expressive product design you prefer?

I think these are a new development. They show what *could* happen. I think that what Philips and the Japanese are doing, this kind of technical design, is all right, but it has nothing to do with culture. Their television sets are not pieces of furniture, they are simply there in the room with you.

You look at the programmes the television transmits, but not at the machine itself. The television's shell is a kind of packaging. This is fine, but I don't think it belongs in the *International Design Yearbook*, which should offer a cultural portrait of the moment.

What are the priorities for designers now?

I don't know. I'm not really interested in the future. What concerns me is that design risks losing contact with ordinary people. We saw it in the 1980s, especially in high tech, where the main concern was formal beauty and the designers forgot that their objects are made for people to use. In fact, 99 per cent of what we do as designers is unnecessary. The world does not actually need any new chairs – there are quite enough marvellous designs already. The only real justification for the designer to create another chair is if he treats it like a work of art and uses it to express or interpret the culture of the moment. Too many designers take themselves too seriously and fool themselves into thinking that their designs can somehow save the world. They imagine that their task is to come up with something that completely shatters the mould. They think that design is a kind of research. But you cannot, in any fundamental sense, reinvent the chair. It will remain forevermore a raised surface for sitting on which offers the sitter at least a degree of extra support. So the impetus for new designs comes from changes in culture, not from changes in the nature of the chair.

The most significant designs in this edition of the *Yearbook* almost invariably come from well-established names. The young "unknowns" you hoped to find making interesting work seemed quiet this year. How do you account for this?

Shoebaloo,
Amsterdam (1991).

At this point it is very difficult for young designers to create something so genuinely unexpected that it stops us in our tracks. Maybe the key issue now, above all others, is one of quality; but it is very difficult to achieve quality when you are young because it comes from experience – the very thing you lack. It has always been much easier for young designers to create something extreme or experimental. In architecture it takes years for people to come into their own, because the discipline is so complicated, not just technically but philosophically. You need to have achieved a state of inner quiet, to be sure about what you think, and this is much more difficult for young people. If you look at the most important architects, there is no one younger than fifty. I think this also holds true for design.

The work that seems most impressive at present, and the most in keeping with the points you made at the beginning of our conversation, is actually the most restrained: people like Antonio Citterio and Jasper Morrison. But I had the impression that you did not particularly like this kind of design – that you did not find it eventful enough.

I've often thought about Jasper Morrison and I like his seriousness very much. For me, though, his pieces are too simple and too similar to designs from the Bauhaus. But perhaps I'm wrong. Perhaps he really is someone who could be the father to the new style. I am certainly convinced that we need a quieter period, so that we can discover a new exuberance.

Do we also need a verbal cooling off period? Has there been too much talk about design, when the key issues are, in fact, fairly straightforward?

I don't think that we speak too much about design. If you ask people on the street, they know very little about it. We're a very small society of people.

And is that the way it should be?

Yes, and I think it is designers who need to look out to the world, rather than the world that needs to look into design. We should be better educated in philosophy and the humanities. Philosophy gives you self-awareness and helps you to think through the consequences of your actions. It helps you to see how your work fits into the wider social and cultural picture. I think theatre and literature are also important because they enter society's bloodstream much quicker than design. Designers work five or ten years behind literature, which is much more powerful, more abstract and less dependent on the material world. I also listen to modern music and opera, and I love ballet. I'm much more interested in these things than in art or design. When I was twenty or thirty I went to exhibitions all over Europe and I took in so much information that I'm full to the brim now. It is the narrative quality of these other art forms that interests me, and how I can apply it to my work. Sometimes, though, when you witness the terrible events that happen in the world – the terror in Bosnia, or seeing your friends die from AIDS – it seems impossible to express your reactions through design. Designers can only really work for a positive world and leave the negative things to literature. This is another reason why I think it may be time now for design to speak more gently, to place the emphasis once again on humanism.

FURNITURE

Sergi and Oscar Devesa
Armchair,
Bravo
Steel tubing, kip leather
H 71cm (28in)
W 64cm (25¹⁄₈in)
D 64.6cm (25⁴⁄₈in)
Manufacturer: Oken, Spain

It was B&B Italia, in a description of Antonio Citterio's *Compagnia delle Filippine* collection, which seemed best to capture the spirit of furniture design in 1992. According to B&B, Citterio's armchairs and chaise-longue in interlaced leather "intend to be decidedly reassuring and tasteful at a moment of great uncertainty". The precise nature of the uncertainty was left unspecified, but it appeared to encompass everything from the state of the furniture industry – gritting its teeth and hoping – to a European political scene rife with resurgent nationalism, endemic corruption (in Italy itself), and civil war across the Adriatic in the territory that used to be Yugoslavia.

Who knows? In circumstances such as these, perhaps the last thing anyone really wants is furniture that insists on posing a challenge instead of sitting there quietly until it is needed. Another Italian stalwart, Moroso, came bearing essentially the same therapeutic message. "The proposal is comfort-first upholstery," said the company, announcing Massimo Iosa Ghini's *Mama* armchair and *Big Mama* sofa. And the names, quite apart from the generous upholstery, said it all: furniture as maternal consolation.

The Milan Furniture Fair remains the most reliable international barometer, and the readings it gave did not differ markedly from those of 1991. The pressure of invention was low, the mood cautious and conservative. A few designers continued to treat furniture design as though it were primarily a cultural activity, or an offshoot of sculpture, and only incidentally about such mundane issues as saleability or comfort, but these were the fêted names of the 1980s, their reputations as innovators already secure. A Starck, a Šipek or an Arad can command enviable freedom to express his own vision, but the chances of less developed talents breaking through with similarly personal or experimental work in the present climate are slim. The most ambitious initiative to forge a working bond between younger designers and manufacturers, Nuovo Bel Design, produced much that was worthy, but little that was truly exceptional. It was left to the celebrity mavericks, and to elder statesmen such as Achille Castiglioni, designer of the masterful *Polet* folding bed-chair for Interflex, to provide the year's most satisfying ideas and enduring moments.

Vicente Soto
Armchair,
Sevilla
*Chromed steel,
wood
H 78cm (30¾in)
Seat H 45cm
(17¾in)
W 60cm (23½in)
D 52cm (20½in)
Manufacturer:
Andreu World,
Spain*

**Sergi and Oscar
Devesa**
Armchair,
Sara
*Steel tubing,
aluminium, wood
H 81cm (31⅞in)
W 53cm (29⅞in)
D 53cm (29⅞in)
Manufacturer:
Oken, Spain*

**Francesca
Anselmi**
Dining chair,
Pompadour
*Steel, fabric
H 92cm (36⅛in)
W 44cm (17¼in)
L 46cm (18⅛in)
Manufacturer:
Bieffeplast, Italy*

Jorge Pensi
Armchair,
Maya
Cherry heartwood,
cherry plywood,
foam, leather
H 84cm (33in)
Seat H 45cm
(17¾in)
W 54cm (21¼in)
D 57cm (22⅜in)
Manufacturer:
Driade, Italy

5

6

Toshiyuki Kita
Folding chair,
Rondine
Steel tube, ABS
H 45cm (17¾in)
folded 80cm
(31½in)
W 40cm (15¾in)
D 50cm (19⅝in)
Manufacturer:
Magis, Italy

8

Pietro Arosio
Chair,
Rosetta
Metal
H 80cm (31½in)
W 45cm (17¾in)
L 45cm (17¾in)
Manufacturer:
Airon, Italy

Josep Lluscà
Stacking chair,
Telenda
Metal, beech or
cherry plywood
H 85cm (33½in)
W 42cm (16½in)
D 51cm (20⅛in)
Manufacturer:
Ciatti, Italy

7

9

Enzo Mari
Dining chair,
Marina
Satin-finished
aluminium,
cherrywood,
uncovered nylon

or polyurethane,
cowhide, alcantara
or leather
H 83cm (32¾in)
W 40cm (15¾in)
D 47cm (18½in)
Manufacturer:
Zanotta, Italy

James Irvine
Chair,
R/1** from the **Piceno
collection
Beechwood
H 70cm (27½in)
W 60cm (23½in)
D 57cm (22⅜in)
Manufacturer:
Cappellini, Italy

10

James Irvine *is a British designer resident in Milan, who caught the design world's eye as a contributor to Solid's first collection of table-top pieces in 1987. Irvine worked for Olivetti under the tutelage of Ettore Sottsass and Michele De Lucchi in the 1980s and put in a year with Toshiba in Japan, where his geometrical stylizations went some way to enlivening the company's gadget-fixated approach to design. Returning to Milan in 1988, he produced pieces for Alessi, Fantoni, Olivetti and Solid's second collection, but was equally at home designing rugs for the Design Gallery, the uncompromisingly avant-garde base of Sottsass and Andrea Branzi.*

Irvine admires masters like Achille Castiglioni and Enzo Mari, and his Piceno *collection for Cappellini exhibits the same controlled sense of a line unfurled to exactly the right point, then held with dignified poise. Like other regular Cappellini collaborators – Tom Dixon, Jasper Morrison and Marc Newson – Irvine is able to sculpt bold, unpredictable shapes that are full of warmth and character, while avoiding the decorative flamboyance and formal excesses of less confident talents. Piceno encompasses chairs, tables and clothes-hangers in dyed white beechwood or aluminium, lacquered green, blue or orange. In their beechwood form in particular, the pieces have the lightness and delicate profile of constructions folded out of paper. This is the most substantial project to date from a designer committed to responsibility and the traditional virtues of humanist design, and it suggests Irvine will be a figure to watch in the years ahead.*

13

André Vandenbeuck
Three-seater sofa,
Ondula
Natural rattan,
hardwood, steel,
polyurethane,
Dacron
H 92cm (36½in)
Seat H 42cm
(16½in)
W 216cm (85in)
D 82cm
(32½in)
Manufacturer:
Strässle Söhne,
Switzerland

Martin Szekely
Clothes stand,
M.P.
MDF, Faia laurel
veneer, heartwood
H 120cm (47¼in)
L 36cm (14⅛in)
D 45cm (17¾in)
Manufacturer:
Noto, Italy

Oscar Tusquets
Blanca
Rocking chair and
chair with sliding
base,
Extra de Varius
Iron, moulded
polyurethane foam,
leather, steel
H 78cm (30¾in)
W 62cm (24⅜in)
D 72cm (28⅜in)
Manufacturer:
Casas, Spain

11

12

**Jane Dillon and
Peter Wheeler**
*Modular seating
system,*
Multipla
*Upholstered
polyurethane, steel
H 80cm (31½in)
W 74cm (29⅛in)
D 75cm (29½in)
Manufacturer:
Kron, Spain*

14

15

Emilio Ambasz
Office seating,
Vertair
Steel, plastic, foam,
leather, fabric
H 84cm (33in)
W 58.5cm (23in)
D 68.5cm (27in)
Manufacturer:
Castelli, Italy

14

16

Dan Friedman
Bed,
Day Dream 5
*Lacquered wood,
velvet
H 100cm (39½in)
W 240cm (94½in)
D 249cm (98in)
Manufacturer:
Arredaesse, Italy*

**Massimo Iosa
Ghini**
*Bed with
attachments,*
Speaking
*Cherrywood, die-
cast aluminium,
polyurethane,
Dacron, cotton
Bed:
H 69cm (27⅛in)
W 168cm (66⅛in)
L 214cm (84¼in)
Low cupboard:
H 45cm (17¾in)
W 190cm (74⅞in)
D 60cm (23½in)
Manufacturer:
Poltronova, Italy*

17

18

Achille Castiglioni
Bed-chair,
Polet
*Beech, polished
brass, PVC, cotton
or alcantara
Chair:
H 177cm (69¾in)
W 70cm (27½in)
D 85cm (33½in)
Bed:
H 35cm (13¾in)
W 70cm (27½in)
L 190cm (74⅞in)
Manufacturer:
Interflex, Italy*

18

Enzo Mari
Armchair,
Danubio
*Expanded
polyurethane,
polyurethane,
Nappa Soft leather,
Dacron Hollofil Du
Pont
H 85cm (33½in)
Seat H 45cm
(17¾in)
W 100cm (39½in)
D 92cm (36⅛in)
Manufacturer:
Zanotta, Italy*

19

Vico Magistretti's Sindbad *armchair,
created for Cassina in 1982, was
inspired by a traditional horse
blanket which he came across in a London
shop. Magistretti threw it over a high-backed
frame to create a seat with informality as its
keynote. Sculptural interest came from the
way in which the blanket, secured by Velcro
fasteners, bunched over the arms and hung
down the back. It was a simple but effective
gesture that had much in common with
Achille Castiglioni's earlier, "ready-made"
use of a bicycle saddle and a tractor seat in
the Sella and Mezzadro stools.*

*With his prototype for the Incisa swivel
chair for De Padova, Magistretti has
returned to the stable for inspiration, this
time directing his attention to a horse's
saddle. The quilted cotton and leather
saddle, turned through ninety degrees on to
its side, forms the backrest and arms of the
chair, and these predetermined curves are
repeated with great elegance in the twin
arcs of the Incisa's legs. For Magistretti, the
idea of the ready-made has been given a
new meaning by the ecological concerns of
the day. The Incisa is a proposition about
how, with a little lateral thought, one object
can be made to substitute for another of
related function. Even if the saddles are not
literally recycled, one workshop can be used
to manufacture both, without the need for
costly additional skills or tooling.*

Vico Magistretti
Swivel chair,
Incisa
*Steel, rigid
polyurethane,
leather, quilted
cotton material,*

*polyester wadding
H 85cm (33½in)
Seat H 49cm
(19¼in)
W 60cm (23½in)
D 54cm (21¼in)
Manufacturer:
e De Padova, Italy*

20

21

21

Antonio Citterio
Armchairs,
Compagnia delle
Filippine
Interlaced leather
Above and top:
H 70cm (27½in)
W 70cm (27½in)
D 65cm (25⅝in)
Right:
H 80cm (31½in)

W 72cm (28⅜in)
D 108cm (42½in)
Above:
H 80cm (31½in)
W 66cm (26in)
D 83cm (32¾in)
Above right:
H 82cm (32¼in)
W 54cm (21¼in)
D 62cm (24⅜in)
Manufacturer:
B & B Italia, Italy

Motomi Kawakami
Table,
Ashi
Light walnut, gun metal
H 72cm (28³⁄₈in)
W & D 120/100cm (47¹⁄₄/39¹⁄₂in)
Manufacturer: Acerbis, Italy

22

24

**Manuel Bañó and
Marcelo Lax**
Caxon
Ash or pearwood
H 60cm (23½in)
W 50cm (19⅝in)
D 50cm (19⅝in)
*Manufacturer: Bañó
& Asociados, Spain*

**Trix and Robert
Haussmann**
Sideboard,
Bibbona
American cherry
H 101cm (39¾in)
W 60cm (23½in)
L 200cm (78¾in)
*Manufacturer:
Unitalia Domestic
Design, Italy*

23

26

Alfredo Arribas
Dining chair,
Fregoli
Beechwood, leather
H 97cm (38¼in)
Seat H 46cm
(18⅛in)
W 46cm (18⅛in)
D 50cm (19⅝in)
Manufacturer:
Carlos Jané
Camacho, Spain

**Elisabetta Gonzo
and Alessandro
Vicari**
Chair,
Drella
*Metal, wood,
polyurethane foam,
fabric*
H 72cm (28⅜in)
W 55cm (21¾in)
D 50cm (19⅝in)
*Manufacturer:
Moroso, Italy*

25

*I*n one of the most ambitious projects to
be aired at Milan in 1992, one hundred
young designers were invited to create
some two hundred prototypes for a group
of Italy's leading companies – Cappellini,
Interflex, Artemide and Luceplan, among
them. It was a bold initiative, organized by
one of the contributing designers, Anna Gili,
and in a year not otherwise very notable for
new ideas, it was perhaps unsurprising
that a few incautious voices were heard
predicting a new Italian design movement
to rival that of Memphis.

Nuovo Bel Design fell quite a long way
short of that level of vision, originality or
impact, but it did throw up some worthwhile
examples of design produced with the still
too-little heeded needs of manufacturing
and the showrooms kept squarely in mind.
Typical of these was **Elisabetta Gonzo** and
Alessandro Vicari's collaboration on the
Drella chair for Moroso. The chair is not
perhaps hugely original in either its use of
the single back leg (virtually a Philippe
Starck trademark) or the way in which the
seat drops to form a screen across the front.
Nevertheless, it is a strong, carefully
resolved and attractive piece of design,
which bodes well for future initiatives from
the group (see also 2.25 and 3.20, 27, 42).

27

Massimo Iosa Ghini
Stacking chair,
Yè-Yè
Satin-finished steel tube, rigid polyurethane painted with liquid rubber
H 81cm (31⁷⁄₈in)
Seat H 44cm (17¼in)
W 41cm (16⅛in)
D 52cm (20½in)
Manufacturer: BRF, Italy

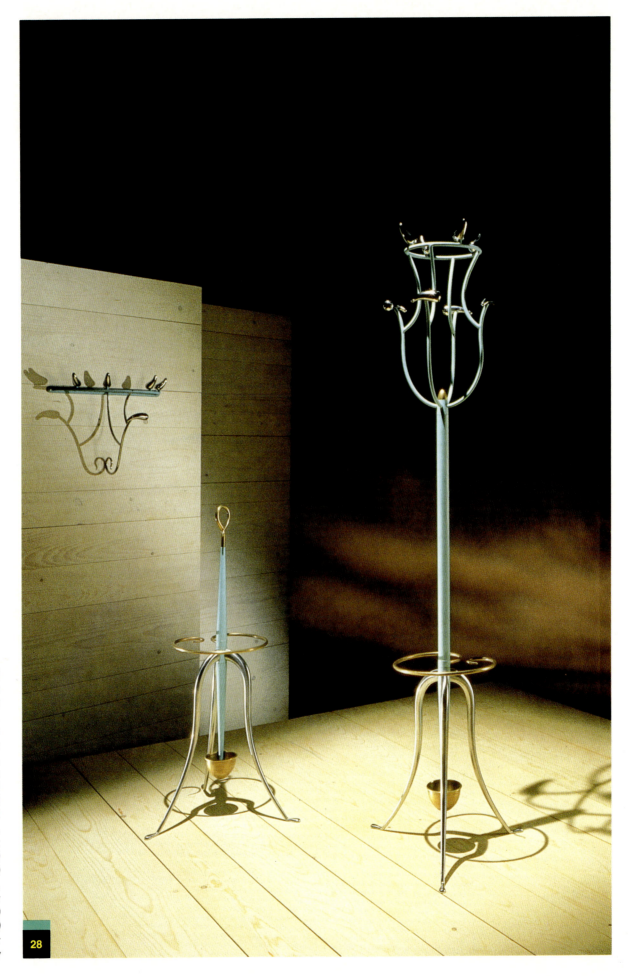

Roberto Lazzeroni
Rolling Home
*Metal, die-cast
polished aluminium,
brass
Left to right:
Clothes rack,*
Polly*:
H 43cm (16⅞in)
W 54cm (21¼in)
D 27cm (10½in)
Umbrella stand,*
Ruby*:
H 100cm (39½in)
Di 52cm (20½in)
Clothes stand,*
Snake-Pit*:
H 177cm (69¾in)
Di 52cm (20½in)
Manufacturer:
Cidue, Italy*

Bohuslav Horák
Cabinet,
Soumĕrná
Beechwood
Limited batch
production
H 240cm (94½in)
W 55cm (21¾in)
D 47cm (18½in)

30

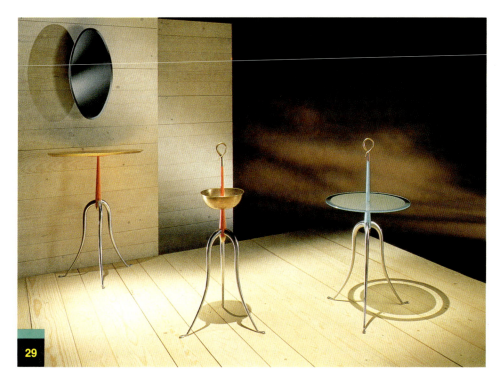

29

Roberto Lazzeroni
Rolling Home
Metal, die-cast
polished aluminium,
gold-painted wood,
frosted glass, brass
Left to right:
Mirror,
Big Chin:
H 64cm (25⅛in)
W 30cm (11⅞in)
D 8cm (3⅛in)

Telephone table,
Egg:
H 86cm (33⅞in)
Di 52cm (20½in)
Ashtray,
Fred:
H 100cm (39½in)
Di 52cm (20½in)
Cocktail table,
Soon:
H 100/67cm
(39½/26⅜in)
Manufacturer:
Cidue, Italy

31

Riccardo Dalisi
Sofa-bed,
Slalom
Metal, cherrywood,
foam, cotton fabric
Sofa:
H 85cm (33½in)
W 195cm (76⅞in)
D 90cm (35½in)
Bed:
H 85cm (33½in)
W 195cm (76⅞in)
D 160cm (63in)
Manufacturer:
Playline, Italy

31

Metal, cherrywood, foam, cotton fabric
The single sheet baldachin is attached to a self-winding roller and can extend to 200cm (78¾in).

Sofa:
H 95cm (37½in)
W 210cm (82⅝in)
D 90cm (35½in)
Bed:
H 95cm (37½in)
W 200cm (78¾in)
D 163cm (64⅛in)
Manufacturer:
Playline, Italy

The sofa-bed is quite possibly the most intractable of furniture types. Designing it to look acceptable when closed is comparatively simple – though many sofa-beds contrive, even then, to look bulbous and ungainly. Unfolded, however, the average sofa-bed is a structural disaster. Invariably, the bed will appear to jut like a broken limb from the frame. Stranded between the two possibilities, the sofa-bed looks like the temporary arrangement it is: neither one thing nor the other.

Riccardo Dalisi's two sofa-beds for the Italian company Playline show how it should be done. *Slalom* is the simpler of the two: a sofa which folds open to make a bed, without losing any of its character as a piece of furniture. *Alato*, the other design, shows that Dalisi has not only solved the problem, but made himself its master. As the sofa is opened, a sheet unwinds from the roller at the back to form an angled canopy covering the length of the bed. In a second version, three triangular pieces of fabric can be attached to the ceiling to create an exotic tent. In neither design does Dalisi make any attempt to conceal one apparatus or function inside another. The elements you see when the bed is fully extended are the same elements you see when it is folded away. Only the arrangement has changed, giving Dalisi's design the sense of inevitability most sofa-beds so conspicuously lack.

Siggi Fischer
Clothes stand
Steel, wood
H 178cm (70in)
Di 59cm (23in)
Manufacturer:
Thomas Schulte,
Germany

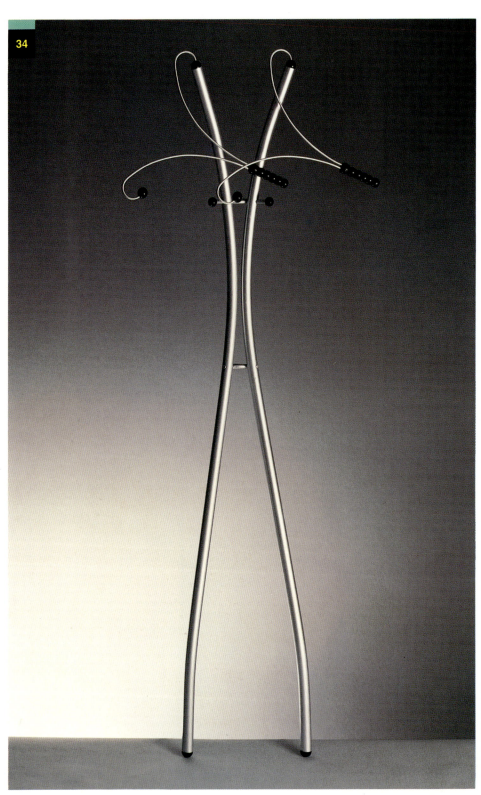

34

33

Siggi Fischer
Clothes stand
Steel, wood
H 178cm (70in)
W 59cm (23in)
Manufacturer:
Thomas Schulte,
Germany

De Pas, D'Urbino and Lomazzi
Clothes stand,
Octopus
Zinc-plated or black soft coated steel, beechwood
H 156cm (61½in)
Di at base 63cm (24⅞in)
Di at top 55cm (21¾in)
Manufacturer: Zerodisegno, Italy

Enzo Mari
Hat rack,
Museo
Stove-enamelled steel, beech
H 187cm (73⅝in)
W 209cm (82⅜in)
D 52cm (20½in)
Manufacturer: Zanotta, Italy

36

Enzo Mari
Clothes stand,
Museo
Stove-enamelled steel, beech
H 185cm (72⅞in)
W 49cm (19¼in)
D 38cm (15in)
Manufacturer: Zanotta, Italy

37

Design 134
Salon chair
Wood, aluminium,
leather
Prototype
H 76cm (30in)
W 55cm (21¾in)
D 48cm (18⅞in)

Jochen Henkels
Nomad's Wardrobe
*MDF, steel, steel
tube, glass
H 120cm (47½in)
W 55cm (21¾in)
D 50cm (19⅝in)
Manufacturer:
Jochen Henkels,
Germany*

39

40

38

Fumio Enomoto
Chair,
Caldia
*Wood, fabric,
leather
H 74cm (29⅛in)
W 62.5cm (24½in)
D 65cm (25⅝in)
Manufacturer:
Artifort/Wagemans
Maastricht, The
Netherlands*

Achille Castiglioni
Central sofa,
825 Hilly
*Polyurethane,
polyester, black-
lacquered wood,
acrylic
H 60cm (23½in)
W 240cm (94½in)
D 137cm (54in)
Manufacturer:
Cassina, Italy*

41

*O*ne of the most disarming new
designs at the 1992 Milan
Furniture Fair was on show outside
the fair itself, in the domed showroom of
Cassina on the Via Durini. There, a relaxed-
looking **Achille Castiglioni** was to be found
demonstrating a range of sofas and tables
called Hilly which could hardly have lived
up to their name more accurately. For Hilly
looks like nothing so much as the contour
lines and variegated colour bands on a
map depicting a low-lying range of hills.
Castiglioni's aim, realized with a literalness
that few except an old master of his stature
would dare to attempt, was to bring a sense
of the surrounding landscape into the home.
If furniture can encourage certain types of
social behaviour by dictating the way in
which the body comes to rest, and by
establishing an overall mood, then Hilly's
low armrests and stepped backrests are
defiantly informal – a virtual incitement to
lounge about and to loll.

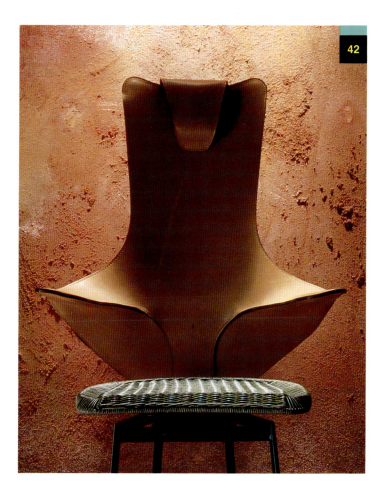

42

Paolo Deganello
Armchair,
Regina
*Stove-enamelled
steel, interlaced
wicker, cowhide*
H 115cm (45¼in)
W 69cm (27⅛in)
D 65cm (25⅝in)
*Manufacturer:
Zanotta, Italy*

43

43

Paolo Deganello
Armchair,
Re
*Stove-enamelled
steel, interlaced
wicker, cowhide*
H 90cm (35½in)
*Seat H 47.5cm
(18¾in)*
W 58cm (22⅞in)
D 58cm (22⅞in)
*Manufacturer:
Zanotta, Italy*

Andrea Dichiara
Table,
Tavolini
Steel, aluminium
H 60.5cm (23⅞in)
Di 40cm (15¾in)
Manufacturer:
Bar Metals, Italy

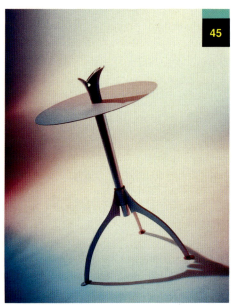

45

Jorge Pensi
Table,
Toledo
*Anodized cast
aluminium,
aluminium tube
H 72.5cm (28½in)
Di 70cm (27½in)
Di of base 58.5cm
(23in)
Manufacturer:
AMAT, Spain*

44

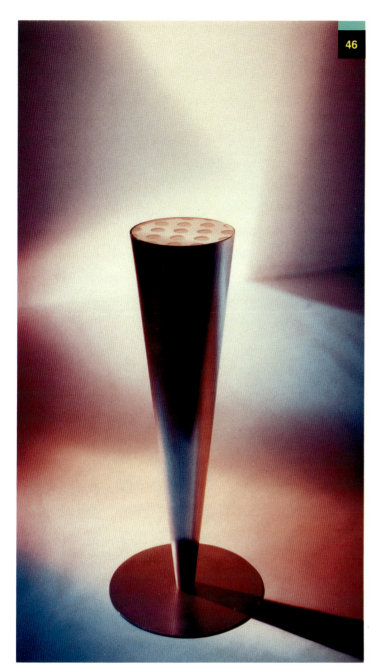

46

Massimo Morozzi
High table
Steel, glass
H 116.5cm (45⅞in)
Di at top 31.5cm
(12⅜in)
Di of base 50cm
(19⅝in)
Manufacturer:
Bar Metals, Italy

Piero Fornasetti
High table,
Pranzinpiedi
Steel, brass
H 75–105cm
(29½–41⅜in)
Di of tubing 1.5cm
(⅝in)
Di of base 35cm
(13¾in)
Di of stand 2cm
(¾in)
Manufacturer:
Bar Metals, Italy

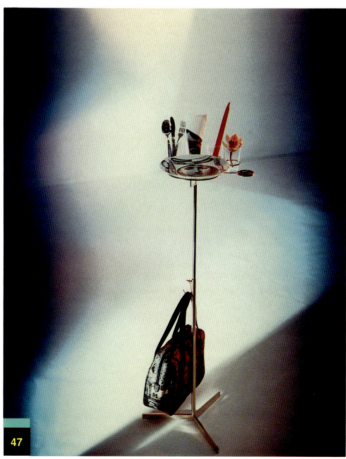

47

48

Mario Botta
Screen,
Nilla Rosa
Flattened sheet metal
H 140cm (55⅛in)
W 140cm (55⅛in)
D 70cm (27½in)
Manufacturer:
Alias, Italy

Michele De Lucchi
Book shelf,
**Pensiero Libero
(1303)**
*Evaporated beech,
aluminium
H 135cm (53⅛in)
W 162cm (63¾in)
D 30cm (11⅞in)
Manufacturer:
Alias, Italy*

Lodovico Acerbis
Table,
San Tomè
*Pearwood, light
walnut, crystal,
chrome-plated
metal
H 74cm (29⅛in)
W 190cm (74⅞in)
D 82cm (32¼in)
Manufacturer:
Acerbis, Italy*

51

*Anodized
aluminium,
galvanized steel,
grooved aluminium
sheet, pearwood,
mirror glass
The system
consists of wall-
fixed uprights to
which shelves, wall
cabinets, consoles
and other fittings
can be attached.*

*Uprights:
H 186cm (73¼in)
218cm (85⅞in)
Back panels:
H 224/192cm
(88⅛/75⅝in)
W 90/60/45/30cm
(35½/23½/17¾/
11⅞in)
Vertical frames:
H 234/202cm
(92⅛/79½in)
Manufacturer:
Driade, Italy*

51

51

51

Philippe Starck
Stacking chair,
Louis 20
Blasted
polypropylene,
aluminium
H 84cm (33in)
W 47cm (18½in)
D 58cm (22⅞in)
Manufacturer:
Vitra, Switzerland

52

Fumio Enomoto
Chair,
Tokiko
Metal, fabric
H 91cm (35⁷/₈in)
W 50.5cm (19⁷/₈in)
D 63cm (24⁷/₈in)
Manufacturer:
Artifort/Wagemans
Maastricht, The
Netherlands

53

Andrea Branzi
Amnesie collection
Cupboard,
Piccola Gabbia
*Punched and
sanded steel,
lacquered wood,
''Pelle di pesca''
finishing*
H 175cm (68⅞in)
W 75cm (29½in)
D 55cm (21¾in)
Manufacturer:
Design Gallery
Milano, Italy

Andrea Branzi *likened an earlier
collection of furniture to ''domestic
animals''. With his latest collection of
furniture, vases and lamps for the Design
Gallery in Milan, his metaphor is urban
rather than organic. Branzi's cupboards look
like buildings and sometimes whole sections
of skyline imprisoned within dark cages of
scaffolding, and he explicitly compares
these ''micro-environments'' to certain kinds
of architecture. They are cold and hard on
the outside, warm and welcoming within.
When opened, they reveal rich finishes
in velvet and lacquer. Branzi calls his
collection Amnesia. Partly, he is referring to
forgetfulness and the betrayals of memory,
but also to the pools of emptiness that
amnesia opens up in an otherwise densely
packed mental landscape. And this, in more
than just a metaphorical sense, is one of the
purposes that the cages fulfil: they hold
other objects and pieces of furniture at bay,
creating a protective stillness around the
towers inside.*

55

Andrea Branzi
Amnesie collection
Divisional furniture,
Grande Gabbia
Lacquered wood with "Pelle di pesca" finish, steel and net with metallic sanded finish
H 192cm (75⅝in)
W 200cm (78¾in)
D 48cm (18⅞in)
Manufacturer:
Design Gallery
Milano, Italy

Andrea Branzi
Amnesie collection
Divisional furniture,
Grande Arco
Natural wood, lacquered and serigraphed wood With halogen spots and a raw, turned wooden vase.
H 210cm (82⅝in)
W 290cm (114⅛in)
D 50cm (19⅝in)
Table,
Grande Piano
Serigraphed crystal, chrome
H 73cm (28¾in)
W 181cm (71⅜in)
D 85cm (33½in)
Manufacturer:
Design Gallery
Milano, Italy

56

57

Frank Gehry
*The Gehry
Collection*
*Laminated
bentwood maple
Left to right:
Club chair,*
Power Play:
*H 83.5cm (32⅞in)
Seat H 40.5cm
(16in)
W 79.5cm (31⅜in)
D 76.5cm (30⅛in)
Ottoman,*
Off Side:
*H 20.5–34.7cm
(8⅛–13⅞in)
W 59.7cm (23⅜in)
D 59.7cm (23⅜in)
Chair,*
High Sticking:
*H 110cm (43⅜in)
Seat H 45.5cm
(17⅞in)*

*W 51cm (20⅛in)
D 60.5cm (23⅞in)
Armchair,*
Hat Trick:
*H 85cm (33½in)
Seat H 45.7cm
(18in)
W 59.8cm (23⅜in)
D 56.3cm (22¼in)
Table,*
Face Off:
*H 73.5cm (28⅞in)
W 91.5cm (36in)
Armchair,*
Cross Check:
*H 85.5cm (33⅝in)
Seat H 46cm
(18⅛in)
W 72.5cm (28½in)
D 63cm (24⅞in)
Manufacturer: The
Knoll Group, USA*

Frank Gehry designs furniture for production only occasionally, but his inventions are always highly original and deeply thought out. In 1992 Vitra re-editioned four pieces from Gehry's Easy Edges collection of 1972, in which the Californian architect experimented with layers of bonded corrugated cardboard (see the Wiggle Side Chair and Low Table Set on page 59). We may be accustomed to thinking of the material as ephemeral and disposable, but the effect produced is one of remarkable solidity and strength.

The same refusal to take anything for granted in the conventional use of a material underpins Gehry's bentwood collection for Knoll. "Bentwood furniture, until now, has always relied on a thick and heavy main structure for the seating," notes Gehry. "The difference in my chairs is that the structure and the seat are formed of the same incredibly lightweight slender wood strips which serve both functions." Gehry has

created seven sinuous maplewood shapes – four chairs, two tables and a chaise-longue – in which weave and structure are one and the same. Where a bentwood master such as Alvar Aalto opted for sculptural simplicity, Gehry's forms loop and curve and double back on themselves to form lightweight arabesques of breath-taking grace. It took Gehry more than a hundred prototypes to achieve the precise spatial relationships he required. These are pieces in which the negative spaces defined by the strips of maple carry as much visual weight as the structure itself.

Christoph Seyferth
Box,
Wandvitrine SC6
Ashwood
Limited batch
production
H 88cm (34⅝in)
W 62cm (24⅜in)
D 24cm (9⅜in)
Manufacturer: Franz
Schatzl Design
Werkstätte, Austria

58

Niek Zwartjes
Folding table,
Wylie
Wood
H 75cm (29½in)
W 167.5cm (65⅞in)
D 71cm (28in)
Manufacturer:
Artifort/Wagemans
Maastricht, The
Netherlands

59

Tadao Shimizu
Table series,
Screw
*Aluminium, wood,
plastics, glass
The table tops
come in various
sizes and shapes;
the legs are
detachable.
Limited batch
production
H 45–55cm
(17³⁄₄–21³⁄₄in)
Manufacturer:
Design Studio
TAD, Japan*

60

60

Milan Knizak
*Table
Steel, glass,
wood, foam
rubber, leather,
fluorescent light
H 82cm (32¹⁄₄in)
Di 150cm (59in)*

61

Christophe Pillet
Dining chair,
So what
*Welded steel slats
and tubing,
anthracite,
mahogany
H 77cm (30³⁄₈in)
Seat H 46cm
(18¹⁄₈in)
W 58cm (22⁷⁄₈in)
D 52cm (20¹⁄₂in)
Manufacturer:
XO, France*

62

Bořek Šípek
Stacking chair,
Sedlak
Natural cast
aluminium, stained
pear or beech,
foam
H 87cm (34¼in)

Seat H 47cm
(18½in)
W 40cm (15¾in)
D 51cm (20⅛in)
Manufacturer:
Vitra, Switzerland

The pressure of expectation on the handful of stars who monopolize the pages of the design magazines is immense. Will they startle their admirers with creations that are genuinely new? Or will they disappoint by repeating themselves? Even if they are on form, can they impress the demanding international hothouse of Milan? At this level of attention and saturation, even the brilliant one-off can lack impact. It is the collection which offers designers the opportunity to make a mark.

Last year, **Massimo Iosa Ghini** made an unexpected foray into wood, a material that sat rather oddly, and not altogether convincingly, with his synthetic, science-fiction tastes. This year's collection for BRF, his fifth to date, sees a return to the more literal cartoon futurism that has sustained him since he laid down his manifesto in 1987 with the Dinamic collection for Moroso. Tran Tran (the words are Italian for ''routine'' or ''everyday'') is bright, comfortable and almost childishly emphatic. Its nonsense names – the Pon-Pon armchair, Bla-Bla bookcase and Toc-Toc table – might suggest a Futurist call to arms, but the liquid rubber-coated reality of many of the pieces has more in common with Mickey Mouse than Marinetti. For BRF, the collection represents an attempt to move, if not down-market, then into a very much wider market, with prices held as low as possible. For Iosa Ghini, it embodies an attempt to locate a kind of domestic ''heroism'' in the details and practicalities of everyday life. (See also page 29.)

Massimo Iosa Ghini
Small table,
Jo-Jo
Fibreglass, liquid rubber
H 46cm (18⅛in)
Di 60cm (23½in)
Manufacturer:
BRF, Italy

64

**Massimo Iosa
Ghini**
Bookcase,
Bla-Bla
*Wood, mirrors,
liquid rubber,
crystal, satin-
finished steel
H 210cm (82⅝in)
L 210cm (82⅝in)
D 40.5cm (16in)
Manufacturer:
BRF, Italy*

65

66

Paola Navone
Screen from the
Mobili del Mondo
*collection
Wood, iron wire,
handmade
decorations
H 170cm (66⅞in)
W of each panel
46cm (18⅛in)
Manufacturer:
Mondo, Italy*

Michele De Lucchi
Armchair,
Elia
Metal, polyurethane
foam
H 84cm (33in)
Seat H 43cm
(16⅞in)
W 83cm (32¾in)
D 95cm (37½in)
Manufacturer:
Arflex, Italy

67

68

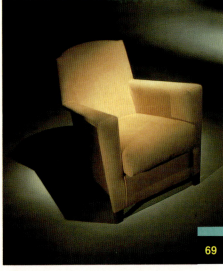

69

Alberto Lievore
Armchair,
Calvino
Beechwood, foam,
Dacron, fabric
H 100cm (39½in)
W 74cm (29⅛in)
D 82cm (32¼in)
Manufacturer:
Divano, Spain

Josep Lluscà
*Chair from **Solo**
seating system
Metal, flexible
foam-injected
polyurethane, low
pressure injected
chrome inox*

*aluminium alloy
H 80cm (31½in)
W 66/63/60cm
(26/24⅞/23½in)
D 68cm (26¾in)
Manufacturer:
Oken, Spain*

Jasper Morrison
Sofa
Anodized
aluminium, fabric,
PU foam
H 81cm (31⁷⁄₈in)
Seat H 43cm
(16⁷⁄₈in)
W 170cm (66⁷⁄₈in)
D 80cm (31¹⁄₂in)
Manufacturer:
Vitra, Switzerland

70

Jasper Morrison
Benches
Chromed steel,
fabric, PU foam
H 51cm (20¹⁄₈in)
W 135/90/45cm
(53¹⁄₈/35¹⁄₂/17³⁄₄in)
D 35cm (13³⁄₄in)
Manufacturer:
Vitra, Switzerland

71

Frank Gehry
Wiggle Side Chair
and *Low Table Set*
Corrugated
cardboard edged
in hardboard
Chair:
H 82cm (32¼in)
Seat H 43cm
(16⅞in)

W 36cm (14½in)
D 61cm (24in)
Tables:
H 50cm (19⅝in)
W & D 63/52/40cm
(24⅞/20½/15¾in)
Manufacturer:
Vitra, Switzerland

73

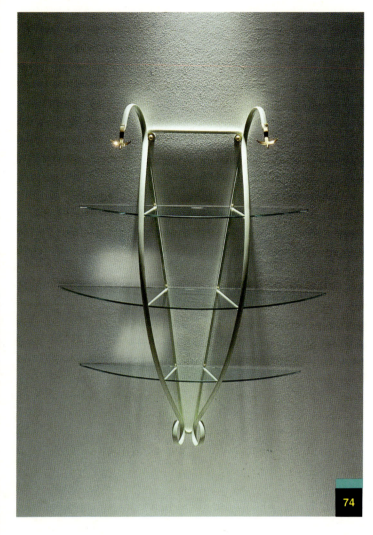

74

Riccardo Dalisi
Mirror with shelves,
Vesuvio
Cast iron, wood
painted with
scratch-resistant
embossing
H 195cm (76⅞in)
W 49cm (19¼in)
D 42cm (16½in)
Manufacturer:
Zanotta, Italy

Riccardo Dalisi
Shelf unit,
Peltrera
Drawn steel stove-
enamelling, 24K
gold-plated cast
bronze, 6mm
(¼in) tempered
plate glass
H 123cm (48⅜in)
W 100cm (39½in)
D 24cm (9⅜in)
Manufacturer:
Zanotta, Italy

Riccardo Dalisi
Table,
Giocondo
*Drawn steel stove-
enamelling, 24K
gold-plated cast
bronze, 12mm
(¹⁄₂in) tempered
plate glass,
stainless steel
H 84cm (33in)
Di 70cm (27¹⁄₂in)
Manufacturer:
Zanotta, Italy*

76

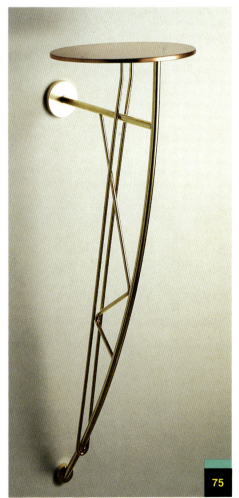

75

Elliott Littmann
Wall bracket,
Arco
*Brass tube, glazed
copper sheet
H 100cm (39¹⁄₂in)
Di 31cm (12¹⁄₄in)
Manufacturer:
Driade, Italy*

77

Ron Arad
Stool,
Hotel Zeus
*Sheet steel, cherry
plywood or black-
painted wood
H 74cm (29¹/₈in)
W 43cm (16⁷/₈in)
D 50cm (19⁵/₈in)
Manufacturer:
Noto, Italy*

Ron Arad
Chair,
Hotel Zeus
*Sheet steel, cherry
plywood or black-
painted wood
H 78cm (30³/₄in)
W 47cm (18¹/₂in)
D 68cm (26³/₄in)
Manufacturer:
Noto, Italy*

78

Matteo Thun
Table,
Clitunno
*Turned pearwood,
polished 10mm
(⅝in) glass
H 72cm (28⅜in)
Di 55cm (21¾in)
Manufacturer:
Friedrich Vorlaufer,
Germany*

Matteo Thun
Stool,
Montepulciano
*Turned Awong,
leather
H 42cm (16½in)
Di 30cm (11⅞in)
Manufacturer:
Friedrich Vorlaufer,
Germany*

Ron Arad
TV stand,
Hotel Zeus
*Sheet steel,
extruded rubber
H 70cm (27½in)
Di 60cm (23½in)
Manufacturer:
Noto, Italy*

Nigel Coates
Bar stool,
Taxim
Lacquered steel,
foam, fabric
H 102cm (40⅛in)
W 45cm (17¾in)
D 43cm (16⅞in)
Manufacturer:
Bros's, Italy

82

83

Nigel Coates
Armchair,
Taxim
Lacquered steel,
foam, fabric
H 81cm (31⅞in)
W 82cm (32¼in)
D 79cm (31in)
Manufacturer:
Bros's, Italy

Massimo Iosa Ghini `84`

Armchair,
Mama

Wood, polyurethane foam, goose down, lacquered maple
H 81cm (31⅞in)
L 103cm (40½in)
D 94cm (37in)
Manufacturer: Moroso, Italy

`85` **Luigi Serafini**

Sofa,
Kingfisher

Metal, cold moulded polyurethane foam, velvet
H 104cm (41in)
W 90cm (35½in)
L 255cm (100⅜in)
Manufacturer: Sawaya & Moroni, Italy

Shigeru Uchida
Chest of drawers,
Kagu 1991
Oak, bubinga
Prototype
H 160cm (63in)
W 55/25cm
(21¾/9⅞in)
D 25cm (9⅞in)
Manufacturer:
UMS-Pastoe,
Holland

The idea of free-standing furniture is still relatively new in Japan. Before the Second World War there were no movable chairs and tables in ordinary homes, only fully integrated spaces that derived from house construction and the traditional Japanese way of life. After 1945, there was an urgent need to become more Westernized, and designers like **Shigeru Uchida** had everything to learn. Uchida, who designs both interiors and furniture (he supervised the interior programme at the Il Palazzo Hotel, Fukuoka), took much of his original inspiration from artist-designers such as Donald Judd, and echoes of Judd's severe, rectilinear forms can still be seen in his own.

Lately, however, Uchida and other colleagues of his generation have found themselves drawn once again, almost unconsciously, to the Japanese tradition and spirit. "Slowly we are finding our identity," he says. "We are now more confident about our own culture." His cherry and steel Chest of Drawers somehow manages to contain a sense of both new and historic Japan, though this, he notes, was not his intention – it is something that observers continually point out. Uchida's towering grid of drawers (there are ninety-six in all) looks like the kind of modern building one might come across on any street in central Osaka or Tokyo, but it also resembles the wooden drug cabinets used by traditional Japanese chemists.

88

Shigeru Uchida
Chest of drawers
Steel, cherrywood
Prototype
H 132cm (52in)
W 132cm (52in)
D 25cm (9⅞in)
Manufacturer:
Chairs, Japan

87

88

**Hans Bauer and
Kay Saamer**
Filing cabinet,
Aktei
Powder-coated
sheet steel
H 193cm (76in)
W 39cm (15⅜in)
D 35cm (13¾in)
Manufacturer:
Moormann,
Germany

Tom Dixon
Chair,
Pylon
Steel wire
Prototype
H 135cm (53⅛in)
W 50cm (19⅝in)
D 55cm (21¾in)
Manufacturer:
Space, UK

There has always been something of the amateur engineer about the British designer **Tom Dixon**. In his early "salvage" furniture he welded found metal objects with an intuitive understanding of the way in which their particular shapes could be combined to form larger, load-bearing structures. In the last year or so, Dixon's designs have taken a more explicitly structural turn – that is to say, the structures have become more symmetrical, regular and exposed. For Cappellini's latest collection, he has created two glass-topped tables and a chair with cross-braced frames of spellbinding intricacy. Indeed, the Pylon chair consists of nothing but open wire, zig-zagging skywards in a crazy matrix of welds, until its backrest appears to hover above the sitter like a mantis.

This new structural virtuosity seems to be the direction that Dixon is most likely to pursue. In the summer of 1992 he announced that he was planning to take a course in engineering (as a designer and craftsman he is entirely self-taught). His aim, he said, was to attempt a kind of "expressionist engineering" using the latest alloys, but he was only too aware of the danger of whimsy without a proper understanding of materials and structure. A 30-foot steel pylon sculpture erected on the roof of Joseph Ettedgui's shop in South Kensington, London, bore an obvious family relationship with the Cappellini pieces and suggested Dixon's designs for the Italian company could be only the beginning.

Tom Dixon
Table,
Pylon
Steel wire, glass
Prototype
H 50cm (19⅝in)
W 50cm (19⅝in)
L 135cm (53⅛in)
Manufacturer:
Space, UK

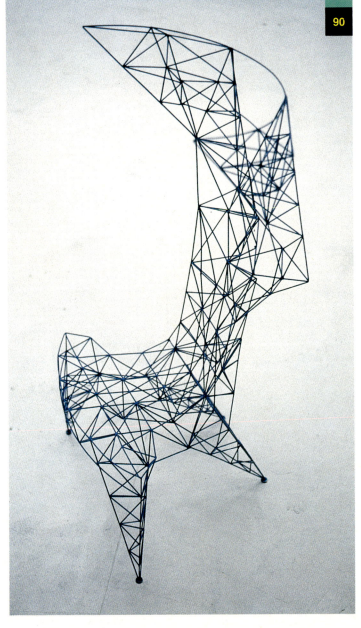

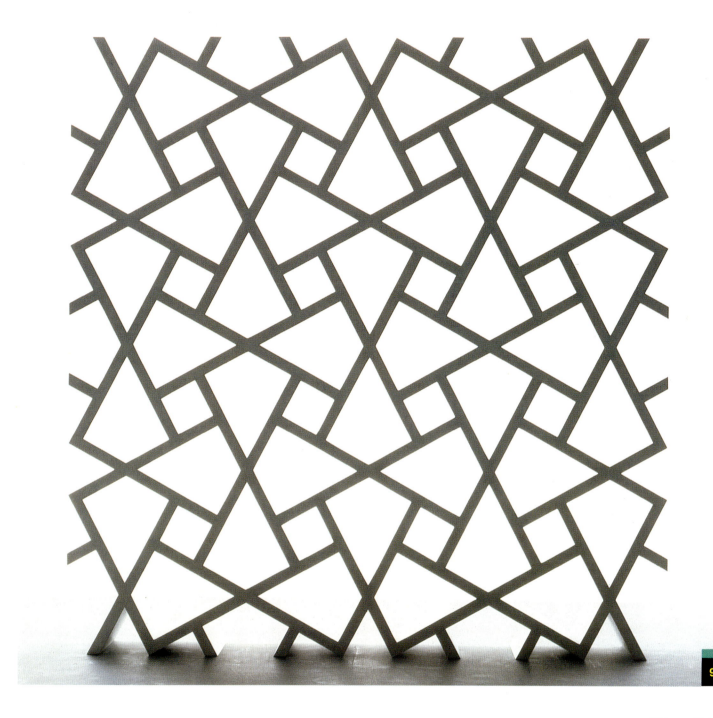

91

Shigeru Uchida
Shelves,
Kagu 1991
Melamine resin
veneer sheet, wood
H 163cm (64¹/₈in)
W 163cm (64¹/₈in)
D 25cm (9⁷/₈in)
Manufacturer:
Chairs, Japan

Lella and Massimo Vignelli
Shelving system,
System Fax
*Lacquered panel,
corrugated plate
finished with
polyurethane paint
H 210cm (82⅝in)
W 96cm (37⅞in)
Manufacturer:
Poltronova, Italy*

92

Fax technology now plays such an intimate role in the development of most international design projects that it is already hard to imagine a time without it. No furniture company has ever paid a more explicit homage to the indispensable nature of the fax machine, however, than **Poltronova**. The company's new shelving system, like fax paper itself, is a tabula rasa, in this case in the form of a perforated screen, on which five design teams – Remo Buti (whose idea the project was), Ettore Sottsass, Lella and Massimo Vignelli, Prospero Rasulo and Lisa Krohn – were invited to project an assortment of shelves, cabinets, drawers and cubby holes. With all the flexibility and speed we have come to expect from the fax as a communication device, these parts can be moved into whatever configuration or composition the user prefers. The additions themselves are nothing if not true to form. Sottsass's varnished pearwood is boxy and almost overpoweringly hieratic, while the minimalist Vignellis' corrugated plate has the hard graphic line and unswerving precision of pencil on tracing paper. If the system is a success, further designers will be invited to fax Poltronova their proposals.

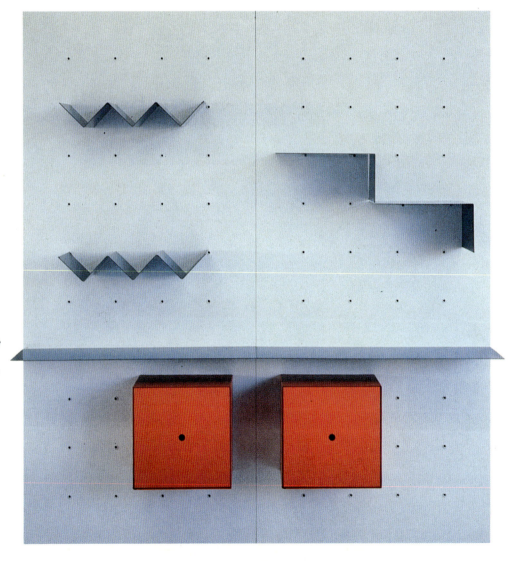

94

Remo Buti
Shelving system,
System Fax
*Lacquered wood,
mirror with sanded
decorations
H 96cm (37⁷⁄₈in)
W 210cm (82⁵⁄₈in)
Manufacturer:
Poltronova, Italy*

93

Ettore Sottsass
Shelving system,
System Fax
*Lacquered wood,
varnished
pearwood
H 96cm (37⁷⁄₈in)
W 210cm (82⁵⁄₈in)
Manufacturer:
Poltronova, Italy*

Bořek Šípek
Desk
Wood, pear
veneer, steel
H 75/68/52cm
(29½/26¾/20½in)
W c.300cm
(118⅛in)
D c.150cm (59in)
Manufacturer:
Vitra, Switzerland

95

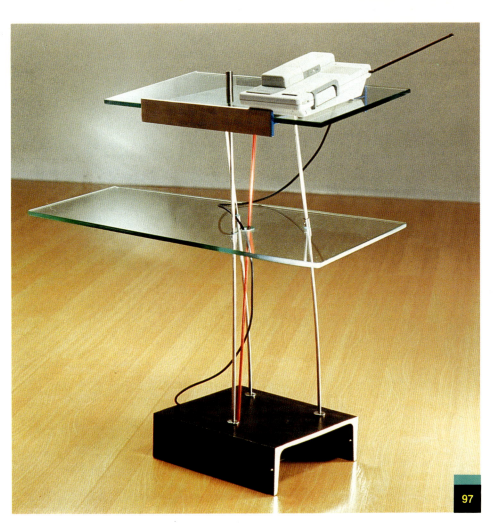

Bořek Šípek
Stand-up desk
Wood, pear veneer
H 115cm (45½in)
W 131/112cm
(51⅝/44⅛in)
D 42cm (16½in)
Manufacturer:
Vitra, Switzerland

96

Coop Himmelblau
Meeting table,
Pich
Lacquered U-
section, chrome,
stainless steel,
aluminium rods,
10mm (³⁄₈in) glass
H 87.8cm (34½in)
W 81cm (31⅞in)
D 31.5cm (12³⁄₈in)
Manufacturer:
Friedrich Vorlaufer,
Germany

97

Philippe Starck
Table,
Chameleon
*Multi-layered wood
with pear veneer,
cast aluminium,
crystal
H 73cm (28¾in)
Di 140cm (55⅛in)
Manufacturer:
Aleph UBIK, Italy*

98

**Toshiko
Kawaguchi**
Chest,
**Paulownia
Furniture No. 2**
Paulownia, steel
*Limited batch
production*
H 58cm (22⅞in)
W 26cm (10¼in)
D 24cm (9⅜in)
*Manufacturer:
Kingirikōgei, Japan*

99

100

**Toshiko
Kawaguchi**
Table,
**Paulownia
Furniture No. 1**
Paulownia, steel
*Limited batch
production*
H 70cm (27½in)
W 120cm (47¼in)
D 48cm (18⅞in)
*Manufacturer:
Kingirikōgei, Japan*

Ettore Sottsass
Bedhead,
Notte di Luna Piena
Wood, brass, brass
dipped in 24K gold,
enamelled pottery
H 197cm (77⅝in)
W 190cm (74⅞in)
D 15cm (6in)
Manufacturer:
Interflex, Italy

101

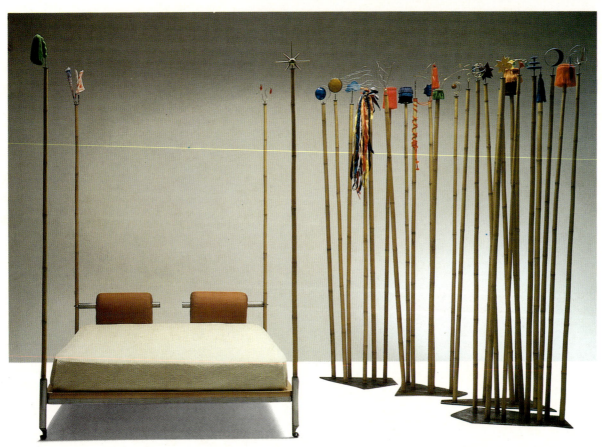

Toni Cordero
Bed,
Sōspir
Metal, canes
The canes are
interchangeable.
H of canes 210cm
(82⅝in)
W 164cm (64⅝in)
L 194cm (76⅜in)
Manufacturer:
Sawaya & Moroni,
Italy

102

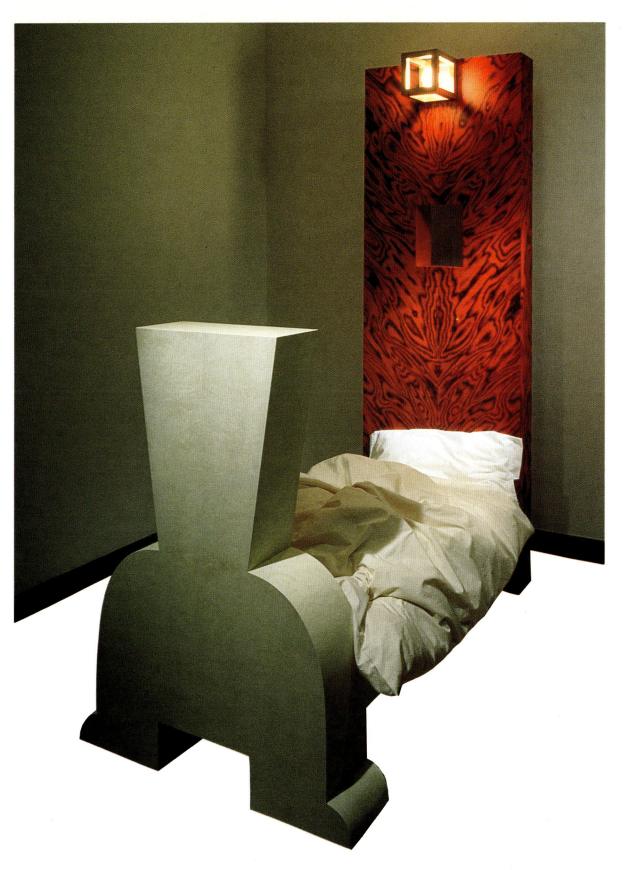

Ettore Sottsass
Bed,
Misteriosa
*Lacquered wood,
natural briarwood,
gilded cube
H 250cm (98¾in)
W 110cm (43⅜in)
D 233cm (91¾in)
Manufacturer:
Design Gallery
Milano, Italy*

103

104

Michael Clapper
Cabinet,
Anasazi
Beech veneer,
plywood, glass
One-off
H 211cm (83in)
W 63.5cm (25in)
D 35.5cm (14in)
Manufacturer:
Michael Clapper
Design, USA

104

Remo Buti
Table,
Maggio
*Lacquered metal,
sand-blasted glass*
H 74cm (29⅛in)
W 200cm (78⅜in)
D 90cm (35½in)
*Manufacturer:
Arredaesse, Italy*

106

105

105

Nazanin Kamali
Chaise-longue,
Flying Carpet
*Steel mesh woven
with elastic rope
Prototype*
H 55cm (21¾in)
W 175cm (68⅞in)
D 150cm (59in)
*Manufacturer: Royal
College of Art, UK*

Bořek Šípek
Garden table,
Dalibor
Marble, aluminium
H 80cm (31½in)
Di 80cm (31½in)
Manufacturer:
Steltman Editions,
The Netherlands

107

Ettore Sottsass
Table,
Aspic
Aluminium,
transparent Pirex,
15mm (⁵⁄₈in) ground
polished glass
H 73cm (28³⁄₄in)
Di 130cm (51¹⁄₈in)
Manufacturer:
FontanaArte, Italy

108

110

Luigi Serafini
Table,
Tabulino
Lacquered metal,
silken fabric
H 64cm (25¹⁄₈in)
W 74cm (29¹⁄₈in)
D 60cm (23¹⁄₂in)
Manufacturer:
Edra, Italy

Pucci de Rossi
Table,
Cactus
Glass, steel
H 74cm (29¹⁄₈in)
W 120cm (47¹⁄₄in)
L 120cm (47¹⁄₄in)
Manufacturer:
Néotù, France

109

Karim Azzabi
Inflatable armchair,
Floating Matilda
PVC, metal, non-deformable elastic, metallic lacquered wood
H 90cm (35½in)
W (inflated) 118cm (46½in) (deflated) 70cm (27½in)
Manufacturer: Edra, Italy

111

Philippe Starck
W.W. Stool
Lacquered and sand-blasted aluminium
H 97cm (38¼in)
W 56cm (22in)
D 53cm (20⅞in)
Manufacturer: Vitra, Switzerland

113

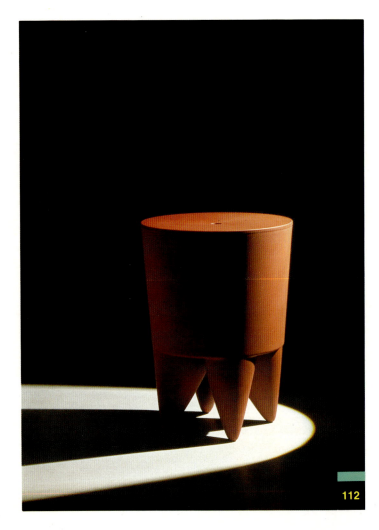

112

Philippe Starck
Stool/coffee table,
Bubu 1er
Plastic
H 43cm (16⅞in)
Di 32.5cm (12¾in)
Manufacturer: 3 Suisses, France

114

With the W.W. Stool for Vitra, **Philippe Starck** has created his most sculptural piece of furniture to date. The stool formed part of a project to design an imaginary office for Wim Wenders, director of the film Wings of Desire in which angels descend on Berlin, and there is something of the fallen angel in W.W.'s soaring lines and haughty mien. W.W. is emphatically not a stool for sitting on, as anyone who has tried to perch on this sand-blasted aluminium spine-crusher will know. Vitra describes it as an exercise in ''purpose-free aesthetics'' and will sell it as part of its Vitra Edition, where comfort has always taken second place to art. At a time when sensible, functional, saleable furniture has become a recession-driven cri de coeur for many companies, Starck has produced a compelling claim for his own creative autonomy. Le Paravent de l'Autre (''The Screen of the Other'') is a similarly uncompromising and introspective essay in artistic celebrity, featuring photographic portraits of a diabolical-looking Marcel Duchamp, Salvador Dali seen as a moustachioed cyclops, and a naked Starck in body-builder pose.

Philippe Starck
Screen,
**Le Paravent de
l'Autre**
*Cast aluminium,
wood, glass
H 190cm (74⁷⁄₈in)*

*W 150cm (59in)
D 3cm (1¹⁄₈in)
Manufacturer:
Driade/Aleph, Italy*

*I*f the original, hugely ambitious Memphis project now seems the epitome of early 1980s fashion-design, a look so striking and seductive that it was bound eventually to collapse under the weight of its own success, the early 1990s find the company that continues to bear the group's name setting its sights on more modest goals. The new **Memphis Extra** collection is dedicated to the slightly forlorn hope that it might be possible to go beyond "style", to break once and for all with the idea of "trends" – to produce work, in short, that lasts. Memphis may, or may not, have achieved that aim, but it has come up with a set of designs that could have been conceived at almost any point in the last twenty-five years.

As if to underline its rejection of all the trappings of fashion, Memphis publicity material presents the pieces in the street, in a builder's yard, and surrounded by discarded packing in casually empty rooms. Do Brandi's Transworld Siren is a hulking leatherette pouffe that looks like a pump or a globular can. Andrea Anastasio's Chanoyu is an otherwise unassuming wood and iron cabinet whose one muted flourish is a series of wiggly glass canes. The most unusual feature of Luigi Serafini's Ros coffee table is the scent of camphor that wafts from its surface. Compared to the candystripe optimism and exuberance of ten years ago, the effect is chastened, even downbeat. Like a number of other designers from the worlds of furniture and fashion, Memphis has put its money on the anti-style card. The obvious risk is that when the economic climate finally improves, and style undergoes the inevitable resurgence, this too will seem dated.

115

Andrea Anastasio
Cabinet,
Chanoyu
Painted wood, iron,
coloured glass
H 105cm (41⅜in)
W 60cm (23½in)
D 39cm (15⅜in)
Manufacturer:
Memphis, Italy

Do Brandi
Pouffe,
Transworld Siren
Sky leatherette
H 78cm (30¾in)
Di 55cm (21¾in)
Manufacturer:
Memphis, Italy

Luigi Serafini
Coffee table,
Ros
Wax-finished,
camphor-scented
rosewood, painted
iron
H 70cm (27½in)
Di 45cm (17¾in)
Manufacturer:
Memphis, Italy

Jiří Pelcl
Cabinet,
Kvete
Wood
H 220cm (86⅝in)
W 50cm (19⅝in)
D 30cm (11⅞in)
Manufacturer:
Atelier Pelcl,
Czechoslovakia

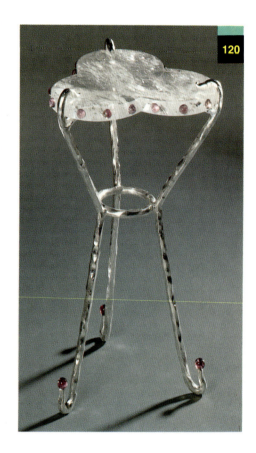

Elizabeth Garouste and Mattia Bonetti
Side-table,
Petit Nuage
Rock crystal, amethysts, silver-plated wrought iron
Limited batch production
H 60cm (23½in)
Di 35cm (13¾in)
Manufacturer: Eva-Maria Melchers, Germany

120

119

Danny Lane
Chair,
Rocking Dwarf
Bellfry oak, leaf springs, birch balls, cast iron
One-off
H 160cm (63in)
W 75cm (29½in)
D 65cm (25⅝in)

121

**Elizabeth
Garouste and
Mattia Bonetti**
Lyre Chair
Wood
H 94cm (37in)
W 42cm (16½in)
D 46cm (18⅛in)
*Manufacturer:
Bros's, Italy*

**Elizabeth
Garouste and
Mattia Bonetti**
Side-table,
Petite Etoile
*Rock crystal,
amethysts, gilded
wood
Limited batch
production
H 60cm (23½in)
W 42cm (16½in)
D 42cm (16½in)
Manufacturer: Eva-
Maria Melchers,
Germany*

122

Garouste and Bonetti's designs
have come a long way from the
intentional "barbarisms" of their
early work for Parisian galleries such as En
attendant les Barbares ("Waiting for the
Barbarians"). But while the couple may have
shed their primitive edge, they retain a
sense of the mysterious and magical that
few other designers can match. Garouste
and Bonetti pieces look like props for a
feature film of a fairy-tale to be shot by
Jean Cocteau. Of their recent furniture
designs, the Lyre Chair for Bros's must rank
as one of the most restrained, though the
classical/mythological links are apparent
enough. The material is wood, pure and
simple; the expressive flourishes are limited
to the gazelle-like curve of the legs and the
musical tension of the lyre-string backrest.

Two new tables for Eva-Maria Melchers
show Garouste and Bonetti on more familiar
ground. The luxurious aim of the German
company's collection, which also includes
pieces by Massimo Iosa Ghini (see pages
126, 127) and Alessandro Mendini, was to
reclaim precious stones from the exclusive
preserve of the jewellers, and bring them
back into interior design. Garouste and
Bonetti's Petit Nuage and Petite Etoile tables
are accordingly studded with amethysts
and glistening hunks of rock crystal. As so
often with these designers, the pieces come
dangerously close to kitsch, but never quite
cross the line.

Hironen
Armchair,
Unichair
Foam, fabric
Prototype
H 100cm (39½in)
W 100cm (39½in)
Manufacturer:
Hironen, Japan

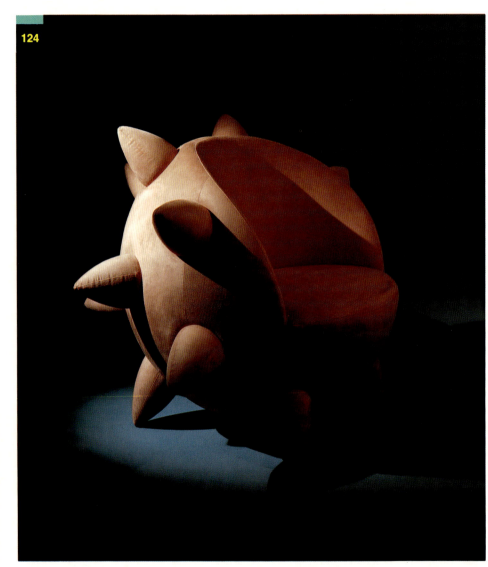

124

Milan Knizak
Table,
Romantic Still Life
Bronze
H 130cm (51⅛in)
W 80cm (31½in)
D 70cm (27½in)

123

Elizabeth
Garouste and
Mattia Bonetti
Dreaming Room
Lacquered wood,
fabric (cotton,
viscose, polyester
by Rohleder,
Germany)
Bed with movable
side-tables:
H 120cm (47¼in)

L 210cm (82⅝in)
D 180cm (70⅝in)
Chair:
H 85cm (33½in)
L 42cm (16½in)
D 42cm (16½in)
Manufacturer: Ligne
Roset, France &
Philips Consumer
Electronics,
Germany

LIGHTING

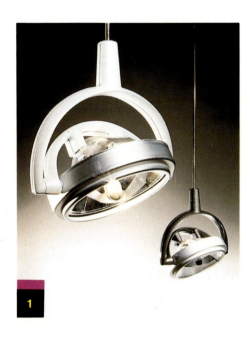

Matteo Thun
Spotlight,
Archetto Intensa
Stanyl of "DSM",
Ryton Phillips
Petroleum
Available with six

special reflectors,
giving a different
beam spread.
Takes one 35,
50 or 75W 12V
halogen bulb.
H 12cm (4³⁄₄in)
W 7cm (2³⁄₄in)
Manufacturer:
Flight, Italy

At a time when furniture companies are playing safer than they have in years, much of the impetus to experiment seems to have shifted into lighting design – and with good reason. Lighting is intrinsically richer in sculptural possibility than furniture. Unlike a sofa or dining chair, a lamp is not expected to provide "comfort" in the intimate, bodily sense, but simply to shed light in the way that its function (task light, uplighter etc.) leads us to expect. Its form is bound to be related to this purpose, but the opportunities for expression and individual statement are still vast.

As in previous editions, this *International Design Yearbook* features designs that push the light-fitting to weird, and sometimes almost savage, extremes. Nick Crowe's *Electric Medusa* is a writhing tangle of naked bulbs on chemically treated brass stalks, while Marre Moerel's *Miss Universe* chandelier is an aerial cluster of thirteen low-wattage bulbs beneath two great wings of beaten steel. At what point does a light break free from its typological moorings and begin to take flight as sculpture? Certainly when it is as large and inaccessible to the average home, and taste, as Ingo Maurer's six-metre light vessel, *Flatterby*.

Yet, at the other extreme, there are lamps whose greatest ambition is to sink back unnoticed into the corner of a room. As selecting editor, Bořek Šípek was amused to

discover the number of fittings still featuring variations on the time-honoured conical shade. Here, as so often, it is Philippe Starck who provides the *reductio ad absurdum*. Starck's *Miss Sissi* table lamp sounds like a doll, and the one-piece plastic fitting comes in an open-fronted box, like a padded boudoir, of which Barbie herself would be proud. The novelty lies not so much in the lamp, even though the zig-zag detail is striking, as in the unusual lengths that have been taken to make it a consumer product with the broadest possible appeal. One can imagine a shopper who knows nothing of Starck, or indeed of contemporary design, coming across a display of *Miss Sissi* lamps in a department store and immediately buying a couple on impulse.

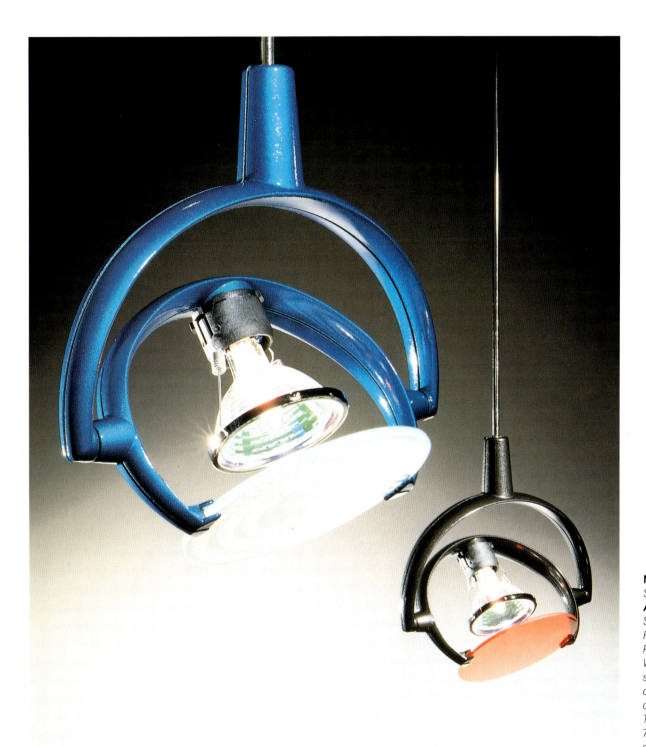

Matteo Thun
Spotlight,
Archetto Più
Stanyl of "DSM"
Ryton Phillips
Petroleum
With coloured or
silkscreen glass
diffuser and
directional lenses.
Takes one 35, 50 or
75W 12V bulb with
dichroic reflector.
H 12cm (4¾in)
W 10cm (4in)
Manufacturer:
Flight, Italy

2

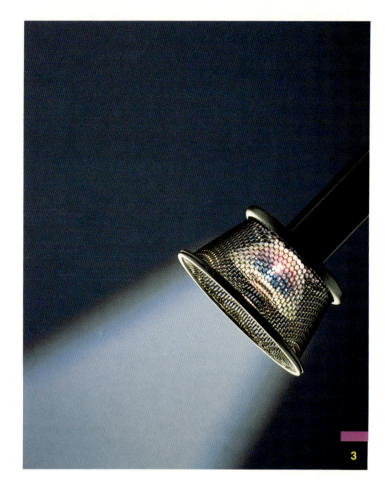

3

Sottsass Associati
Spotlight range
Aluminium
Takes low-voltage,
cool-beam dichroic
reflector bulbs.
H 30cm (11⅞in)
W 5cm (2in)
L 10cm (4in)
Manufacturer:
Zumtobel Lighting,
Italy

Spotlights are the one area of lighting design that least requires, and seems least to receive, a highly personal touch. In most cases the lamps will be used as a system rather than singly, and the main considerations are that they should be functional, readily adjustable and, given the size of their aerial presence, reasonably unobtrusive. High-tech, unsurprisingly, is the favoured look.

Sottsass Associati's new range for Zumtobel is far from retiring, however, and anyone familiar with the company's output will probably identify them immediately as Associati products. In contrast with other spotlight systems that make a virtue of lightness, the delicacy of the dichroic fittings is partially concealed, if not entirely overwhelmed, by heavy reflectors of straight-sided glass and thick-rimmed mesh; one is even square. These are ceremonial pieces which demand to be integrated into settings on their own terms. They enshrine the Associati's conviction that design is a search for "new and original metaphors" and a cultural task of the utmost importance to society. "Ours is an anthropological and linguistic operation," they say, "which aims to create not only new signs, but new messages."

3

3

Sigeaki Asahara
Spotlights,
S.A. Spot
*Aluminium, die-cast
aluminium, glass
Takes one 75W
halogen bulb.
D 12cm (4³/₄in)
Di 10.5cm (4¹/₈in)
Manufacturer:
Yamada Shomei,
Japan*

4

4

Hannes Wettstein
*Floor, table and
wall lamp,*
Soirée
*Satined metal,
silkscreened
polycarbonate
Takes one 60W
opaline bulb.
Floor:
H 160cm (63in)
W 12–34cm
(4¾–13⅜in)
Table:
H 28cm (11in)
W 12–34cm
(4¾–13⅜in)
Wall:
W 12–34cm
(4¾–13⅜in)
D 28cm (11in)
Manufacturer:
OLuce, Italy*

5

Leonardo Marelli
Wall bracket,
Model A-1161
Steel, hardwood
Takes one halogen
bulb.
H 32cm (12½in)
W 21cm (8¼in)
Manufacturer:
Estiluz, Spain

7

Massimo Sacconi
Spotlight,
Dese
(semi-recessed)
Technopolymers,
metal
Takes a single- or
double-ended 150W
metal halide bulb,
a high-pressure 50
and 150W sodium
bulb, a max 250W
halogen bulb or a
compact fluorescent
18W bulb, each
giving different
light intensities.
H 29cm (11⅜in)
Di 20cm (7⅞in)
Manufacturer:
Unione Plastiche,
Italy

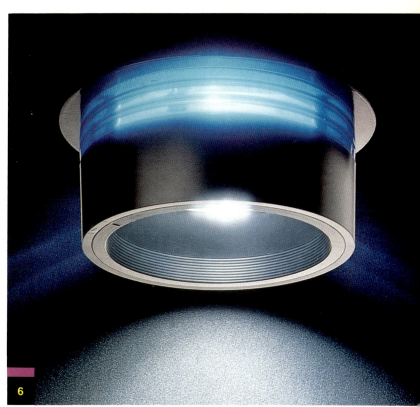

6

Masayuki Kurokawa

Lamp,
Ieris
Painted steel, milk-white glass
Takes one krypton bulb.
Left:
H 22cm (8⅝in)
Di 25cm (9⅞in)
Right:
H 31.7cm (12½in)
Di 36.3cm (14⅜in)

Archivio Storico

Floor lamp,
Zodiaco
Nickelled brass, blown glazed white milk glass
The diffuser is decorated with a silkscreen print of the signs of the zodiac.
Takes four 60W 220V filament bulbs.
H 210cm (82⅝in)
Di 64cm (25⅛in)
Manufacturer: FontanaArte, Italy

9

Prospero Rasulo

Wall lamp,
Alcea
Blown glazed glass, silver-lacquered metal
Takes one 150W incandescent bulb.
H 30cm (11⅞in)
W 19cm (7½in)
D 24cm (9⅜in)
Manufacturer: Foscarini Murano, Italy

8

Jorge Garcia Garay

Picture light,
Clipper
*Chromed iron,
anodized aluminium
Takes one 20W
compact fluorescent,
60 or 200W bulb.
W 42cm (16½in)
D 18cm (7⅛in)
Manufacturer:
Garcia Garay,
Spain*

Piero Castiglioni
Wall lamp,
Belem
*Steel
With a built-in
transformer.*

*Takes one dichroic
50W 12V bulb.
H 13.5cm (5⅜in)
W 13.5cm (5⅜in)
D 6cm (2⅜in)
Manufacturer:
FontanaArte, Italy*

12

13

Piero Castiglioni
Wall lamp,
Dicroshelve
*Brass, Pirex glass
sheet with sand-
blasted stripe and
opening*

*With a built-in
transformer.
Takes one dichroic
50W 12V bulb.
H 22cm (8⅝in)
W 11cm (4⅜in)
D 11cm (4⅜in)
Manufacturer:
FontanaArte, Italy*

Gae Aulenti and Piero Castiglioni
Wall or ceiling lamp,
Aldabra
Pressed glass, externally sanded and vacuum-treated with aurora borealis or aluminium finish Takes one non-reflecting 100W 220V bulb.
D 14cm (5½in)
Di 34cm (13⅜in)
Manufacturer: FontanaArte, Italy

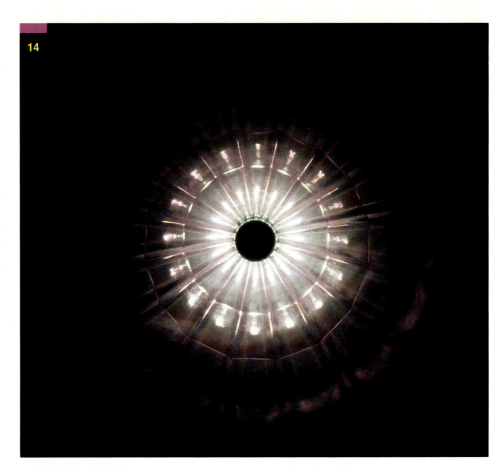

David Palterer
Wall or ceiling lamp,
Timete 43/53
Painted metal, sand-blasted diffuser Takes one 100W opaline or one 150W halogen bulb.
Left:
H 25cm (9⅞in)
Di 55cm (21¾in)
Right:
H 24cm (9⅜in)
Di 65cm (25⅝in)
Manufacturer: Artemide, Italy

16

Jorge Pensi
Wall light,
Farol
*Translucent plastic,
cast aluminium
Takes 80, 125,
250 or 400W
mercury vapour
components; 70,
100, 130 or 250W
high-pressure
sodium vapour
components; or
100, 250 or 400W
metal halogens.
H 67cm (26³⁄₈in)
W 46cm (18¹⁄₈in)
Manufacturer:
Santa-Cole
Ediciones de
Diseño, Spain*

Charlotte Packe
Table lamp,
Calyx
Farmed tulip wood,
gesso, gilt
Limited batch
production
Takes one max
60W candle bulb.
Left to right:
H 49cm (19¼in)

Di 14cm (5½in)
H 70cm (27½in)
Di 17cm (6⅝in)
H 79cm (31in)
Di 20cm (7⅞in)
Manufacturer:
Christopher Nevile
Design Partnership,
UK

Philippe Starck
Table lamp,
Miss Sissi
Plastic
Takes one 40W
bulb.
H 30cm (11⅞in)
Di 14.5cm (5¾in)
Manufacturer:
Flos, Italy

17

18

Daniela Puppa
Floor lamp,
Terra
Blown glass
Takes four 60W
220V filament
bulbs.
H 190cm (74⁷⁄₈in)
W 60cm (23¹⁄₂in)
D 27cm (10¹⁄₂in)
Manufacturer:
FontanaArte, Italy

Daniela Puppa
Table lamp,
Small
Transparent lexan,
nickel-plated brass,
blown glazed glass
Takes one spherical
60W 220V bulb in
the lampshade and

two tubular 15W
220V lamps in the
base.
H 40cm (15³⁄₄in)
W 29cm (11³⁄₈in)
D 10cm (4in)
Manufacturer:
FontanaArte, Italy

20

19

21

Christophe Pillet
Floor lamp,
Paris Dancing
(Sheherazade
lamp)
Solid mahogany,
opalescent

polyphane
Takes one 40W
bulb.
H 150cm (59in)
Di 32cm (12¹⁄₂in)
Manufacturer:
XO, France

Marco Zanuso
Table and floor lamps,
Olivella
*Stone or marble,
polycarbonate,
metal
Takes one 150W
incandescent bulb.
Table:
H 75cm (29½in)
Di 35cm (13¾in)
Floor:
H 160/120cm
(63/47¼in)
Di 35cm (13¾in)
Manufacturer:
Ultima Edizione,
Italy*

22

23

Jorge Pensi
Table lamp,
Lorea
*Metal, sanded
glass
Takes one 50W 12V
halogen bulb.
H 44cm (12in)
W 15cm (6in)
Manufacturer:
B. Lux, Spain*

23

Jorge Pensi's Toledo chair has
become an icon of the new Spanish
design, one of the handful of images
invariably called on to express the country's
creative vigour and new-found commercial
acumen. There is something of the same
spareness and bold definition of form in the
designer's new halogen lamp for B.Lux.
But while Toledo found such widespread
acclaim because it was the quintessence
of a type – the metal café chair – Lorea is
such a departure from our expectations of
what constitutes a table lamp, and so rich
in unexpected associations, that it seems
to aspire to the condition of table-top
sculpture. You might read its cylindrical

diffuser and dish as a church candleholder
or a torch, were it not for the flex that issues
from its base like a fuse and curves down to
a switch like a detonator, giving the lamp a
strangely ballistic air. Commercially, Lorea is
much too idiosyncratic to equal the impact
of Toledo. Artistically, it confirms Pensi as
a designer of imaginative daring, who lets
nothing go to waste.

24

Luigi Serafini
Table lamp,
Plumelia
Metal, silk,
Marabou feathers
Heat from the lamp
rises and moves
the feathers.
H 58cm (22⁷/₈in)
W 15cm (6in)
Manufacturer:
Edra, Italy

25

**Francesco
Castiglione Morelli**
Table lamp,
Afrodisia
Metal, glass
With dual-intensity   illumination.
adjustable light for   Takes one 20W 12V
reading or indirect   halogen bulb.
H 38cm (15in)
Di 14cm (5¹/₂in)
Manufacturer:
Artemide, Italy

Andrea Branzi
Table lamp,
Pavillon
Glass, metal
The stem
supporting the bulb
has three positions
providing different
sources of light.

Takes one 35W
bulb with dichroic
reflector.
H 44cm (17¼in)
Di of base 30cm
(11⅞in)
Manufacturer:
Arteluce, Italy

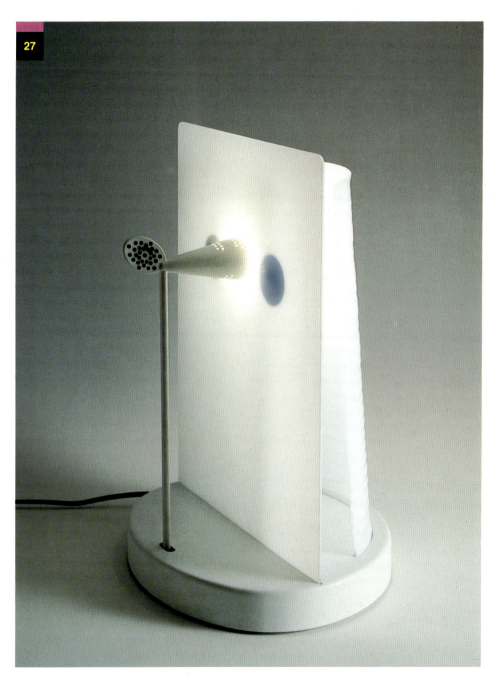

27

**Ingo Maurer and
team**
Wall sconce,
Zero One
White Corian,
frosted adjustable
mirror
Takes one 75W 230
or 125V halogen
bulb with protective
glass disc.
H 5cm (2in)
W 5cm (2in)
D 27cm (10½in)
Di of mirror 17cm
(6⅝in)
Manufacturer: Ingo
Maurer, Germany

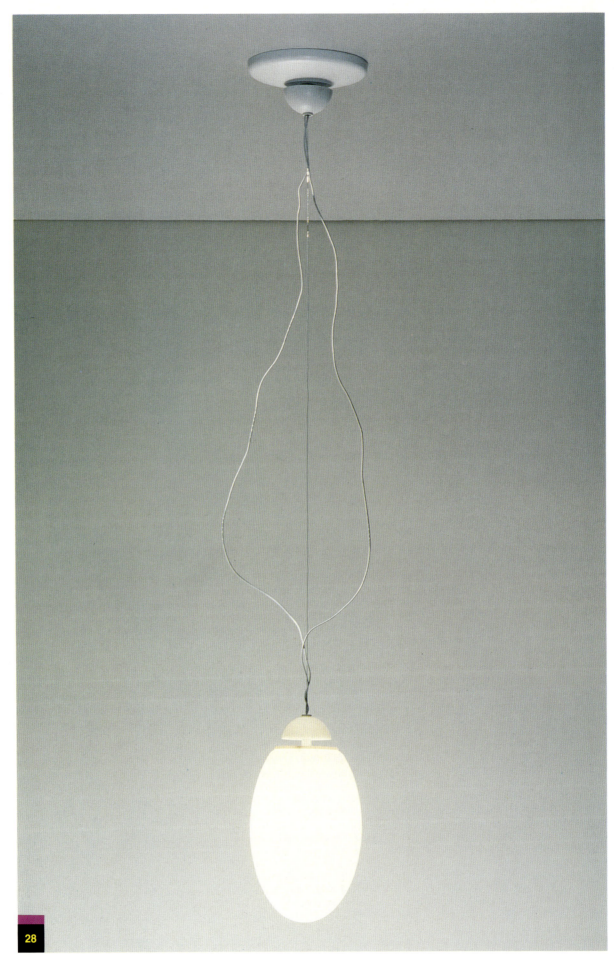

Achille Castiglioni
Pendant lamp,
Brera Sospensione
Blown glass
Takes one max
100W bulb.
Di 16.8cm (6½in)
Manufacturer:
Flos, Italy

28

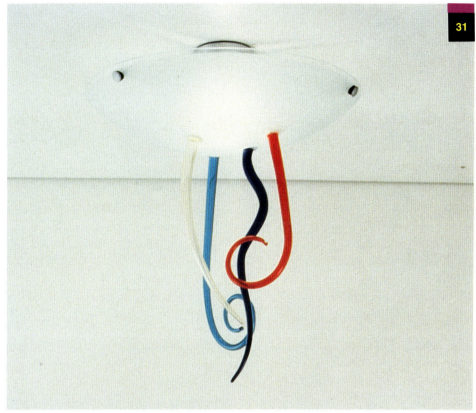

Andrea Anastasio
Ceiling lamp,
Efesto Plafoniera
*Painted metal,
blown multi-
coloured glass
Takes one 150W*

*opaline halogen
bulb or one 100W
opaline bulb.
H 60cm (23½in)
Di 51cm (20⅛in)
Manufacturer:
VeArt, Italy*

29

Andrea Anastasio
Suspended lamp,
Efesto Sospensione
*Painted metal,
chrome, blown
multi-coloured
glass
Takes one 150W*

*opaline halogen
bulb or one 100W
opaline bulb.
H min 115cm
(45¼in) max 170cm
(66⅞in)
Manufacturer:
VeArt, Italy*

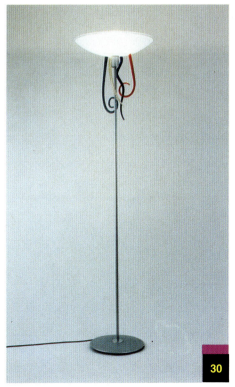

30

Andrea Anastasio
Floor lamp,
Efesto Terra
*Painted metal,
chrome, blown
multi-coloured
glass
Takes one 250W
opaline halogen
bulb.
H 190cm (74⅞in)
Di 51cm (20⅛in)
Manufacturer:
VeArt, Italy*

David Palterer *has made occasional appearances in* The International Design Yearbook, *but this edition sees the designer represented by some of his strongest conceptions to date. Palterer, an Israeli, is a partner with Bořek Šípek in Alterego (see page 140) and he shares Šípek's love of a quality that can only be described as poetic enchantment. These are pieces that reject everyday routine, that utterly despise the humdrum or ordinary. Like props from a play, they seem to demand that the life around them should be lived on a higher plane, at theatrical levels of intensity. For Driade, Palterer has used Murano glass to fashion a ceiling light, Borea, and a wall light, Boucher, with pipes clustering together like saxophones of melting crystal. Another ceiling lamp, Barine, a combination of glass, brass and copper, testifies to Palterer's feel for the way in which surfaces and textures interact. These are less feverish creations than Šípek's, without his sense of delirious invention, but they are no less assured for that.*

David Palterer
Wall lamp,
Boucher
*Murano glass,
brass
Includes 110VA
transformer.
Takes three 35W
12V halogen bulbs.
H 65cm (25⅝in)
Di 45cm (17¾in)
Manufacturer:
Driade, Italy*

David Palterer
Ceiling lamp,
Barine
*Glass, copper-
plated brass
Takes two
incandescent bulbs
for indirect lighting
and one halogen
bulb for direct
lighting.
H 45cm (17¾in)
Di 60cm (23½in)
Manufacturer:
Driade, Italy*

33

34

David Palterer
Ceiling lamp,
Borea 1
*Murano glass,
brass
Includes 450VA
transformer.
Takes eight 50W
and one 20W 12V
halogen bulbs.
H 140cm (55½in)
Di 50cm (19⅝in)
Manufacturer:
Driade, Italy*

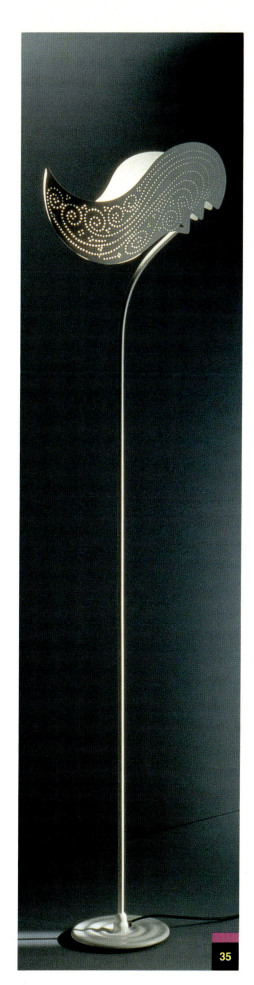

Riccardo Dalisi
Floor lamp,
Zèfiro 366
*Satined or matt
white lacquered
metal
Takes one max
300W halogen
bulb.
H 200cm (78¾in)
W 24cm (9⅜in)
L 52cm (20½in)
Manufacturer:
OLuce, Italy*

35

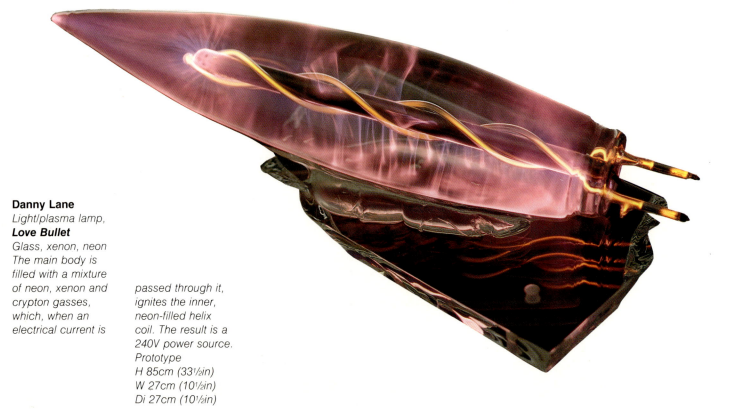

Danny Lane
Light/plasma lamp,
Love Bullet
*Glass, xenon, neon
The main body is
filled with a mixture
of neon, xenon and
crypton gasses,
which, when an
electrical current is*
*passed through it,
ignites the inner,
neon-filled helix
coil. The result is a
240V power source.
Prototype
H 85cm (33½in)
W 27cm (10½in)
Di 27cm (10½in)*

*T*he most interesting lamps in 1992
are those that play with the freedom
brought by lightweight electrical
fittings, while avoiding the now rather passé
temptation to emphasize technological
image above all else. New designs by
Danny Lane, **Ezio Didone** and **Karim
Azzabi** show their designers exulting in
outline, transparency and the lamp's
structural possibilities as a diffuser of light.
Lane's Love Bullet is a racy sculpture on the
theme of a light bulb in which a coil of neon
stands in for the filament; Didone's Papalla
is an adaptable, double-ended bulb like a
truncated barbell, which can lie on its side,
sit upright on a blown-glass stand, or lean
casually against it; and Azzabi's Elastic is a
collection of luridly radiant plastic inflatables
in a range of wriggling shapes. These lamps
may be the products of ''high'' design, but
none of them takes itself too seriously.

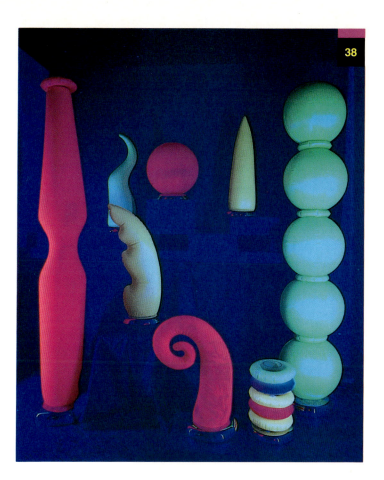

Karim Azzabi
Floor and table lamps,
Elastic
Aluminium, inflatable PVC
Floor lamps each take one 58W fluorescent bulb, table lamps take one 20W fluorescent bulb. Left to right:

Anfora:
H 164cm (64⁵⁄₈in)
W 30cm (11⁷⁄₈in)
Fiaccola:
H 65cm (25⁵⁄₈in)
W 22cm (8⁵⁄₈in)
Piuma:
H 65cm (25⁵⁄₈in)
W 22cm (8⁵⁄₈in)
Sfera:
H 30cm (11⁷⁄₈in)
W 22cm (8⁵⁄₈in)
Merlino:
H 65cm (25⁵⁄₈in)
W 22cm (8⁵⁄₈in)

Siluro:
H 65cm (25⁵⁄₈in)
W 22cm (8⁵⁄₈in)
Anelli:
H 30cm (11⁷⁄₈in)
W 22cm (8⁵⁄₈in)
Pallottoliere:
H 164cm (64⁵⁄₈in)
W 30cm (11⁷⁄₈in)
Manufacturer: Oceano Oltreluce, Italy

Ezio Didone
Table lamp,
Papalla
Blown glass, metal, plastic
Takes one 7W and one 11W fluorescent bulb.
H 35cm (13³⁄₄in)
Manufacturer: Arteluce, Italy

Ingo Maurer and team

39

Electronic transformer/dimmer,
Golden Nugget
Plastic
H 4cm (1½in)
W 10cm (4in)
L 15cm (6in)
Manufacturer: Ingo Maurer, Germany

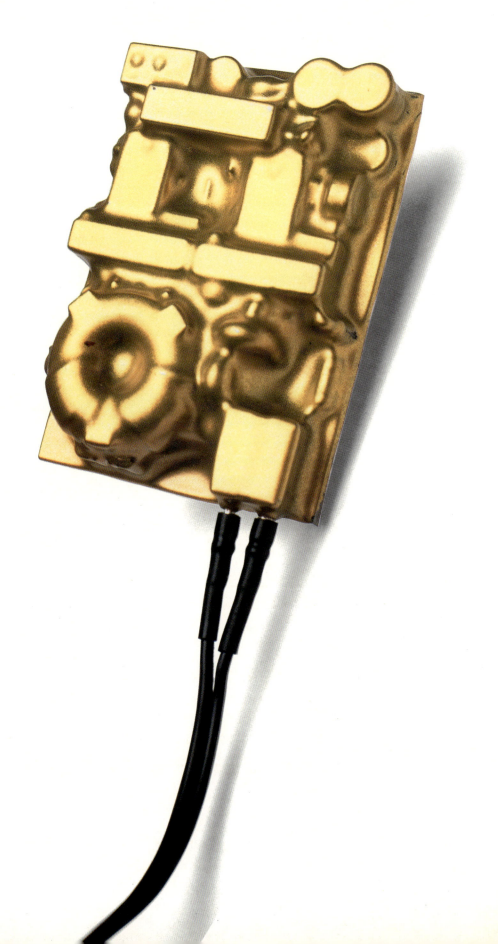

*I*n 1991, an American publisher which specializes in collections of graphic ephemera and commercial memorabilia brought out a book on toy ray guns, from the 1930s to the present. It made for an amusing, nostalgic browse, but it seemed unlikely that such goofy predictions could have much to teach designers in the 1990s. Their charm lay in the way in which naïve dreams of future technology have been overtaken by reality.

Yet, intentionally or not, it is toy ray guns such as these that **Philippe Starck**'s prototype for Flos's Doctor Life floor lamp most vividly evokes – in its gun-like profile and cartoonish phallic aggression, but above all, in the way that its crude aluminium mouldings appear to hug the shape of its interior components (a similar approach can be seen in Ingo Maurer's Golden Nugget transformer/dimmer). This is not "retro" design in the sense in which the cars and cameras designed by Water Studio in Tokyo are retro: an attempt to conjure up a past that never quite happened for jaded consumers who would much prefer to stay in the present. It is Starck's way of underlining the point that the miniaturization of lighting technology frees designers to create almost any image they choose for a lamp. Doctor Life has fun with this by housing new technology (a motor inside turns a coloured disk to project different coloured light) in what could have seemed a hopelessly outdated shell. The curious thing to anyone coming across this throwback for the first time in Milan was how fresh, and even avant-garde, it looked.

Philippe Starck
Floor lamp,
Doctor Life
*Aluminium, steel,
moulded and
etched glass,
cast iron
The top section
houses a motor
which turns the
coloured disc, and*
*a low-voltage
halogen bulb for
projecting the
colours.
Takes one max
300W and one
max 20W bulb.
H 197cm (77⅝in)
W 40cm (15¾in)
Manufacturer:
Flos, Italy*

Jiří Pelcl
Floor lamp,
Iris
Metal
One-off
Takes one 100W
bulb.
H 230cm (90½in)
Di 35cm (13¾in)

41

Marre Moerel
Chandelier,
Miss Universe
Stainless steel
One-off
Takes 13 15W
bulbs.
H 120cm (47¼in)
W 110cm (43⅜in)
D 30cm (11⅞in)
Manufacturer: Royal
College of Art, UK

**Ingo Maurer and
team**
*Floating light
sculpture,*
Flatterby
*Glass, plastic,
carbon fibre,
painted paper
(silver or*

*gold-plated)
Limited batch
production
Takes neon,
halogen bulbs and
incandescent tubes.
L up to 6m (237in)
Manufacturer: Ingo
Maurer, Germany*

43

44

Hironen
Lamp,
Bellissima
Steel, stained glass, brass
Prototype
Takes two 40W halogen bulbs.
H 180cm (70⅝in)
W 100cm (39½in)

H*ironen is a two-man design team formed in London in the mid-1980s. Ronen Levin, an Israeli, was studying at the Architectural Association and Hiroyuki Okawa had recently arrived from New York. Like other "salvage" designers of the time, they would cobble together bits of junk and scrap into objects for the interior, which they could sell at markets in Camden and the Portobello Road. Levin and Okawa were early beneficiaries of Japan's insatiable appetite for Western design and designers. The Seibu department store selected them for a "London Fair", featuring the work of Nigel Coates and others, and Hironen found themselves invited to stay. A stream of commissions for objects, interiors and exteriors has kept them in Tokyo ever since.*

Most of Hironen's work is jointly conceived, developed and credited, though occasionally one of the designers will go off on a tangent of his own. They want their work to be comfortable to live with and inviting to touch. "In the 1980s, design was very cool, sharp and solid, and excluded people," they say. "Everything was designed for the eye." Hironen's solution is organically inspired pieces with an unapologetically handmade look. Seen in one way, the Poko lamps bring to mind mushrooms nudging their way through the earth, while Bellissima has the lilt of a dancing plant. Yet there is also a darker, more disturbing quality, a kind of medieval futurism reminiscent of the brooding sets in David Lynch's science fiction film epic Dune.

Nick Crowe
Table lamp,
Electric Medusa
Brass, chemicals
Limited batch
production
Takes 15W "flicker"
bulbs.
H 40cm (15¾in)
W 40cm (15¾in)
D 40cm (15¾in)
Manufacturer: Nick
Crowe Design, UK

46

Hironen
Table lamp,
Poko
FRP, glass, gold
leaf
Prototype
Takes one 40W or
one 10W halogen
bulb.
Left:
H 33cm (13in)
Di 33cm (13in)
Right:
H 80cm (31½in)
Di 37cm (14½in)

45

TABLEWARE

1

**Anthony
Theakston**
Jug,
Bird
*Salt-glazed ceramic
Limited batch
production
H 25.5cm (10in)
W 20.3cm (8in)
Manufacturer:
Theakston
Ceramics, UK*

As with the previous *Yearbook* editor, Andrée Putman, tableware was an area of design which drew strong opinions from Bořek Šípek, and this is hardly surprising given his own commitment as a designer to the medium. In making his selection, Šípek was wary of designers who were concerned with surface patterning or texture at the expense of structure and shape. "It's decoration, not design," he said emphatically of a vase by Alessandro Mendini for Alessi, which a hundred designers had been asked to pattern, illustrate, or otherwise cover with motifs. Šípek rejected work that seemed too obviously bound up in an "arts and crafts" aesthetic. While his own designs have a highly ornamental quality, he insists that he is still a functionalist at heart. "I don't like things that are unfunctional," he says.

Yet this remains a selection in which the ornamental pieces – vases, bowls and candlesticks – considerably outnumber more prosaically useful types of tableware. Even the designs by a newcomer to this area, such as Massimo Iosa Ghini, and by regular tableware designer Philippe Starck, fall into the category of not strictly necessary ornament. If there *is* a trend here, it is one exemplified by Šípek and his colleagues in Alterego, David Palterer and Niek Zwartjes: great formal daring, breath-taking technical accomplishment, but the ever-present risk that, for some palates, a diet of such exotic

flavours will prove simply too strong to digest. As Šípek himself has sometimes observed, this is a kind of design which demands that the spectator comes down either for or against.

For quieter pleasures, turn to Oscar Tusquets Blanca, who has created glasses and a decanter of enormous elegance and refinement, or to the Danish silversmith Allan Scharff, who points out how "tiny nuances" can often be deployed to disproportionately large effect. And for signs that a younger generation of designers is capable of similar sensitivity, consider Alessio Pozzoli and Sam Ribet's oil and vinegar cruets for the Nuovo Bel Design project – the simple armature is perfectly judged in both looks and tone.

Vivianne Karlsson
Bowl,
Sarek black
Crystal
Limited batch
production
H 12.5cm (5in)
Di 28cm (11in)
Manufacturer:
Orrefors, Sweden

3

Vivianne Karlsson
Bowl,
Sarek blue
and white
Crystal
Limited batch
production
H 14cm (5½in)
Di 24.5cm (9⅝in)
Manufacturer:
Orrefors, Sweden

2

Guido Niest
Candleholder,
Pachanga
Extra strong silver-plated brass alloy
One-off
H 27cm (10½in)
Di 9cm (3½in)
Manufacturer:
Atelier Canaima,
Italy

5

**Giuliano
Malimpensa**
*Champagne bucket
Silver-plated brass
Limited batch
production
H 20cm (7⅞in)
Di 20cm (7⅞in)
Manufacturer:
Mesa, Italy*

Dieter Sieger
Vase,
Rose
*Glass
H 23cm (9in)
W 25cm (9⅞in)
Manufacturer:
Marsberger
Glaswerke
Ritzenhoff,
Germany*

6

**Massimo Iosa
Ghini**
Vase,
Diana
*Rose quartz,
rhodonite
Limited batch
production
H 5.5cm (2⅛in)
W 10cm (4in)
L 44cm (17¼in)
Manufacturer: Eva-
Maria Melchers,
Germany*

Olivier Gagnère
*Vase
Japanese porcelain
H 36.4cm (14⅜in)
Di 12cm (4¾in)
Manufacturer:
Galerie Maeght,
France*

8

9

Massimo Iosa Ghini
Vase,
Salome
*Silver, aventurine
Limited batch
production
H 40cm (15¾in)
Di 8cm (3⅛in)
Manufacturer: Eva-Maria Melchers,
Germany*

10

Marie-Christine Dorner
*Champagne bucket
Silver-plated metal
Limited batch
production
H 19cm (7½in)
W 22.5cm (8⅞in)
Di 17cm (6⅝in)
Manufacturer: Au
Bain Marie, France*

Wolf Karnagel
Water jug,
Agua
Stoneware
H 22cm (8⅝in)
W 9cm (3½in)
L 13cm (5⅛in)
Capacity .75 litre
Manufacturer:
Manufactura Toro
Ceramica Valencia,
Spain

11

Greg Daly
Vase
Porcelain clay,
lustres
One-off
H 33cm (13in)
W 35.5cm (14in)

13

Guglielmo Berchicci
Napkin ring
Aluminium
H 13cm (5⅛in)
W 18cm (7⅛in)
L 9cm (3½in)
Manufacturer:
Bar Metals, Italy

12

Lino Sabattini
Tea service,
New Angels
*Extra strong silver-
plated brass alloy*
One-off
Teapot:
H 15cm (6in)
Di 12.5cm (5in)
Sugar bowl:

H 8cm (3¹⁄₈in)
Di 9cm (3¹⁄₂in)
Cream jug:
H 7cm (2³⁄₄in)
Di 9.5cm (3³⁄₄in)
Manufacturer:
*Sabattini
Argenteria, Italy*

14

15

Lino Sabattini
Pot and tray,
New Angels
*Extra strong silver-
plated brass alloy*
One-off
*Teapot or water
pot:*
H 12cm (4³⁄₄in)
Di 12cm (4³⁄₄in)

Tray:
H 3cm (1¹⁄₈in)
Di 30cm (11⁷⁄₈in)
Manufacturer:
*Sabattini
Argenteria, Italy*

O ne day someone will write a study
of why at the end of the twentieth
century, in an increasingly secular
age, the traditional image of the angel
continues to supply artists and designers
with such a rich seam of inspiration. John
Hejduk, dean of the school of architecture
at the Cooper Union and a Vorwerk
collaborator, is one admirer of these
heavenly beings. Another is Paolo Pallucco,
the enigmatic designer who based an entire
collection of furniture on angelic themes for
one notorious launch in Milan (see The
International Design Yearbook 1989/90).
Now **Lino Sabattini**, a Yearbook regular for
his elegant silverware, has designed two
new collections, a pot and tray, and a tea
service, which he calls New Angels. And
true to their name, in place of conventional
handles, his pieces have long, silver-plated
wings – perkily raised in one case; sharp,
drooping and slightly sinister in the other –
to balance their equally exaggerated spouts.

**Masahiko
Uchiyama**
Ashtray,
Leaf
*Aluminium ladle,
lemon squeezer
and ball
Prototype
H 4cm (1½in)
W 13cm (5⅛in)
D 7cm (2¾in)
Manufacturer: Step
Design, Japan*

17

**Giancarlo
Montebello**
Serving spoons,
Alligators
*Silver
L 30cm (11⅞in)
Manufacturer:
Hop-Là, Italy*

16

18

Allan Scharff
Scent bottle and sculpture,
Falcon
Sterling silver, crystal
H 15.5cm (6¹⁄₈in)
Manufacturer: Royal Copenhagen, Denmark

20

**Alessio Pozzoli
and Sam Ribet**
*Oil and vinegar
cruets*
Steel, glass, plastic
Prototype
H 17cm (6⅝in)
W 22cm (8⅝in)
D 8cm (3⅛in)

19

William Sawaya
Carafe,
Le Diable en Tête
Silver
H 27cm (10½in)
Di 14cm (5½in)
Manufacturer:
Hop-Là, Italy

**Michal Froněk and
Jan Němeček**
Espresso cup,
Kalíšek
China
*Limited batch
production*
H 10cm (4in)
Di 7cm (2¾in)
Manufacturer:
*Epiag – Porcelan
Dalovice,
Czechoslovakia*

21

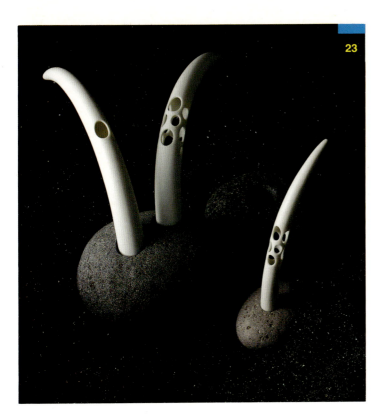

Makoto Komatsu
Vase,
Tsuno *from the*
Kaseki *series*
Natural stone,
porcelain
Limited batch
production

Left:
H 29cm (11³/₈in)
Di 2.5cm (1in)
Right:
H 18cm (7¹/₈in)
Di 1.5cm (⁵/₈in)
Manufacturer:
Makoto Komatsu,
Japan

Olivier Gagnère
Dish,
Petite Coupe
Carrée
Silver-plated and
hammered metal,
oak
H 14cm (5¹/₂in)
Di 15cm (6in)
Manufacturer:
Galerie Maeght,
France

22

Marcello Panza
Vase,
Carilla
Ceramic
Limited batch
production
H 19cm (7¹/₂in)
W 22cm (8⁵/₈in)
L 14cm (5¹/₂in)
Manufacturer:
Anthologie Quartett,
Germany

24

Andrea Branzi
Vases,
***"Amnesie e
Altri Luoghi"***
*collection
Turned and
brushed aluminium
Produced on
numerically
controlled lathes.
Limited edition of
50 signed pieces
Left to right:
Vase A 56:
H 44cm (17¼in)
Di 12cm (4¾in)*

*Vase A 38:
H 28cm (11in)
Di 14cm (5½in)
Vase A 28:
H 22cm (8⅝in)
Di 14cm (5½in)
Vase A 51:
H 40cm (15¾in)
Di 14cm (5½in)
Vase A 46:
H 34cm (13⅜in)
Di 15cm (6in)
Manufacturer:
Design Gallery
Milano, Italy*

25

27

**Pierangelo
Caramia**
*Salt and pepper
containers,*
Rio
*18/10 stainless
steel, wood
H 9.5cm (3¾in)
W 12.5cm (5in)
D 8cm (3⅛in)
Manufacturer:
Alessi, Italy*

26

**Oscar Tusquets
Blanca**
Crystalware,
Victoria
*Left to right:
Champagne flute:
H 23cm (9in)
Di 6.5cm (2½in)
Red wine glass:
H 20cm (7⅞in)
Di 9.3cm (3⅔in)
White wine glass:
H 17.7cm (6⅞in)
Di 7.4cm (2⅔in)
Water glass:*

*H 12.6cm (5in)
Di 7cm (2¾in)
Dessert wine glass:
H 16.5cm (6½in)
Di 6.2cm (2⅜in)
Liqueur glass:
H 13.7cm (5⅜in)
Di 5cm (2in)
Liqueur glass:
H 17.5cm (6⅞in)
Di 4.8cm (1⅞in)
Sherry glass:
H 15.5cm (6⅛in)
Di 5.2cm (2⅛in)
Manufacturer:
Driade, Italy*

Oscar Tusquets Blanca
Decanter,
Victoria
Crystal
H 33cm (13in)
Di 9cm (3½in)
Manufacturer:
Driade, Italy

Lharne Shaw
Bowl,
Prickly Descent
Lead crystal, glass
Limited batch
production
H 12.5cm (5in)
Di 33.5cm (13½in)
Manufacturer:
Tobias Associate
Design, UK

30

Bořek Šípek
Bowls,
Nos. 503 and 504
Lacquered wood
Limited batch
production
H 20cm (7⅞in)
Manufacturer:
Alterego, The
Netherlands

29

31

Bořek Šípek
Bowl,
Urushi-Arai, No. 1
Lacquered wood
Limited batch
production
H 50cm (19⅝in)
Manufacturer:
Alterego, The
Netherlands

32

David Palterer
Decanter, glasses
and vase
Crystal, cobalt
Limited batch
production
Decanter, **No. 602**:
H 35cm (13¾in)
W 15cm (6in)

Glasses, **Nos. 113A**
& **113B**:
H 9/15cm (3½/6in)
Vase, **No. 209**:
H 46cm (18⅛in)
Manufacturer:
Alterego, The
Netherlands

33

Since its formation in 1984 by Bořek Šípek and David Palterer, the Dutch company **Alterego** has established itself as one of the most inventive and, at times, startling manufacturers of glass, porcelain and ceramics. Working with the finest glass-blowers from Bohemia, porcelain makers from Czechoslovakia and potters from Delft, Alterego aims to create objects which bear witness not to the cold imprint of the production line, but to the irreplaceable skills and individual attention of the craftsman's hand.

The imagery that Šípek and Palterer favour as art directors of Alterego is overridingly organic. In some pieces it is as though the outcrops and growths which bud from the objects' surfaces are compromises between internal forces and the intentions of the shaping hand. Zwartjes's ceramic centrepiece No. 408 stands on caterpillar legs (see page 143); Palterer's cobalt and crystal vase No. 222 is tenderly treasured by plant-like stems of glass. There is nothing sentimental, though, about Alterego's approach to design. The company is just as likely to withdraw successful as unsuccessful pieces from its catalogue in a bid to spur new production. "The objects may well attract the eyes of many beholders," says Alterego. "They can't, however, fulfil the desires of many hands."

David Palterer
Vase,
No. 222
Crystal, cobalt
Limited batch
production
H 28cm (11in)
W 18cm (7⅛in)
Manufacturer:
Alterego, The
Netherlands

David Palterer
Vase,
No. 223
Amber, cobalt
Limited batch
production
H 32cm (12½in)
W 17cm (6⅝in)
Manufacturer:
Alterego, The
Netherlands

34

David Palterer
Centrepiece,
No. 411
Amber, cobalt
Limited batch
production
H 37cm (14½in)
W 38cm (15in)
Manufacturer:
Alterego, The
Netherlands

35

Niek Zwartjes
Vase,
No. 220
Glass
Limited batch
production
H 30cm (11⅞in)
W 15cm (6in)
with decoration
25cm (9⅞in)
Manufacturer:
Alterego, The
Netherlands

36

Niek Zwartjes
Centrepiece,
No. 408
Ceramic
Limited batch
production
H 10cm (4in)
W 35cm (13¾in)
Manufacturer:
Alterego, The
Netherlands

Niek Zwartjes
Beer glass,
No. 115
Glass
Limited batch
production
H 20cm (7⅞in)
W 10cm (4in)
Manufacturer:
Alterego, The
Netherlands

Niek Zwartjes
Centrepiece,
No. 410
Ceramic
Limited batch
production
H 30cm (11⅞in)
W 30cm (11⅞in)
Manufacturer:
Alterego, The
Netherlands

Radovan Hora
40

Water candle,
Descartes
Metal, mahogany
H 40cm (15¾in)
W 12cm (4¾in)
D 12cm (4¾in)
Manufacturer:
Dobro,
Czechoslovakia

Annalisa Cocco
Kernos
Wood, glass
H 9cm (3¹/₂in)
Di 45cm (17³/₄in)
Manufacturer:
Cappellini, Italy

42

41

Vít Lukas
Vase,
Vertu
Metal, teak
H 50cm (19⁵/₈in)
W 30cm (11⁷/₈in)
L 30cm (11⁷/₈in)
Manufacturer:
Dobro,
Czechoslovakia

3

Andrea Anastasio
Cheprer Glass
Blown glass
H 24cm (9³⁄₈in)
W 54cm (21¹⁄₄in)
Manufacturer:
Memphis, Italy

44

43

Andrea Anastasio
Vase,
Moribana
Blown glass
H 55cm (21³⁄₄in)
W 37cm (14¹⁄₂in)
Internal Di
10cm (4in)
Manufacturer:
Memphis, Italy

Andrea Anastasio
Vase,
Morimono
Blown glass
H 60cm (23¹⁄₂in)
Di 19cm (7¹⁄₂in)
Manufacturer:
46
Memphis, Italy

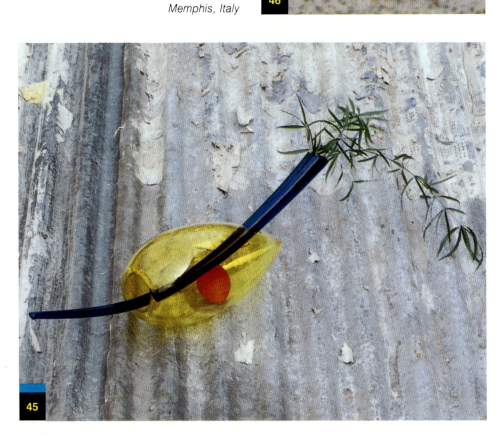

Andrea Anastasio
Vase,
Ikebana
Blown glass
H 14cm (5¹⁄₂in)
L 60cm (23¹⁄₂in)
Manufacturer:
45
Memphis, Italy

Andrea Anastasio
*Centrepiece/
candlestick,*
Bhakti and Mukti
*Blown glass
H 40cm (15¾in)
Di 8cm (3⅛in)
Manufacturer:
Hop-Là, Italy*

47

Some of the most striking new work
in glass design in 1992 came from
the hand of the Italian designer
Andrea Anastasio, who produced
collections for Memphis Extra and Hop-Là,
the new objects division of Sawaya &
Moroni. In contrast to the encrusted
ornamentation and baroque detailing of
Alterego, Anastasio favours smooth
surfaces (whether transparent or opaque),
uncomplicated outlines, and blocks of
strong, contrasting colour, frequently
primaries. Forms are reduced to a handful of
well-considered elements which play against
each other in a way that makes the objects
easy to read, and this enhances the sense
of gentleness and whimsy. Anastasio has a
particular liking for waving tendrils of glass,
which also feature in her jellyfish-like lamps
for VeArt (see page 111).

Bořek Šípek
Bowl,
Fafala-Ajeto
Glass
Limited batch
production
H 21cm (8¼in)
W 23cm (9in)
Di 20cm (7⅞in)
Manufacturer:
Alterego, The
Netherlands

50 **Bořek Šípek**
Bowl,
Šaral
Glass
Limited batch
production
H 28cm (11in)
W 18cm (7⅛in)
Manufacturer:
Alterego, The
Netherlands

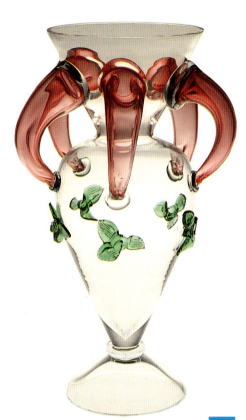

51

Bořek Šípek
Vase,
Ajeto
Glass
Limited batch
production
H 45cm (17¾in)
W 24cm (9¾in)
Di 19cm (7½in)
Manufacturer:
Alterego, The
Netherlands

Bořek Šípek
Vase,
Barkovsky-Ajeto
Glass
Limited batch
production
H 40cm (15¾in)
W 25cm (9⅞in)
Manufacturer:
Alterego, The
Netherlands

49

52

*N*ow in his mid-seventies, **Ettore Sottsass** *continues to generate new designs with prodigious energy. His latest collection, introduced during the 1992 Milan Furniture Fair, in the tiny but packed rooms of the Design Gallery on Via Manzoni, consisted of forty-seven pieces, ranging from vases in ceramics and blown glass, to monumental sideboards in plastic laminate, and ceremonial beds of haunting mysteriousness and beauty. Sottsass called his exhibition* Ruins, *and the bleakness of the title was reflected in a short statement in which he seemed almost to despair of explaining the meaning of his creations, or the forces that drive him. "I feel as if I had wandered deeper and deeper into an immense desert of ruins and everything I do, whatever project comes into my mind, seems to turn immediately into a ruin . . . a solitary presence whose reasons I understand less and less."*

It was a confession of personal estrangement that found only the subtlest of echoes in the objects themselves. As with a painting or sculpture, it was the title that often provided the most decisive clue to interpretation, as in the autobiographical vases Non Conoscerò *("Never Known to Me") and* E Così Facevo Cose *("So I Did Things"). A briarwood and gilded bronze vase,* Le Logiche *("Logic"), could perhaps be seen, with a little stretch of the imagination, as an antique tower, or the metaphorical "ruin" of some lost civilization, but in fabrication and finish its most pronounced characteristics are its solidity and strength. In an exhibition that recapitulated many of Sottsass's favourite themes, some pieces harked back to the bold colourations of Memphis, others to the more recent influence of India. All of them looked, pace Sottsass, as though they had been constructed to last.*

Ettore Sottsass
Vase,
Non Conoscerò
"Rosso di Francia"
and "bianco P"
marble, gilded
brass
H 76cm (30in)
W 40cm (15¾in)
D 40cm (15¾in)
Manufacturer:
Design Gallery
Milano, Italy

Ettore Sottsass
Vase,
Le Logiche
Natural briarwood,
gilded bronze,
marble
H 110cm (43³⁄₈in)
Di 60cm (23¹⁄₂in)
Manufacturer:
Design Gallery
Milano, Italy

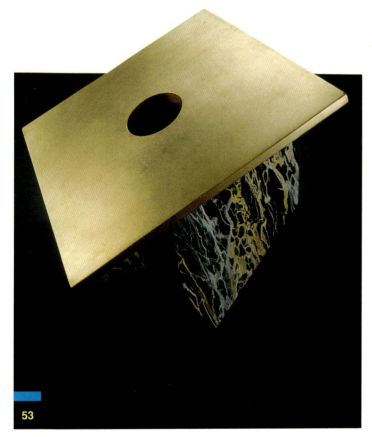

Ettore Sottsass
Vase,
***E Così Facevo
Cose (3)***
"Portoro" marble,
gilded bronze
H 45cm (17³⁄₄in)
W 50cm (19⁵⁄₈in)
D 50cm (19⁵⁄₈in)
Manufacturer:
Design Gallery
Milano, Italy

Ettore Sottsass
Vase,
Voglio Dire
Ceramic
H 44cm (17¹⁄₄in)
W 43cm (16⁷⁄₈in)
D 16cm (6¹⁄₂in)
Manufacturer:
Design Gallery
Milano, Italy

3

57

Philippe Starck
Vase,
Gilbert
Transparent crystal
H 48cm (18⅞in)
Di 26cm (10¼in)
Manufacturer:
Driade, Italy

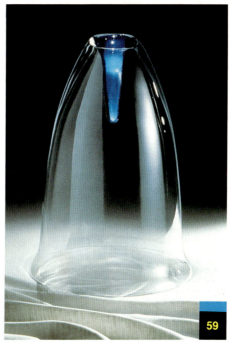

59

Philippe Starck
Vase,
Garnier
Transparent crystal
H 57cm (22⅜in)
Di 34cm (13⅜in)
Manufacturer:
Driade, Italy

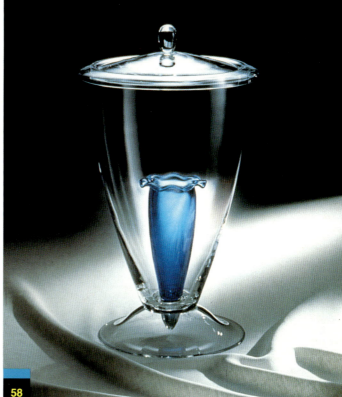

58

Danny Lane *(in
conjunction with
Daniele Minetto)
Drinking glass,*
Gingerino
*Stained glass, lead
came, silicon,
Gingerino bottles
Prototype
H 35cm (13¾in)
W 7cm (2¾in)
D 7cm (2¾in)*

Philippe Starck
Vase,
Gerome
*Transparent crystal
H 55cm (21¾in)
Di 35cm (13¾in)
Manufacturer:
Driade, Italy*

Bořek Šípek
*Salt and pepper
grinders,*
Savini
*Left to right:
Pepper mill
Porcelain, oak
L 22cm (8⅝in)
Di 3.5cm (1⅜in)
Small saltmill
Porcelain, oak*

61

*L 26cm (10¼in)
Di 5.5cm (2⅛in)
Pepper mill
Oak
H 23cm (9in)
W 5cm (2in)
L 6.5cm (2½in)
Large saltmill
Porcelain, ebony
L 33cm (13in)
Di 8cm (3⅛in)
Manufacturer:
Driade, Italy*

Bořek Šípek
*Oil and vinegar
cruets,*
Savini
*Left:
Oil cruet
Bohemian crystal,
amber, brass,
nickel-plated brass
L 34cm (13⅜in)
Di 10cm (4in)*

*Right:
Vinegar cruet
Bohemian crystal,
brass, nickel-plated
brass
L 36cm (14⅛in)
Di 8cm (3⅛in)
Manufacturer:
Driade, Italy*

60

Bořek Šípek
Vase,
Leonora
Bohemian crystal,
brass
H 56cm (22in)
Di 18cm (7⅛in)
Manufacturer:
Driade, Italy

Bořek Šípek's Savini collection for
Driade is so exotic in appearance
that it comes as a surprise to
discover that its purpose is simply to apply
condiments to food. On closer inspection,
the six pieces, which look like something
from the kit-bag of a medieval court jester,
are revealed to be two salt shakers, a
pepper shaker, a pepper mill (the least
abstract of the group) and cruets for oil
and vinegar. Is this a case, aesthetically
speaking, of using a hammer to crack open
(or salt) an egg – of burdening essentially
simple tasks with a weight of ritual they can
hardly be expected to support? The answer,
in both senses, is a matter of taste. As
always with Šípek, the pieces are an
invitation to look at routine actions in
unfamiliar ways and, at the very least, to
concede that there may be times when
social events deserve to be charged with
a much greater sense of occasion than
conventional tableware can supply.

TEXTILES

As in previous years, it is the Japanese who make the greatest impact in this year's selection. From the pioneers of an earlier generation, such as Junichi Arai and Hiroshi Awatsuji, still at the height of their powers, to younger talents like Koji Hamai and Yoshiki Hishinuma, these designers approach their task with a minimum of preconceptions about the way that a textile should look, or indeed how it should be made. Their designs set out to obliterate the sense of surface and where the material begins and ends, with non-repeat patterns and fields of abstract texture revealing only the barest traces of their figurative and usually natural origins. The boffins among them tinker restlessly with the composition of the fabric itself, with new kinds of fibre and innovative techniques. While European designers, such as Ulf Moritz and Finn Sködt, excel at conventional pattern-making, often with a strongly traditional basis (Sködt, for instance, has a fabric inspired by ornamental borders from the ancient books of Kells and Durrow), the Japanese are propelling textile design into the twenty-first century.

Fewer rugs were submitted for selection this year, but this is a field that Vorwerk, already well known for its three earlier *Dialog* carpet collections, has now entered with conviction. The company gave twenty architects and artists complete freedom to pursue their own vision, and the wildly divergent results, in a collection pitched somewhere in the hazy borderland between art and design, range from Coop Himmelblau's scratchy, almost autistic line drawings, to the exuberant paintbrush daubs of David Hockney. Yet even in this area of textile design there are those who prefer to look back. From New York comes a vibrant, though largely monochrome, hand-tufted rug on the theme of city traffic, created by Ken Cornet for Schumacher, which pulses with convincingly rendered Art Deco forms.

Yoshiki Hishinuma
Fabric,
Rose and Number
Polyester Jacquard
W 112cm (44⅛in)
Repeat 20cm
(7⅞in)

2

Yoshiki Hishinuma
Fabric,
Planet
Polypropylene
W 75cm (29½in)
Repeat 50cm
(19⅝in)

As textile designer and fashion
designer, **Yoshiki Hishinuma** is in
the unusual position of being the
first and most critical consumer of his own
fabrics. His first fashion collection, shown in
Paris in the spring of 1992, featured clothes
made from cassette tape woven into cloth,
vinyl, metallic net and Plexiglas. ''Material
is the keystone of my design,'' he told
American Elle. ''And since the choice of
material is so important, I try to develop it
myself.'' The Hishinuma designs shown here
are by no means as iconoclastic, but they
give a good sense of his unpredictability
and range. Rose and Number, a Jacquard,
is a peculiar Pop Art combination of floating
flowers and digits, while Planet is a transfer
print which can work on any polyester
material (here it is seen on coated paper).
Both suggest that Hishinuma's inspirations
lie as much in the synthetic textures and
energy of contemporary life as in the
traditional domain of nature, which he
also cites.

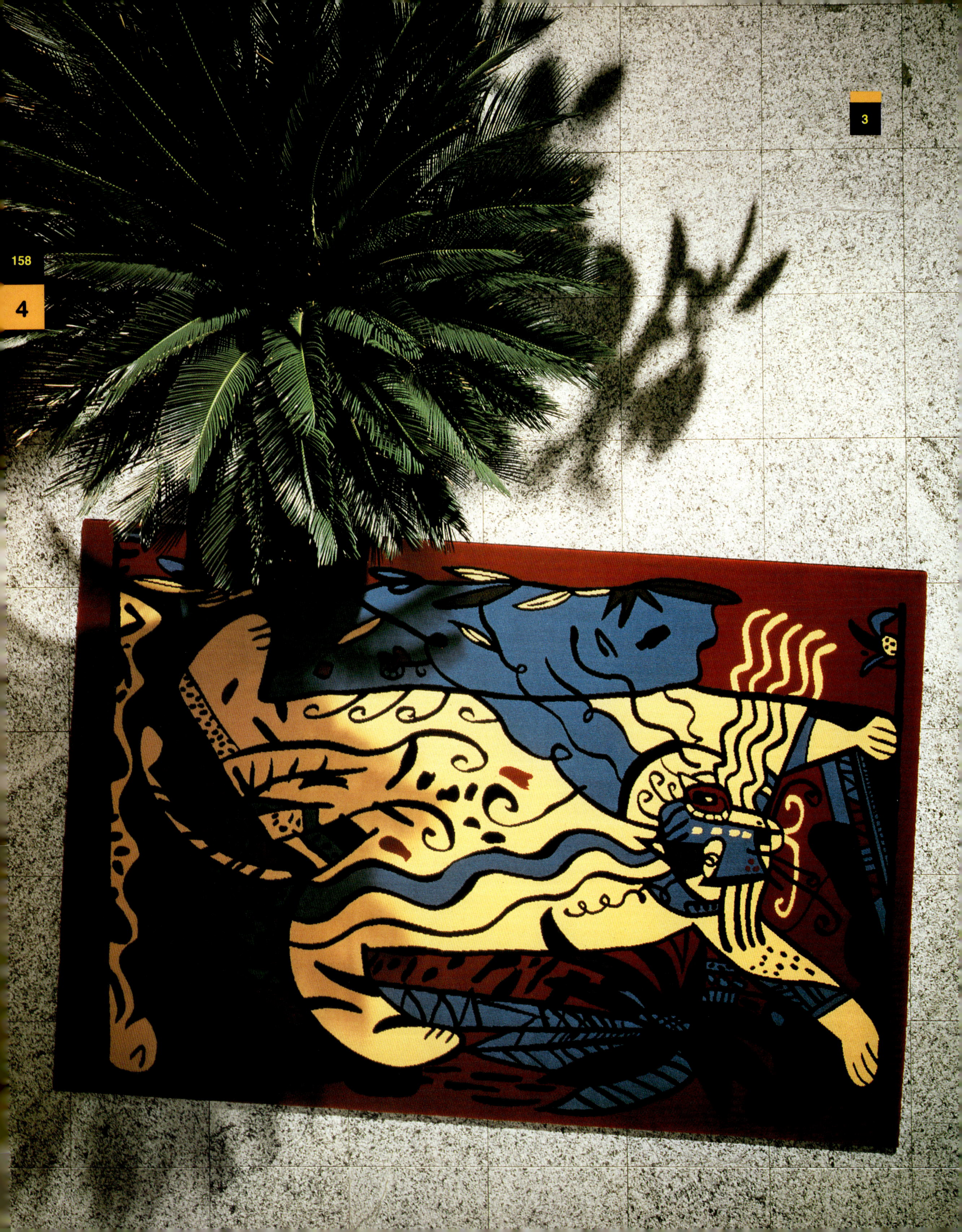

Javier Mariscal
Rug,
Arterior *collection*
Wool
W 200cm (78¾in)
L 300cm (118⅛in)
Manufacturer:
Vorwerk, Germany

Since 1988 when **Vorwerk** introduced its first range of carpets designed by architects and artists, its Dialog collections have become a regular event. With Arterior, the company readapts the original concept and turns its attention to rugs. Twenty artists and architects, including regular Vorwerk collaborators such as David Hockney, Sam Francis, Mimmo Paladino and Zaha Hadid, have created highly personal floorshows that make few, if any, concessions to the blandly decorative conventions of most floor-coverings.

Vorwerk's Dialogs have all featured heavily in The International Design Yearbook, but this year's guest editor, Bořek Šípek, was in two minds about including the company. The rugs are intriguing, but are they strictly speaking examples of design? There is nothing intrinsically "rug-like" about many of the images, or their means of generation. Sam Francis's spattered paint trails have been meticulously tufted in a way that positively denies their new medium: wool. Zaha Hadid's rug looks exactly like one of her architectural panoramas cast on to the floor. For Vorwerk, these freedoms are precisely the point. "Each of these 2 by 3 metre rugs conveys an individual artistic message created without making compromises and concessions solely on the basis of decorative requirements," says the company. Whether Arterior is described as design or applied art, the real status of the rugs is the same. These are industrial artefacts, not isolated one-offs, manufactured in quantities as large as the public will buy.

4

**Wolf Prix and
Helmut Swiczinsky**
Rug,
Arterior *collection*
Wool
W 200cm (78¾in)
L 300cm (118⅛in)
Manufacturer:
Vorwerk, Germany

Andreas Schulze
Rug,
Arterior *collection*
Wool
W 200cm (78¾in)
L 300cm (118⅛in)
Manufacturer:
Vorwerk, Germany

5

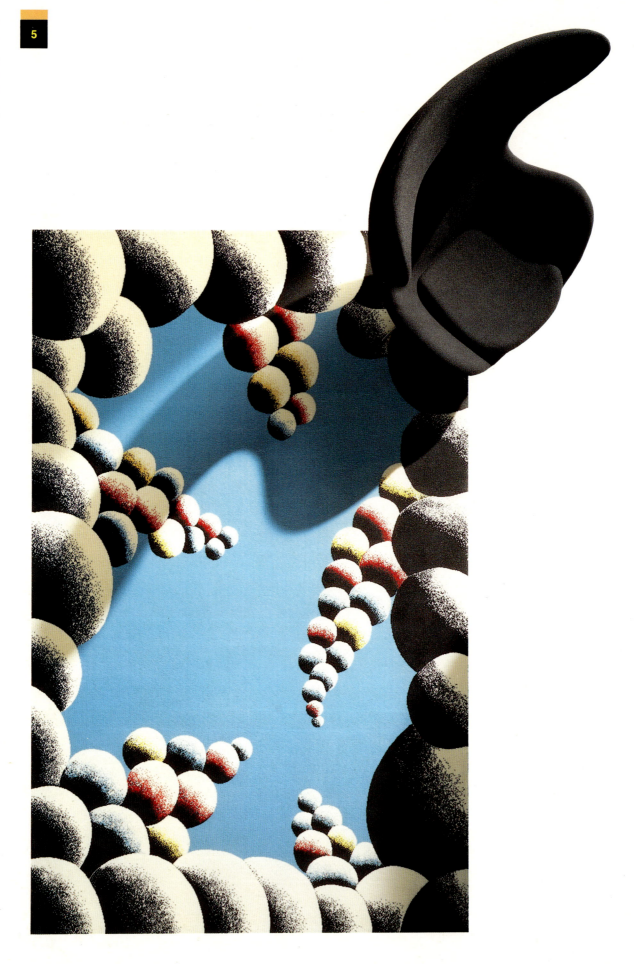

Richard Long
Rug,
Arterior *collection*
Wool
W 200cm (78¾in)
L 300cm (118⅛in)
Manufacturer:
Vorwerk, Germany

6

David Hockney
Rug,
Arterior *collection*
Wool
W 200cm (78¾in)
L 300cm (118⅛in)
Manufacturer:
Vorwerk, Germany

7

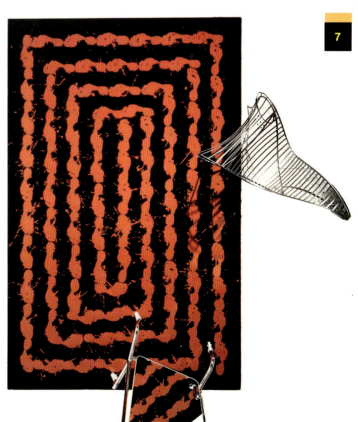

Jiří Dokoupil
Rug,
Arterior *collection*
Wool
W 200cm (78¾in)
L 300cm (118⅛in)
Manufacturer:
Vorwerk, Germany

9

8

Mimmo Paladino
Rug,
Arterior *collection*
Wool
W 200cm (78¾in)
L 300cm (118⅛in)
Manufacturer:
Vorwerk, Germany

10

Sam Francis
Rug,
Arterior *collection*
Wool
W 200cm (78¾in)
L 300cm (118⅛in)
Manufacturer:
Vorwerk, Germany

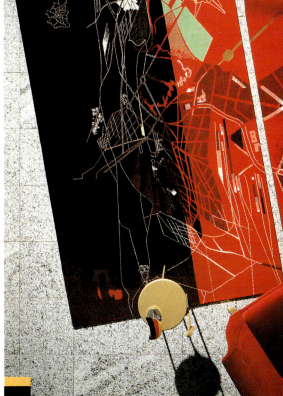

Zaha Hadid
Rug,
Arterior *collection*
Wool
W 200cm (78¾in)
L 300cm (118⅛in)
Manufacturer:
Vorwerk, Germany

11

Hiroshi Awatsuji
Fabric,
Ren
Cotton
W 132cm (52in)
Repeat 97cm
(38¼in)
Manufacturer:
Design House
AWA, Japan

12

Computers are transforming all areas
of design, including textiles, but
Hiroshi Awatsuji, *a pioneer of*
Japanese textile printing now in his sixties,
continues to draw and paint by hand.
Drawing, he says, remains the best way of
developing an idea into a usable motif.
Awatsuji is interested only in the surface of
the cloth, not its composition, and in how
space can be transformed by applied
pattern. He never uses his source images –
a flower, say, or a fish – in their entirety,
preferring to isolate a small detail in order to
allow ambiguity of interpretation. In Kei, a
recent printed cotton, the subject might be
grass, waves or even the wind. In Ren, the
seemingly abstract semi-circular motif is a
flower petal multiplied thousands of times.
Awatsuji uses pattern as a way of hiding
the material, allowing it to grow like a plant
over the surface of the cloth. The lack of
background helps to give the fabric greater
body and make it more three-dimensional.

Kouji Kikuchi
Fabric,
Transparent Cloth
*Wool (50%), nylon
(50%), sirofil yarn
One-off
W 150cm (59in)*

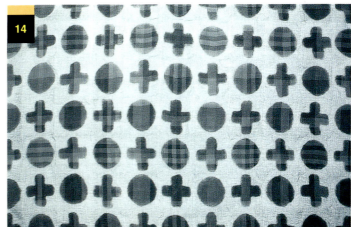

Hiroshi Awatsuji
Fabric,
Paido
*Cotton
W 135cm (53⅛in)
Manufacturer: Fujie
Textile, Japan*

Hiroshi Awatsuji
Fabric,
Kei
*Cotton
W 132cm (52in)
Repeat 116cm
(45⅝in)
Manufacturer:
Design House
AWA, Japan*

16

Kaori Maki
Fabric,
No. 3
*Cotton, rayon, gilt
and synthetic yarn
One-off
W 60cm (23½in)
L 250cm (98⅜in)
Manufacturer:
Maki Textile
Studio, Japan*

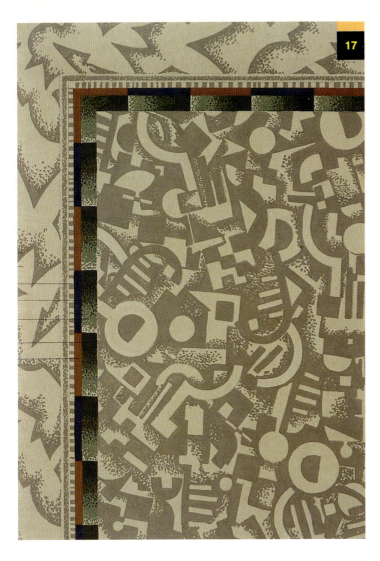

Ken Cornet
Rug,
Traffic
Hand-tufted wool
Prototype
Custom sizes
Manufacturer:
F. Schumacher, USA

Shirley Chang
Rug,
Opera
Wool
W 274cm (108in)
L 412cm (162in)
Manufacturer:
Edward Fields
Carpet Makers,
USA

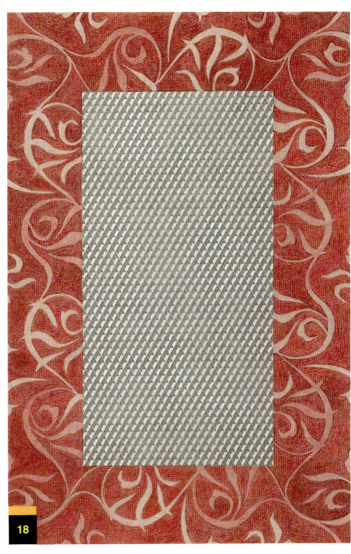

Koji Hamai
Fabric,
Ray Textile
100% polyester
W 100cm (39¹/₂in)
L 100cm (39¹/₂in)

19

Koji **Hamai** *sees himself more as a scientist than a craftsman. For Hamai, as for many other Japanese textile designers, new materials represent the greatest challenge. Hamai wants to overturn the way in which we think about the processes of weaving, knitting and dyeing cloth. His experiments with metals and chemical reactions are bold, typically Japanese, attempts to fuse technology and nature. "Perhaps," he says, "I am not so much a textile designer as a fabric designer." Hamai's creations break so radically with expectation as to be almost other-worldly. His* Combination Polyester *is a cloudy mass tangled with wriggling threads. With his* Crush Polyester, *Hamai's aim was to express the metallic vitality of bonito fish, though there is a wide gap, in this instance, between literal appearance and symbolic representation. Hamai crinkled black polyester at random, then crushed it repeatedly in a press at high temperatures with threads of stainless steel. Even after washing, the treated fabric retains its flinty, three-dimensional form.*

Koji Hamai
Fabric,
Crush Polyester
100% polyester
W 100cm (39½in)
L 100cm (39½in)

21

Koji Hamai
Fabric,
**Combination
Polyester**
100% polyester
Prototype
W 70cm (27½in)
L 70cm (27½in)

20

Junichi Arai
Fabric,
Seaspray
Polyester
Limited batch
production
W 80cm (31½in)
Manufacturer:
K. K. Arai Creation
System, Japan

22

23

Reiko Sudo
Fabric,
Stainless
Polyester
W 115cm (45¼in)
Manufacturer:
Nuno, Japan

Eiji Miyamoto
Scarf
Silk, polyurethane,
nylon
Limited batch
production
W 50cm (19⅝in)
L 180cm (70⅝in)
Manufacturer:
Miyashin, Japan

24

Eiji Miyamoto
Spacy Yarn Scarf
Silk
Limited batch
production
W 120cm (47¼in)
L 180cm (70⅝in)
Manufacturer:
Miyashin, Japan

25

27

Finn Sködt
Upholstery fabrics,
Durrow *and* **Kells**
100% wool worsted
W 144cm (56¾in)
Manufacturer:
Kvadrat, Denmark

Finn Sködt
Fabric,
Xanto
100% cotton satin
Limited batch
production
W 140cm (55⅛in)
Repeat 65cm
(25⅝in)
Manufacturer:
Kvadrat, Denmark

29

Ulf Moritz
Fabric,
Caprice
*21% silk, 14%
linen, 50% viscose,
15% acetate
W 140cm (55⅛in)
Manufacturer:
Sahco-Hesslein,
The Netherlands*

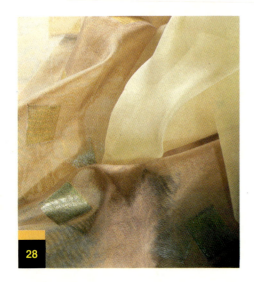

28

Ulf Moritz
Fabrics,
Carnival *and*
Fenice
Left, **Carnival***:
72% acetate, 22%
silk, 6% Lurex
W 150cm (59in)
Repeat 22cm
(8⅝in)
Manufacturer:
Sahco-Hesslein,
The Netherlands*

30

Ulf Moritz
Fabrics,
Fenice *and*
Myosotis
Top left, **Fenice***:
69% silk, 31%
acetate
W 150cm (59in)
Manufacturer:
Sahco-Hesslein,
The Netherlands*

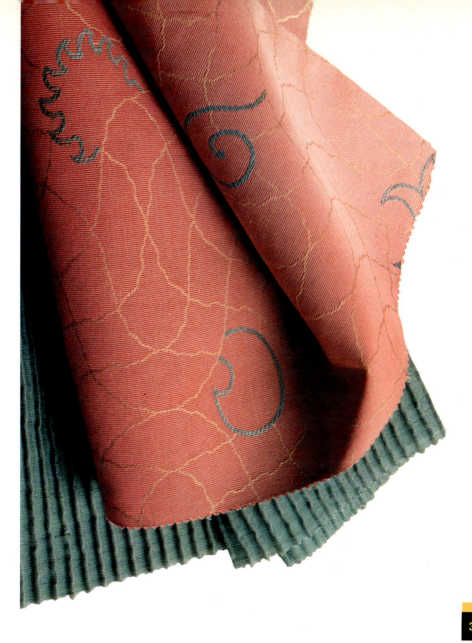

Ulf Moritz
Fabric,
Zenyta
*70% cotton, 30%
viscose*
W 140cm (55⅛in)
Repeat 32cm (13in)
*Manufacturer:
Sahco-Hesslein,
The Netherlands*

32

Ulf Moritz
Fabrics,
Myosotis *and*
Caprice
Left, ***Myosotis****:
70% cotton, 30%
viscose
W 140cm (55⅛in)
Repeat 6.5cm
(2½in)
Manufacturer:
Sahco-Hesslein,
The Netherlands*

31

Ulf Moritz
Fabrics,
Carmyna *and* **Lyra**
Cotton
W 140cm (55⅛in)
Repeat of
Carmyna *(left)*
32cm (13in)
Manufacturer:
Sahco-Hesslein,
The Netherlands

33

Ulf Moritz
Fabric,
Solana
Polyester
W 140cm (55⅛in)
Repeat 130cm
(51in)
Manufacturer:
Sahco-Hesslein,
The Netherlands

34

35 **Leonne Hendriksen**
Napkin,
Peony
Linen, organza silk
Prototype
Two squares of
W 50cm (19⅝in)
L 50cm (19⅝in)
Manufacturer:
Alterego, The
Netherlands

35

Maddalena De Padova
Range of bedroom
textiles
100% cotton
Pillow cases:
W 30/50cm
(11⅞/19⅝in)
L 40/80cm

(15¾/31½in)
Sheet & quilted bed
cover:
W 230cm (90½in)
L 240cm (94½in)
Manufacturer:
e De Padova, Italy

36

The German manufacturer **Rasch** can claim one of the most prestigious histories in modern wallpaper design. In 1928, it was involved in the development of the Bauhaus wall-coverings in association with the Dessau Bauhaus and went on to produce a collection in 1930 which is now seen as a landmark of the medium. Zeitwände, the company's latest collection, shows its continuing commitment to design of the highest quality, with papers by Alessandro Mendini, Ginbande, Berghof/Landes/Rang and a predominance of former Memphis stars: Ettore Sottsass, George Sowden, Nathalie du Pasquier and Matheo Thun. The quality which most obviously unites these designs is their gentleness and restraint. Mendini's columnar motifs are graphically assertive (though soothingly coloured), but most of the designers treat the paper deferentially as a textured backdrop or tint, a way of colouring the atmosphere of an interior rather than dominating its mood. This quality is brought out by Rasch's photographs, in which the designs are shot against architectural settings of decaying splendour. There are eleven designs in all, available in a total of twenty-eight colours.

37

Ettore Sottsass
Wallpaper,
Ercolano
*Limited batch
production
H 6cm (2³⁄₈in)
W 53cm (20⁷⁄₈in)
L 300cm (118¹⁄₈in)
Manufacturer:
Rasch, Germany*

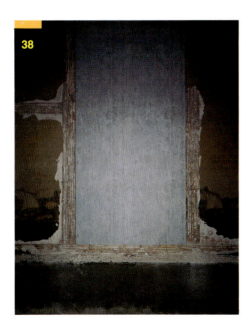

Alessandro Mendini
Wallpaper,
Colonna
Limited batch production
W 53cm (20⅞in)
L 300cm (118⅛in)
Manufacturer:
Rasch, Germany

Ginbande Design
Wallpaper,
B "100"
Limited batch production
W 53cm (20⅞in)
L 1005cm (396in)
Manufacturer:
Rasch, Germany

**Norbert Berghof,
Michael Landes
and Wolfgang
Rang**
Border,
Fries oder Stirb
Paper
Limited batch production
W 26cm (10¼in)
L 1000cm (394in)
Manufacturer:
Rasch, Germany

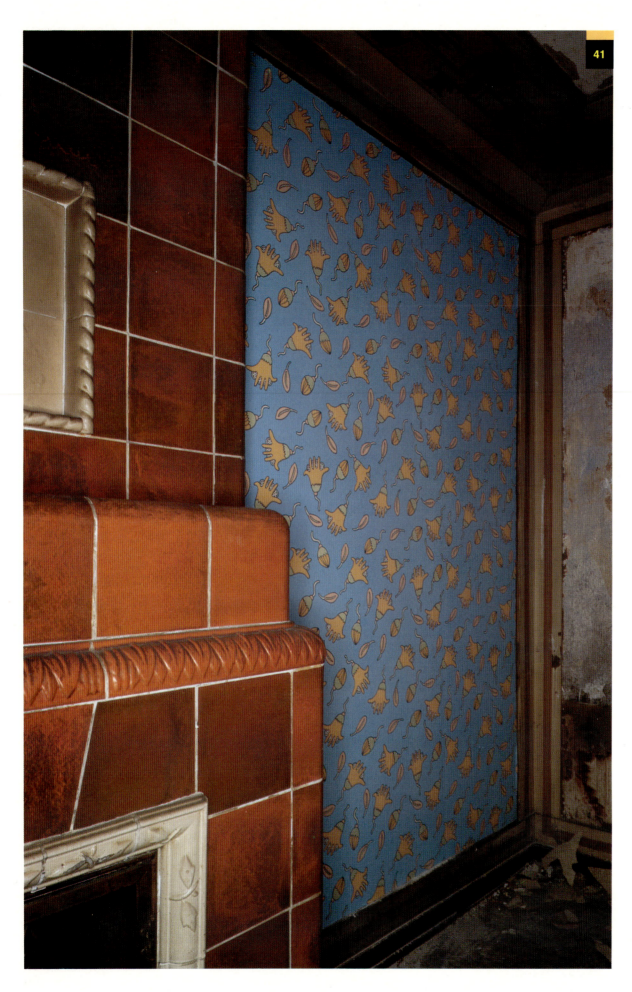

41

Nathalie du Pasquier
Wallpaper,
Piacenza
*Limited batch
production*
W 53cm (20⁷⁄₈in)
L 1005cm (396in)
*Manufacturer:
Rasch, Germany*

Ettore Sottsass
Wallpaper,
Arabia Felix
*Limited batch
production
W 53cm (20⅞in)
L 300cm (118⅛in)
Manufacturer:
Rasch, Germany*

43

George Sowden
Wallpaper,
Mention
*Limited batch
production
W 53cm (20⅞in)
L 1005cm (396in)
Manufacturer:
Rasch, Germany*

42

PRODUCTS

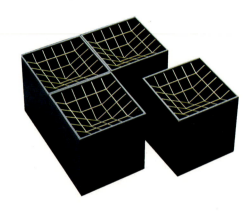

**Antonio Tena and
Vicenç Mutgé**
Ashtray,
Rusc
*Stainless steel,
black Bakelite,
wood
H 9cm (3½in)
W 9cm (3½in)
Manufacturer:
Bd. Ediciones de
Diseño, Spain*

How many new designs of television and telephone does the world actually need? This subversive question – not, perhaps, one that might be expected to arise in a yearbook of design – was posed by Bořek Šípek some way into the selection of products. He was plainly impatient with the infinitesimal styling adjustments and insignificant technical improvements that pass for innovation in the design of cameras, televisions and hi-fi, when in reality their main effect is to keep the customer in a state of dissatisfaction and longing for more. "It is always the same," Šípek observed. "The round corners. There are very few inventions."

In truth, genuine, mould-breaking invention is rare. Few products redefine our conception of the way in which a familiar technology might be contained, transported or applied as boldly as Emilio Ambasz's *Handkerchief TV*. Fewer still combine superb technical innovation with a brilliantly researched design to create an entirely novel device with the life-enhancing potential of IDEO's wearable heart support system for patients awaiting heart surgery.

At a less elevated level, though, many of these products hope to make small but useful enhancements to the texture of our lives, and this is a wholly honourable ambition for design. For the international

traveller, there are 4-inch screen portable televisions from Toshiba and Philips, which can be used anywhere in the world; for the home hair stylist, there is Studio De Lucchi's *Mist Blo* hairdryer, with a liquid spray attachment for water and gel; and for the shaver, there is Winfried Scheuer's pleasingly resolved shaving brush set, with a niche in the handle for the blade.

Bořek Šípek has also selected a number of objects which overlay their practical purpose with an ornamental flourish. Among the most striking is Dan Friedman's *Balbec* wall mirror for Driade, deftly fractured by the designer into a Cubist composition of angles and planes. For the makers of electronic consumer goods there is a lesson in formal ingenuity here which, despite the experimental projects of the 1980s from Memphis to the New British Design, is still all too infrequently applied.

Masanori Umeda
Soap tray
Aluminium, acrylic
resin
H 2.5cm (1in)
W 14.5cm (5¾in)
D 11.5cm (4½in)
Manufacturer:
Uchino, Japan

3

Kyushu Matsushita Electric Co. Ltd
Personal Fax
KX-PW1
ABS, plastic

H 11.2cm (4½in)
W 32.6cm (12¾in)
D 23.2cm (9⅜in)
Manufacturer:
Kyushu Matsushita
Electric, Japan

*A*lthough fax machines have had a huge impact on the way we go about business, they have never been much to look at. The typical fax machine, whether designed for offices in the city or home, looks at best acceptably functional – and at worst, plain clumsy.
Matsushita's Personal Fax KX-PW1 suggests that a new wave of more attractively styled machines could soon be upon us. It also suggests that the Japanese electronics corporations, having largely saturated the businesses of the developed world with faxes, are now looking for ways to turn the technology into a regular household consumer purchase, alongside telephones, hi-fi, cameras and video. To this end, Matsushita's sales literature is full of pictures of grinning schoolboys with Personal Faxes tucked under their arms, while the PW1 logo has a pronounced chalk-on-blackboard quality. But even if the machine is being marketed at this point as a costly toy for the precocious youngster, its smoothly drawn lines and low triangular profile represent a welcome improvement, both ergonomically and aesthetically, on the average fax.

Ninaber/Peters/
Krouwel
Folding key set,
Futuro
Blackened steel,
injection-moulded
plastic

H 4cm (1½in)
W 2.5cm (1in)
L 12cm (4¾in)
Manufacturer:
Beargrip Tool,
The Netherlands

4

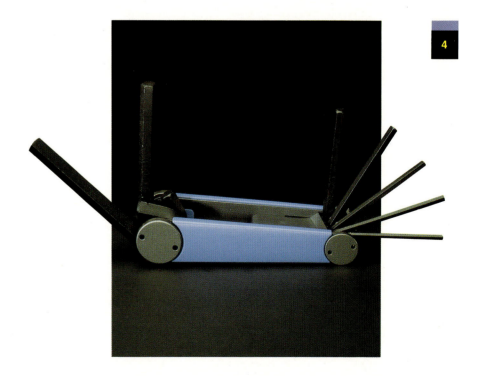

**Ninaber/Peters/
Krouwel**   6

*Ruler
Plastics
W 2.1cm (⁷⁄₈in)
L 35cm (13³⁄₄in)
Manufacturer:
Randstad
Uitzendbureau,
The Netherlands*

**Ninaber/Peters/
Krouwel**

*Paperclip holder
Plastics
H 4.8cm (1⁷⁄₈in)
Di 9.2cm (3⁵⁄₈in)
Manufacturer:
Randstad
Uitzendbureau,
The Netherlands*

7

Geoff Hollington
Pen,
Parker Insignia
*Brass, stainless
steel
L 13.2cm (5¹⁄₈in)
Di 0.8cm (¹⁄₄in)
Manufacturer:
Parker Pen, UK*

5

David Harris,
Mark Dziersk and
Tim Repp
Audiovox
Transmitters
High volume ABS,
polycarbonate
W 4cm (1½in)
L 5.7cm (2¼in)
Manufacturer:
Audiovox, USA

Ninaber/Peters/Krouwel *is one of*
The Netherlands' best established
younger industrial design
consultancies. The company's aim is to
achieve a harmonious bond between the
aesthetics of a design and its technical
potential, a philosophy which places the trio
in a direct line of descent from the Bauhaus.
Inspired by the simplicity and logic of
organic structures, they aim for a similar
clarity in their projects, which range from
medical technology to lighting systems to
paperclip holders. A new water bottle for
cyclists, the Hopper, is a good example
of their ability to rethink a problem and
come up with a more practical solution in
an area which may previously have been
overlooked. Its innovations include a
retractable nozzle, a broad grip and a lid
that can be removed to allow cleaning –
mould caused by stubborn particles of
liquefied food is a perennial problem with
bottles of this kind. The Hopper will fit
into a standard bicycle bottle cage, but
undoubtedly looks best with its own Clip, a
small, rigid bottle-holder.

Ninaber/Peters/
Krouwel
Water bottle,
Hopper
Blow-injected
plastics
H 25cm (9⅞in)
Di 7cm (2¾in)
Manufacturer:
Technische
Industrie Tacx,
The Netherlands

10

Puls Design
Toaster,
Delta 51
Metal, plastic
H 19cm (7½in)
W 12.5cm (5in)
L 21cm (8¼in)
Manufacturer:
Cuisinarts, USA

Winfried Scheuer
Shaving set,
London
*Zinc die-casting
Brush:
H 10cm (4in)
Razor:
L 10.5cm (4¹/₈in)
Manufacturer:
Merkur Solingen,
Germany*

11

Dieter Sieger
Wash basin,
Guilia
Ceramics, wood,
steel
H 85cm (33½in)
W 49cm (19¼in)
Di 57cm (22⅜in)
Manufacturer:
Duravit, Germany

12

14

Dieter Sieger
Waterflow heater,
DHE
Plastic
H 47cm (18½in)
W 20cm (7⅞in)
D 15cm (6in)
Manufacturer:
Stiebel Eltron,
Germany

13

Roberto Marcatti
Tile inlay work,
Halley
Marble
W 30cm (11⅞in)
L 30cm (11⅞in)
Manufacturer:
Up & Up, Italy

15

Christoph Seyferth
Box,
Wandschrank SC3
*Ebonized oak,
white maple
H 20cm (7⅞in)
W 20cm (7⅞in)
D 45cm (17¾in)
Manufacturer: Franz
Schatzl Design
Werkstätte, Austria*

Niek Zwartjes
*Photograph
frame/vase,*
Number 406
*Nickel-plated brass,
mirror
H 50cm (19⁵/₈in)
W 15cm (6in)
Manufacturer:
Alterego, The
Netherlands*

16

17

Christoph Seyferth
Box,
Schlüsselschrank SC7
*American walnut,
white maple
H 36cm (14¹/₈in)
W 27cm (10¹/₂in)
D 20cm (7⁷/₈in)
Manufacturer: Franz
Schatzl Design
Werkstätte, Austria*

18 **Pentax Industrial Design**
Camera,
Pentax zoom 90WR
Polycarbonate
H 7.6cm (3in)
W 14.9cm (5¾in)
D 6.4cm (2½in)
Manufacturer:
Asahi Optical
Company, Japan

Theo Williams
Child's toy camera
Medium impact
ABS plastic
Prototype
H 16.5cm (6½in)
W 7.6cm (3in)
L 20.4cm (8½in)
Manufacturer:
Domus Design
Agency, Italy

19

20

**Pentax Industrial
Design**
Camera,
Pentax Z-1
Polycarbonate,
aluminium

H 9.6cm (3¾in)
W 15.2cm (6in)
D 7.4cm (3in)
Manufacturer:
Asahi Optical
Company, Japan

Chifuyu Tanaka
*8mm video
camcorder,*
Canon UC-10
*ABS plastic
H 13.9cm (5³/₈in)
W 7.9cm (3¹/₈in)
D 16.1cm (6¹/₂in)
Manufacturer:
Canon, Japan*

22

**Yoshifumi
Ishikawa**
*8mm video
camcorder,*
EX-1 Hi
*ABS plastic
H 16.5cm (6¹/₂in)
W 17cm (6⁵/₈in)
D 23.7cm (9³/₈in)
Manufacturer:
Canon, Japan*

21

Bernd Reibl
*Digital projection
system,*
Cyclop
*Plastic
Prototype
H 60cm (23½in)
W 40cm (15¾in)
L 50cm (19⅝in)*

23

Multimedia has become one of the
buzzwords of the early 1990s.
It encapsulates a dream of
seamlessly integrated media that is fast
becoming a reality. **Bernd Reibl**'s prototype
for the Cyclop projection system looks back
to earlier pre-computerized approaches to
multimedia, as typified by the audio-visual
slide-shows that remain a standard feature
of commercial presentations, but combines
them with the enhanced power of digital
technology. Its processor allows both text
and imagery to be projected at large sizes
in a quality twice as good as high-definition
television. The facility to channel two images
through a single collapsible lens or ''eye''
(hence the product's name) means that it is
possible to overlay text and video, text and
graphics, computerized animation and
video, or to devise any other combination
that the user's message demands. The
system is intended for use in schools,
universities, company presentations and
multimedia shows.

23

25

Philips Corporate Industrial Design
Portable liquid crystal display colour TV
Toughlon plastic
H 5.5cm (2¹⁄₈in)
W 14.3cm (5⁵⁄₈in)
D 12.7cm (5in)
Manufacturer:
Philips International,
The Netherlands

Satoko Ito
4-inch liquid crystal display colour TV,
LX410 Multi Top
Plastics, punched metal
H 5.5cm (2¹⁄₈in)
W 17.5cm (6⁷⁄₈in)
D 13.6cm (5³⁄₈in)
Manufacturer:
Toshiba Corporation, Japan

24

GK Design Group
CD player,
GT-CD1
Plastic
H 16cm (6½in)
W 43.5cm (17⅛in)
D 40cm (15¾in)
Manufacturer:
Yamaha
Corporation, Japan

26

Controversial from its inception, the compact disc has transformed the purchase and packaging of sound recordings; but despite the audio revolution it has initiated, CD players still tend to look exactly like any other item of hi-fi hardware – in a word, dull. Tokyo-based **GK Design Group**'s aim in designing the GT-CD1 for Yamaha was to produce nothing less than the "Rolls-Royce" of CD players. The result is a machine for the audiophile who wants everything, with a price tag to match, roughly ten times that of a standard CD player. GK chose to treat the player more as an item of high-quality furniture than as a piece of audio equipment. The machine is handmade in aluminium and glass surmounted by a slab of solid walnut, giving it a top-heavy body weight of 24 kilograms. The usual remote control is supplied, but users of the GT-CD1 are expected to want to touch a machine this tactile and to savour at first-hand the "ceremony" of the moment. And the meaning of the "GT"? Only a Japanese copy-writer fluent in the hybrid language of "Japlish" could have dreamt it up: "Gigantic-Tremendous"

*I*n his book Industrial Design, *Raymond Loewy* included a chart showing how, over the course of time, industrial artefacts become simpler, sleeker and increasingly streamlined. One of the examples, alongside cars, trains and women's footwear, was the telephone. The final drawing, with a question mark next to it to indicate uncertain date, seemed to imply that the phone of the future, in profile at least, would most resemble a hubcap. We know now that Loewy did not go nearly far enough. The hand-held telephone receiver is one of those archetypal industrial forms that has developed about as far as it can go if it is to remain a recognizable – or for that matter, easily usable – member of the genus "telephone". Its limits are defined by the shape of the human face.

Some of the most challenging contemporary designs, such as those by Lisa Krohn or Eric Chan, retain a face-fitting curve, though most other details are suppressed. Others go all the way and reduce the receiver to an undeviatingly straight-sided wafer. One such appliance, shown in last year's International Design Yearbook, was **Hedda Beese**'s T410/T415 for the German company Bosse. Much of the phone's interest lay in the way that Beese had related the receiver to its resting place, which doubled as a speaker – it is here and in the rest of the hardware (if there is any) that designers have the greatest scope for invention. Beese's latest phone for the company, the T315, sees the idea taken a step further, with the two elements connected only by an umbilical cable. The elegantly flared receiver comes with a speaker like a miniature piece of hi-fi, which allows users both to talk and to listen, while working at other tasks with their hands.

27

Hedda Beese
*Compact
telephone,*
T 315
*ABS plastic
H 3.8cm (1³⁄₈in)
W 7cm (2³⁄₄in)
L 24cm (9³⁄₈in)
Manufacturer:
Bosse, Germany*

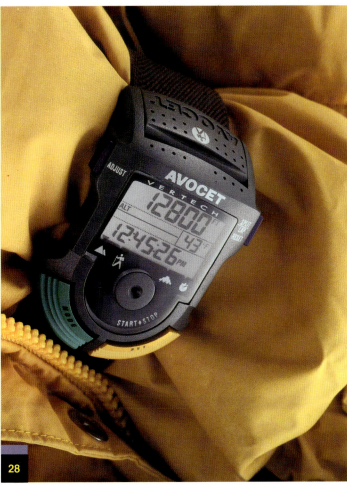

28

Josep Lluscà
Torch,
Argos
ABS
H 27.5cm (10⅞in)
W 12.5cm (5in)
D 15cm (6in)
Manufacturer:
Daisalux, Spain

29

**Naoto Fukasawa
and Peter
Spreenberg
(IDEO)**
*Measuring
instrument for
sports enthusiasts,*
Vertech
*Silicone plastic
In addition to time
of day, calendar,
alarm and stopwatch
functions, it detects*

*and calculates
elevation, rate of
ascent/descent,
barometric
pressure and
temperature.
W 3.5cm (1⅜in)
L 5.6cm (2⅛in)
D 1.2cm (⅜in)
Manufacturer:
Avocet
International, USA*

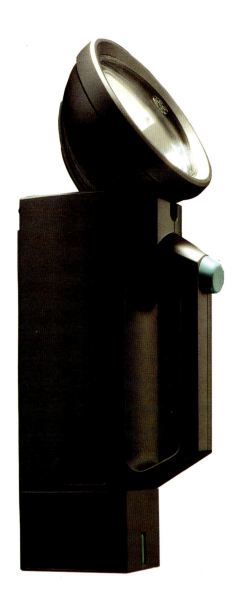

30

Gerhard Fuchs
Glasses,
Minimal Art
*Hardened metal
alloys
Limited batch
production
W 13.5cm (5⅜in)
L 15.6cm (6in)
Manufacturer:
Silhouette
International,
Austria*

30

Guido Niest
Oil lamp,
David
Brass alloy, extra
strong silver-plate
One-off
H 16cm (6½in)
Di 14cm (5½in)
Manufacturer:
Atelier Canaima,
Italy

32

31

Paolo Pedrizzetti
Shower platform,
Nautilus
ABS plastic,
thermoplastic resins
H 2cm (¾in)
Di 60cm (23½in)
Manufacturer:
Saniplast, Italy

31

Sharp Corporation
*Wall-mounted liquid
crystal display
colour monitor,*
9E-H01
*ABS plastic, metal,
glass, aluminium
H 43cm (16⅞in)
W 57cm (22⅜in)
D 13.1cm (5⅛in)
Manufacturer:
Sharp Corporation,
Japan*

33

34

Sharp Corporation
*Wall-mounted liquid
crystal display
colour TV,*
9E-HC2T
*ABS plastic, metal,
glass, crystal-cut
titanium
H 30.8cm (12in)
W 37.7cm (14⅝in)
D 10cm (4in)
Manufacturer:
Sharp Corporation,
Japan*

Sharp *suggests that the styling of its
wall-mounted colour monitor should
bring to mind images of the future,
but it is just as likely to call up images of the
future as visualized in the not-so-distant
past. There is something of the Jetsons –
the early 1960s Hanna-Barbera cartoon
series that went on to become a post-
modern cult in the 1980s – about this
conception of how the future will look. The
liquid-crystal monitor's frame and display
panel have an exaggerated scale and a
space-age flashiness out of all proportion to
the impact of the small rectangular screen,
or most of what it will show. Sharp hopes the
monitor, which is for video playback only
(it is not a TV), will encourage creative
self-expression on the part of its owners.
The company's wall-mounted LCD colour
television, on the other hand, confers the
appearance, if not the status, of fine art on
standard television output by enclosing it
in the kind of aluminium frame one would
usually expect to see on a contemporary
painting or print.*

**Naoto Fukasawa,
Tim Parsey,
Robin Sarre and
Jane Fulton
(IDEO)**
*Left Ventricular
Assist System*
Powder-coated
cast magnesium,
injection-moulded
plastic, PVC,
woven material
Limited batch
production
Control unit:
W 12.7cm (5in)
L 16cm (6½in)
D 3.5cm (1¼in)

Main battery:
W 12.7cm (5in)
L 19cm (7½in)
D 3.4cm (1¼in)
Support battery:
W 13.4cm (5¼in)
L 10.7cm (4¼in)
D 2.5cm (1in)
Manufacturer:
Baxter Healthcare
Corporation,
Novacor Division,
USA

35

36

U ntil now, patients needing care for
a failed heart have been hooked up
to support systems the size of a
small car. With the Left Ventricular Assist
System, a remarkable collaboration between
the Novacor Division of Baxter Healthcare in
California and the design firm **IDEO**, this
technology has been reduced to a trio of
body-hugging units that can be worn on a
harness around the waist. Patients who
would once have been confined to a
hospital bed, can continue to live relatively
normal lives at home, while waiting for a
heart donor and transplant.

The system consists of a mechanical
pump, implanted in the body and controlled
by the rhythms of the heart, an intelligent
unit, a battery and a back-up battery. The
position of the elegantly moulded, gun-metal
coloured units at midriff level allows the
patient to move about freely – to walk, sit,
sleep or take a shower as usual. From the
start of the project, human factors research
played a vital role in ensuring the system's
comfort, safety and ease of use. Indicator
lights are sited accessibly along the top of
the units, and it is impossible for the patient
to unplug both batteries at the same time.

John Lai
Ski goggles
Urethane
mouldings
H 7.3cm (3in)
W 17.8cm (7in)
D 2.5cm (1in)
Manufacturer: Smith
Sport Optics, USA

**Matsushita Seiko
Design Center**
Electric fan,
F-C309J
*ABS resin, wood
H 114cm (44⁷/₈in)
Di 30cm (11⁷/₈in)
Manufacturer:
Matsushita Seiko,
Japan*

37

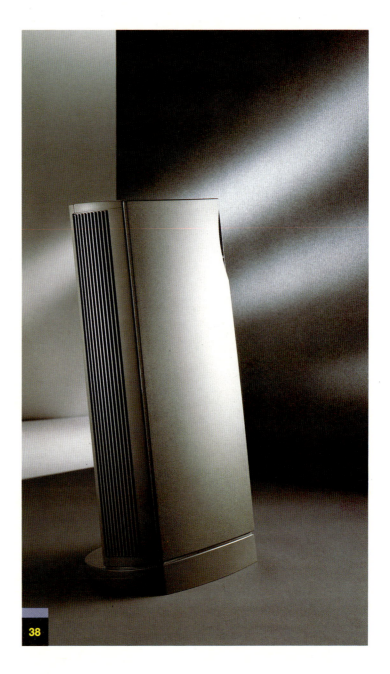

38

**Masahito
Takasuna**
Air purifier,
CAE-501
*ABS, steel
H 75cm (29¹/₂in)
W 36cm (14¹/₈in)
D 31cm (12¹/₄in)
Manufacturer:
Toshiba, Japan*

**Matsushita Seiko
Design Center**
Ceiling fan,
F-V110B
*ABS resin
Di 115cm (45¼in)
Manufacturer:
Matsushita Seiko,
Japan*

**Matsushita Seiko
Design Center**
Humidifier,
FE-05KTF
*PP resin
Generated by an
electric heater and
equipped with a
mood lamp.
H 31cm (12¼in)
W 25cm (9⅞in)
D 25cm (9⅞in)
Manufacturer:
Matsushita Seiko,
Japan*

Studio De Lucchi
*Mirror light, from
the Sintesi range
Aluminium alloy,
frosted glass
H 14.5cm (5¾in)
W 12cm (4¾in)
D 9.8cm (3⅞in)
Manufacturer:
Interform MFG,
Japan*

41

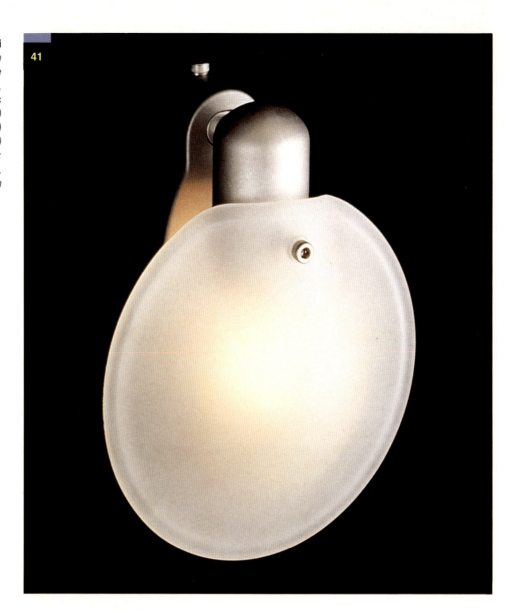

Studio De Lucchi
*Toilet roll holder,
from the Sintesi
range
Aluminium alloy,
stainless steel
H 7.5cm (3in)
W 14.9cm (5⅞in)
Manufacturer:
Interform MFG,
Japan*

42

Studio De Lucchi
*Bathroom
accessories,*
Sintesi
*Aluminium,
aluminium alloy,
stainless steel,
plastic
Hooks:
H 6.5cm (2½in)
W 68.8cm (27in)
D 7.5cm (3in)
Mirror:
H 60cm (23½in)
W 60cm (23½in)
D 2cm (¾in)
Shelf:
H 3cm (1½in)
W 44.9cm (17⅝in)
D 12.7cm (5in)
Toothbrush & cup
holder:
H 3cm (1⅛in)
W 14cm (5½in)
D 11.6cm (4½in)*

*Ashtray:
H 3.8cm (1⅜in)
W 8cm (3½in)
D 11.6cm (4½in)
Towel ring:
H 15.5cm (6⅛in)
W 15cm (5½in)
D 4.9cm (1⅞in)
Soap holder:
H 3cm (1⅛in)
W 14.9cm (5⅞in)
D 13.4cm (5¼in)
Toilet brush holder:
H 48cm (18⅞in)
W 22.2cm (8¾in)
D 24.5cm (9⅝in)
Waste bin:
H 65.5cm (25⅞in)
W 22.2cm (8¾in)
D 20.6cm (8⅛in)
Manufacturer:
Interform MFG,
Japan*

**Masayuki
Kurokawa** `44`
Bottle,
Vittel 1.5l
Acrylic resin
H 29.1cm (11³⁄₈in)
W 10.1cm (4¹⁄₈in)
*Manufacturer: Arrk
Corporation, Japan*

`208`

`5`

PRODUCTS

Tobias Koeppe
*Flask/cigarette
holder,*
Pocket Flask II
*Polished, silver-
and gold-plated
steel
Prototype
H 2.4cm (1in)
W 7.3cm (3in)
L 14.8cm (5¾in)
Manufacturer:
Hip Shing Fat,
Hong Kong*

Studio De Lucchi
Hairdryer,
Mist Blo Zerbino
*Plastic
Includes a liquid
spray attachment.
H 11cm (4⅜in)
L 17cm (6⅝in)
Manufacturer:
Matsushita Electric
Works, Japan*

**Michal Froněk and
Jan Němeček**
Mirror,
Zrcátko
*Aluminium, mirror,
bulbs
Light density is
altered by touching
the frame which
acts as a sensor
switch.
H 80cm (31½in)
W 60cm (23½in)
D 10cm (4in)
Manufacturer:
Olgoj Chorchoj,
Czechoslovakia*

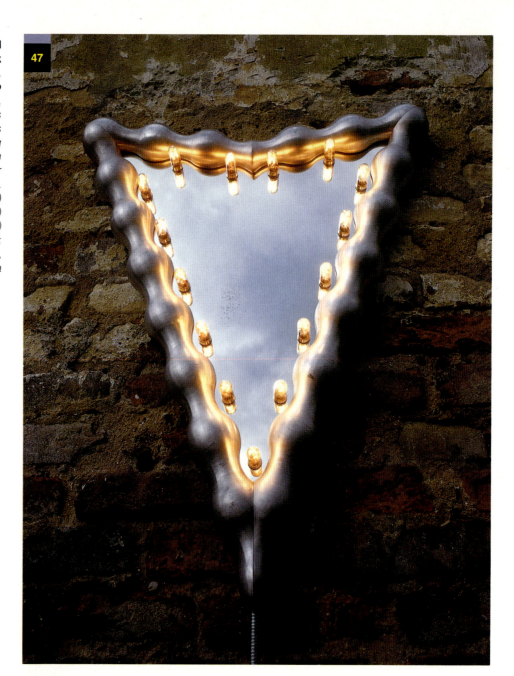

47

André Ricard
Plaque,
Osca
*Bronze
Limited batch
production
H 35cm (13¾in)
L 45cm (17¾in)
Manufacturer: Ocsa
(Cultural Olympics),
Spain*

48

Martin Szekely
Clock,
Crystal
Crystal
Limited batch
production
Di 27cm (10½in)
Manufacturer: Hour-
Lavigne, France

49

Philippe Starck
Wall mirror,
Royalton
Aluminium, crystal
mirror, satin,
transparent glass
H 167cm (65¾in)
W 52cm (20½in)
D 35cm (13¾in)
Mirror:
H 81cm (31⅞in)
W 50cm (19⅝in)
Manufacturer:
Driade, Italy

50

Alessandro Mendini
Mirror,
Specchio di Proust
Mirror, glass
The glass frame is covered in a polychrome pointillist design.
H 100cm (39½in)
L 70cm (27½in)
Manufacturer: Glass Design, Italy

Vittorio Locatelli and William Bertocco
Mirror,
Egeso
Silkscreen-printed mirror glass
H 130cm (51⅛in)
W 65cm (25⅝in)
D 22cm (8⅝in)
Manufacturer: Driade, Italy

**Vittorio Locatelli
and William
Bertocco**
Mirror,
Eos
*Silkscreen-printed
mirror glass
H 73cm (28¾in)
L 67cm (26⅜in)
D 22cm (8⅝in)
Manufacturer:
Driade, Italy*

54

Dan Friedman
Mirror,
Balbec
*Polyurethane, mirror
glass, sand-blasted
decoration
H 100cm (39½in)
L 110cm (43⅜in)
Manufacturer:
Driade, Italy*

53

Emilio Ambasz
Handkerchief TV
*Polycarbonate,
leather, foam,
rubber
Prototype
H 1cm (³⁄₈in)
W 25cm (9⁷⁄₈in)
L 25cm (9⁷⁄₈in)
Manufacturer:
Brion Vega, Italy.*

*D*espite the talk over the last few
years of the dawning era of "soft-
tech" products that are kinder to
the touch, and a degree of softening at the
corners and edges of many appliances,
most industrial objects continue to be
manufactured in hard, bony cases. Why
should this be? Take that most ubiquitous of
late-twentieth century leisure innovations, the
Walkman. As **Emilio Ambasz** has pointed
out, its interior components must meet far
more rigorous standards for impact than
those of its casing; they simply do not need
their inflexible shell. Nor would it make much
sense to encase this shell in something
softer. Instead, in a trio of prototypes for
Brion Vega, Ambasz proposes the Soft
Notebook Computer, a Walkman in a
wallet, and a colour television wrapped in
a handkerchief. In each case, the few
injection-moulded polycarbonate parts are
enfolded in rubber, leather and foam.

The most radical proposal of the three is
the Handkerchief TV, mainly because of the
way it helps to overturn our assumption that
a television is fundamentally a box. Folded
open, the Handkerchief TV has four planes,
each with its own function: screen, antenna,
battery/speaker and external parts. Flat-
screen technology represents the future of
the medium, and Ambasz shows here how
readily such miniaturization can be sculpted
to fit the human form. "Small enough to
fit in a shirt or jacket pocket, or to rest
comfortably on the hip, these products
become an extension of the user," he says.

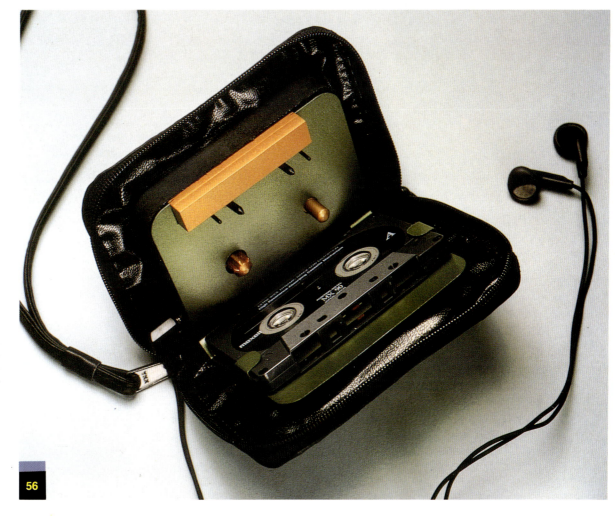

Emilio Ambasz
*Soft, Portable
Radio/Cassette
Player*
*Plastic, leather,
rubber, foam
Prototype
W 9cm (3½in)
L 13cm (5⅛in)
D 3cm (1½in)
Manufacturer:
Brion Vega, Italy*

56

56

57

Emilio Ambasz
*Soft Notebook
Computer*
*Polycarbonate,
leather, foam,
rubber
Prototype
H 5cm (2in)
W 31.7cm (12½in)
L 25.5cm (10in)
Manufacturer:
Brion Vega, Italy*

BIOGRAPHIES

Every effort has been made to obtain details about the designers whose work is featured in this book, but in some cases information was not available. The figures following each entry refer to the illustrations of that designer's work (the number before the full point indicates the chapter number).

Lodovico Acerbis is president of the family-owned furniture design company Acerbis International which was founded in 1870 and was one of the first Italian companies to call on architects for furniture designs. Born in Albino, Bergamo, in 1939, he graduated in economics and business studies from Milan University. He not only takes an industrialist's interest in Acerbis International but, along with Giotto Stoppino, has created some of the company's most important designs. A number of his works have been awarded major international design awards, such as the Milan Compasso d'Oro, and can be seen in the permanent collections of the Victoria and Albert Museum, London, the Neue Sammlung Staatliches Museum für Angewandte Kunst, Munich, the Museum of Contemporary Art, Chicago and in the City Hall of Shanghai. Among the positions he has held is the Presidency of the Gruppo Mobili (the national association of furniture industries). 1.50

Emilio Ambasz was born in Argentina in 1943. He gained a Master's degree in architecture from Princeton University, where he was subsequently made a professor. While still in his twenties, he helped to found New York's Institute of Architecture and Urban Studies, and served as Curator of Design at the Museum of Modern Art. He has received international recognition and won several awards for his work as architect and interior and industrial designer, most recently the 1990 Quaternario Award for high technological achievement. He has exhibited widely, including the 1989 travelling show "Emilio Ambasz: Architecture Exhibition: Industrial and Graphic Design" which appeared at many venues in the USA and Canada. Among his buildings, the Museum of American Folk Art and Houston Center Plaza are especially well known. 1.15, 5.55–7

Andrea Anastasio was born in Rome in 1961. Before becoming a designer, she was involved in various disciplines including the history of art, philosophy, modern Arian languages of India, musical aesthetics and circus performing. Since 1989 she has exhibited jewellery and glassware within Italy, holding a collective exhibition of amulets and jewels with MASSIMO IOSA GHINI, Giorgio Vigna and LUIGI SERAFINI in 1991. Since 1991 she has collaborated with Artemide, Memphis Extra and Sawaya & Moroni. 1.115, 2.29–31, 3.43–7

Francesca Anselmi studied at the Venice University of Architecture. She started her collaboration with Bieffeplast, the furniture division of Bieffe, in 1988. As Assistant to the Design Manager, she is in charge of the company's image, as well as research and product development. 1.4

Ron Arad, a furniture, product and interior designer, was born in 1951 in Tel Aviv. He studied at the Jerusalem Academy of Art and at the Architectural Association, London, graduating in 1979. After working for a firm of London architects, he founded the design company One-Off Ltd in 1981. Ron Arad Associates was formed in 1989. In this year Arad designed the interior of the public spaces for the new Tel Aviv Opera House with C. Norton and S. McAdam. He has exhibited his work widely, both nationally and internationally. 1.77, 78, 81

Junichi Arai was born in 1932 in Gunma Prefecture, Japan. He is a textile manufacturer specializing in sculptural, heavily textured fabrics. In the 1950s he developed the new technique of making and weaving with metallic yarn. He has supplied Issey Miyake and Comme des Garçons, among other leading Japanese designers, and in 1987 he was made an Honorary Member of the Faculty of Royal Designers for Industry. He has exhibited in Japan and the USA, and his work can be found in the permanent collections of the Victoria and Albert Museum, London, the Cooper-Hewitt Museum, New York and the Museum of Applied Arts, Finland. 4.22

Pietro Arosio was born in Lissone, Italy, in 1946 and studied at the Institute of Applied Arts in Monza. He worked as Art Director for AF&F until 1972 when he set up as an independent designer, collaborating with various companies in the field of home furnishings. In 1983 he won first prize in the Casaviva d'Oro for the kitchen *Agrodolce*. He currently collaborates with companies including Airon, Emmebi, Sorgente Dei Mobili, Arkifasem and Piuluce. His designs have been exhibited at the Victoria and Albert Museum, London and the modern art museum Die Neue Sammlung, Munich. 1.8

Alfredo Arribas was born in Barcelona in 1954 and studied architecture at the Superior Technical School of Architecture in Barcelona where he is at present professor. In 1982 he became president of the Spanish interior design organization INFAD. In 1986 he designed Network Café and the Francisco Valiente shop with Eduard Samso. Miguel Morte joined Arribas' practice in 1987, and together they designed the Velvet Bar and the discothèque Louis Vega in Tarragona. In 1990 he began a close collaboration with JAVIER MARISCAL, and they have designed many interiors together including the Torres de Avila bar in Barcelona. In 1990 he showed his first industrial design work at the Vincon gallery in Barcelona in the form of the chair *J. Greystoke*, manufactured by Carlos Jané Camacho. 1.26

Sigeaki Asahara was born in Tokyo in 1948 and educated in Turin. He is at present a freelance designer working in both Japan and Italy, and for the last two years has received the I.F. award from the Hanover exhibition. An example of his work is on permanent show at the Brooklyn Museum, New York. 2.4

Antonia Astori, whilst working primarily in the field of industrial design, considers her architectural projects to be the highest expression of her skill. She graduated from the Athenaeum in Lausanne before starting her collaboration with Driade in 1968. She is at present designing an extension to the firm's museum. 1.51

Gae Aulenti graduated in architecture from the Milan Polytechnic in 1954. As well as her architectural projects, she has designed stage sets and costumes for opera and drama, lectured extensively on architecture, had exhibitions throughout the world and received many awards. She was responsible for the Musée National d'Art Moderne at the Georges Pompidou Centre, and for the interior architecture of the Musée d'Orsay, Paris. In 1977 President Mitterrand conferred on her the title of Chevalier de la Légion d'Honneur. 2.14

Hiroshi Awatsuji, a textile designer, was born in Kyoto, Japan, in 1929 and graduated from the Kyoto Municipal College of Fine Arts, establishing his own design studio in 1958. Since 1964 he has collaborated with the Fujie Textile Company. His principal commissions in Japan include textiles for the government pavilion at Expo'70, and tapestries for the Keio Plaza and Ginza Tokyu hotels. He exhibited at the Victoria and Albert Museum's "Japan Style" exhibition in 1980, and at the "Design since 1945" exhibition in Philadelphia in 1983. 4.12, 13, 15

Karim Azzabi was born in Milan in 1957 and gained a degree in industrial design at the European Institute of Design. He worked in various fields of product design before setting up his own studio, Defacto Design Associati, offering services in design, graphics and packaging, and collaborating with manufacturers such as Oceano Oltreluce and Edra. He recently developed a new recycled plastic called "neolite" which he has used to create a travelling bag for Brics and a collection of telephones for Brondi. 1.111, 2.38

Manuel Bañó and Marcelo Lax were born in Valencia, Spain, in 1959 and 1961 respectively. Bañó studied fine art in Valencia and Barcelona; Lax studied applied art in Valencia. Both industrial designers, they set up Bañó & Asociados in 1985, producing furniture, lighting, toys and household equipment. In addition to their work for Bañó & Asociados, both designers teach in the Superior Technical School of Industrial Engineering at the University and Polytechnic of Valencia and at the School of Design of the CEU San Pablo. 1.24

Hans Bauer and Kay Saamer were born in 1963 and 1960 in Darmstadt and Zürich respectively. Both studied at the Darmstadt Fachhochschule für Gestaltung. They set up a studio together in 1990. 1.88

Hedda Beese was born in Guhrau, Germany, in 1944 and has degrees in educational sciences and industrial design. She became a designer in 1976 and was elected to the board of directors of Design Developments Ltd, London, in 1979. An acclaimed industrial designer, she has lectured in England, Ireland and Germany. From 1981–87 she was Managing Director of Moggridge Associates, London, and became a member of the Chartered Society of Designers, a Fellow of the Royal Society of Arts and a member of the VDID (Verband Deutscher Industrie-Designer e.V). She has received several awards, and her work can be seen in the permanent collection of the Museum of Modern Art, New York. 5.27

Guglielmo Berchicci was born in Milan and graduated with a degree in architecture from the Polytechnic in 1984. In 1986 he opened a shared studio in Milan where he works in architecture, design and visual design. He has collaborated with manufacturers including Lumi, Bonacina, Unitalia, GRF Metals and Dilmos. His architectural projects include a showroom and apartments in Milan and a villa in the provinces. His work has been published in Italian and foreign periodicals and in three books: *New Italian Design* (Rizzoli), *Nuovo bel Design* (Electa) and *Le Nouveau Design Italian* (Terrail). 3.12

Berghof, Landes and Rang was founded in 1981 in Frankfurt by Norbert Berghof, Michael Landes and Wolfgang Rang. All three graduated from the Technical University of Darmstadt, where they now lecture. In 1988 they joined with Albrecht/Jourden/Müller. Notable projects include architecture-orientated furniture for Studio Draenert, and the design of the head office of DEKA/DESPA, as well as interior design work in Frankfurt. 4.40

Mario Botta was born in 1943 in Mendrisio, Switzerland. He attended the Academy of Fine Arts in Milan, then graduated in architecture from the University of Venice. He gained practical experience in Le Corbusier's studio, establishing his own architectural practice in Lugano in 1969. Since 1982 he has been designing furniture for Alias. Two of his chairs are in the study collection of the Museum of Modern Art, New York. 1.48

Do Brandi was born in Modena in 1968 and studied architecture in Florence. She worked in the office of Adolfo Natalini from 1988 to 1990, and is at present working with Sawaya & Moroni. 1.116

Andrea Branzi, who lives and works in Milan, is one of Italy's most renowned avant-garde designers, having been a member of Archizoom Associates until 1974. A frequent exhibitor at the Milan Triennale and the Venice Biennale, he has also exhibited work in one-man shows throughout the world. As a journalist, he collaborates with the leading Italian and foreign magazines, and is at present editorial consultant to Interni Annual, Gruppa Electa and Passigli Progetti. He has lectured as a visiting professor at the main universities in Italy, France, Holland, England, the United States and Canada, Japan, Argentina and Brazil, and has had many books published on his theories of design. In 1983 he founded Domus Academy and in 1984 was awarded a special mention at the Compasso d'Oro for creating the first international post-graduate design and fashion-design school. He has been cultural director of the school and is now its vice-president. He is also vice-president of the Tokyo-based Domus Design Academy which was created to plan and develop design in Japan. Major projects include the Modern Art Gallery in Arezzo. 1.54–6, 2.27, 3.25

Remo Buti started his career as a ceramic designer before graduating in architecture. He is now professor at the University of Architecture in Florence where he teaches interior architecture and design. One of the founder members of Global Tools, he is considered a leading avant-garde architect. He participated in the XIV, XVI and XVII Milan Triennale, and in 1978 was invited to take part in the Venice Biennale. Together with ANDREA BRANZI and a group of younger architects, he won the nation-wide competition for the restoration of Castel di Sangro Historical Centre. His projects are frequently published in Italian and foreign design reviews. 1.94, 106

Pierangelo Caramia was born in 1957 in Cistermino, Italy, and studied under REMO BUTI and ANDREA BRANZI, receiving a Master's degree in "Scenografia Urbana" from the Domus Academy. He is at present professor of design at the École des Beaux Arts in Rennes, and has designed products for Italian and French firms, including XO, Sawaya & Moroni, Arredaesse, Cassina and Alessi. He has exhibited his work widely, most notably at the 3rd International Venice Biennale and at a one-man show for XO in Athens. Major projects include the interior design for a flag factory in Lille and, with Alex Locadia, the Bond Street Café in New York. 3.27

Achille Castiglioni was born in Milan in 1918. He began his work as a designer in partnership with his brothers, Livio and Pier Giacomo, specializing in interiors and furniture, and in lights, for which he is particularly well known. Castiglioni is one of the foremost talents in Italian design, and has been honoured seven times with the Compasso d'Oro, as well as having six of his pieces selected for exhibition at the Museum of Modern Art, New York. He is currently Professor of Industrial Design and Decoration at the University of Milan. 1.18, 41, 2.28

Piero Castiglioni was born in Lierna, Italy, in 1944. He graduated in architecture, and since 1980 has been working as a technical consultant for FontanaArte. He collaborated with his father, ACHILLE CASTIGLIONI, on the *Scintilla System* which FontanaArte has been producing since 1983. He worked on the Musée d'Orsay in Paris with GAE AULENTI, and was involved in the design of structures for the 1992 Olympic Games in Barcelona. 2.12–14

Shirley Chang was born in Hong Kong and moved to the United States where she studied fine art and architecture, receiving a Master of Architecture from the University of Pennsylvania in 1977. After a period spent working for I.M. Pei and Partners and Skidmore, Owings and Merrill Architects, she founded her own design business, Shirley S. Chang Architect, in New York City in 1984. The firm is involved in interior and architectural projects, both residential and commercial, and custom-designed furnishings. Her work has been published in the American edition of *House and Garden* magazine. 4.18

Antonio Citterio was born in Meda, Italy, in 1950. He studied at Milan Polytechnic, and has been involved in industrial and furniture design since 1967. In 1973 he opened a studio with Paolo Nava, and the two have worked jointly and individually for B & B Italia, Flexform and others. In 1979 they were awarded the Compasso d'Oro. In 1987 Terry Dwan became a partner in Studio Citterio Dwan, and the company has undertaken many interior design projects. Citterio has taught at the Domus Academy in Milan and has participated in many exhibitions, including independent shows in Hanover, Rome, Amsterdam, Paris and Weil. In 1992 he was responsible for the original concept and layout of the exhibition "Objects and Projects" in Paris. 1.21

Michael Clapper trained as a cabinet-maker and from 1981–87 was the restoration specialist of the US Department of Interior. He is at present head of the Woodworking Department at the Genoa Institute, New York. His furniture designs are only available through select galleries and by commission. His work has been published in various trade magazines. 1.104

Nigel Coates was born in 1949 in Malvern, England. He studied at the University of Nottingham and at the Architectural Association where he has lectured since his graduation in 1974. In 1985 he co-founded Branson Coates with Douglas Branson. He is known for his belief that architecture can be odd and amusing as well as extremely well-built and durable, and his projects include work for Jasper Conran and Katherine Hamnett. He has also designed restaurants in Japan, and his present plans include the Nishi Acabu Wall in Tokyo and the Sea Hotel in Otaru, Japan. 1.82, 83

Annalisa Cocco was born in Cágliari, Italy, in 1959. She studied in Cágliari and Florence, and since 1983 has lived and worked in Milan as a freelance designer. In recent years she has begun to specialize in the research, development and production of objects for domestic use (flower vases, glasses, tables etc.). She collaborates with various companies, including Alessi, Stil Domus, Cappellini and Bottega dei Vasai. Her works have been published in major design magazines, such as *Casa Vogue*, *Interni* and *Brava Casa*. 3.42

Coop Himmelblau was founded in Vienna in 1968 by the architects Wolf Prix (born 1942, in Vienna) and Helmut Swiczinsky (born 1944, in Poland) and the practice now has offices in Vienna and Los Angeles. Their earlier work consisted of installations, speculative projects and conversions in Vienna such as the Baumann Studio (1985), the Iso-Holding offices (1986), Passage Wahliss (1986), Rooftop Remodelling (1988) and the Funder Factory 1 & 3 (1988). They have now graduated to larger-scale industrial projects in Austria, France, Germany, California and Japan. In 1987 they won two major competitions: the Ronacher Theatre, Vienna and the Melun-Senart city planning project near Paris. Both partners lecture and exhibit internationally; Prix is currently Adjunct Professor at SCIARC, Los Angeles. 1.97, 4.4

Toni Cordero graduated in Turin with a degree in architecture. His most important projects to date are the Alps Stadium (1985) and the Automobile Museum (1987), both in Turin. He has collaborated with European manufacturing houses such as Artemide, Driade and Sawaya & Moroni. 1.102

Ken Cornet is a home furnishings designer. Born in New York, he attended the Fashion Institute of Technology and the New York School of Interior Design. He started by designing fabrics for the fashion industry, but today also designs wallpapers, bed and bathroom furniture, tableware and rugs. In 1982 he set up the design partnership A. Musticorn and Co. which creates fabrics for interior designers and architects. 4.17

Nick Crowe trained in Fine Art at the Cheltenham School of Art and worked as a graphic designer before becoming a partner of The Control Room. He has exhibited his clock designs in the UK. In 1991 he completed the metal lighting and sculpture in "Juliana's" nightclub, Istanbul. 2.46

Riccardo Dalisi, the Italian avant-garde designer, was a member of the experimental design group Global Tools throughout the 1970s. He has written several books on architecture and animation, and teaches architectural composition at the University of Naples. He was awarded the Compasso d'Oro in 1981 for a coffee-maker produced by Alessi. He has also collaborated with Baleri Italia, OLuce, Play Line and Zanotta. He has participated in many exhibitions, including the Venice Biennale and the Milan Triennale. 1.31, 32, 73, 74, 76, 2.35

Greg Daly was born in Melbourne in 1954. He is a member of numerous pottery organizations, including the International Academy of Ceramics, the Arts, Sciences and Letters Academy in France and the Potters Society of Australia. He has exhibited at more than fifty one-man shows and has received international acclaim for his work. His designs are represented in the permanent collections of many leading museums, including the Victoria and Albert Museum, London, and the National Gallery of Victoria, Melbourne. 3.13

Paolo Deganello was born in Este, Italy, in 1940. Whilst working towards his graduation, he began his professional career in a collaboration on the restoration of the Orsanmichele in Florence and in several urban planning projects. In 1966 he founded Archizoom Associates in Florence with ANDREA BRANZI, Gilberto Corretti and MASSIMO MOROZZI. Since the studio closed, he has worked as a freelance in Milan, collaborating with, amongst others, Cassina, Marcatré, Driade, Cidue, Vitra International and Artelano. He has been the subject of many exhibitions, including the one-man show promoted by the two galleries Binnen and Van Krimpen in Amsterdam in 1988, and has lectured throughout Italy and at the Architectural Association in London. His works are widely published. 1.42, 43

Michele De Lucchi was born in Ferrara, Italy, in 1951. He studied first in Padua and then at Florence University, graduating in 1975 and subsequently teaching there. In 1978 he began a close collaboration with ETTORE SOTTSASS. He worked and designed for Alchimia until the establishment of Memphis in 1981. He created some of Memphis' best-known products. In 1979 he became a consultant for Olivetti in Ivrea and, under the supervision of Sottsass, he designed their *Icarus* office furniture. He is currently designing for a range of furniture manufacturers. 1.49, 67, 5.41–3, 46

Maddalena De Padova created the furniture manufacturing company ICF in 1958 along with her husband. The company produced under licence Hermann Miller's furniture by designers such as Eames and Girard. After her husband's death, she set up Edizioni De Padova in 1985, collaborating with designers such as ACHILLE CASTIGLIONI, Dieter Rams and VICO MAGISTRETTI. 4.36

Jonathan de Pas, Donato d'Urbino and Paolo Lomazzi were all born in Milan where they started working together in 1966 in the fields of architecture, design, interior design and urban planning. In the 1960s they created a series of inflatable designs which were shown at the World Exposition in Osaka and at the XIV Triennale in Milan, and which culminated in 1967 in the creation of their inflatable chair *Blow*. They continued with similar designs, working for Acerbis, Artemide, Driade, Disform and others. They have exhibited their work widely and have shown at all the Compasso d'Oro exhibitions since 1979. They recently extended their scope to include architecture, product and lighting design, and their output is documented in historical literature on Italian design, as well as in major international publications on industrial architecture and design. Examples of their work can be found in the permanent collections of the Museum of Modern Art, New York, the Victoria and Albert Museum and the Design Museum, London, the Georges Pompidou Centre, Paris, the Kunstgewerbe Museum, Zurich, the Staatliches Museum für Angewandte Kunst, Munich and the Jerusalem Museum, Israel. Jonathan de Pas died in 1991. 1.35

Pucci de Rossi was born in Verona in 1947. He studied sculpture with the American H. B. Walker, and in 1973 had his first exhibition of works in metal in Paris (Galerie Néotù 1987 and 1989), Los Angeles, Tokyo, Milan, Nice and Cologne. 1.109

Design 134 was founded in 1989 by Bjorli Lundin, Erling Christoffersen and Flemming Steen Jensen, all of whom graduated from the Danish Design School and the Royal Danish Academy of Fine Arts, School of Architecture. They have exhibited their work widely within Northern Europe and have received national recognition. They currently teach at the Danish Design School. 1.38

Sergi and Oscar Devesa were born in 1961 and 1963 respectively in Barcelona. They both studied design, and in 1987 founded the D & D Society with the purpose of collaborating in product design for national and international markets. They have exhibited widely and have worked with Metalarte, Disform, Supergrif-Damixa and Blauet. 1.1, 3

Andrea Dichiara was born in Ancona, Italy, in 1950 and graduated from the Accademia di Belle Arti of Rome. In 1970 he started his career as a furniture designer, drawing on experience he had previously gained working with wood and metal. At the same time he completed various interior design projects nationally and internationally. He has participated in design shows world-wide, and lectures at the Centro Sperimentale di Design in Ancona. 1.45

Ezio Didone was born in 1939 in Milan where he studied architecture, specializing in industrial design. In 1963, together with Studio G14 and the architect Alberto Colombi, he founded Designers Associati Milano which he has since left. He collaborates with Valenti, Gruppo Industrial Busnelli and Arteluce. 2.37

Jane Dillon was born in England in 1943. She studied interior design in Manchester and furniture design at the Royal College of Art. On graduating in 1968 she worked for Knoll International before moving to Milan in 1970 to work for Olivetti under ETTORE SOTTSASS. From 1973 she worked in partnership with Charles Dillon as a consultant, and since 1986 has had a continuing collaboration with PETER WHEELER and Floris van den Broecke on projects for furniture manufacturers in Europe and the USA. She also works independently and is currently involved in a furniture project with the ceramic designer Janice Tchalenko. 1.14

Tom Dixon was born in Sfax, Tunisia in 1959, and moved to the UK in 1963. He has no formal design training but learnt to weld metal as an enthusiast, founding Creative Salvage with Nick Jones and Mark Brazier Jones in 1985. He has exhibited his work in one-man and group shows throughout Europe, the USA and Japan, and examples of his designs can be seen in the permanent collections of the Victoria and Albert Museum and the Crafts Council and Design Museum, London, the Musée des Arts Décoratifs and the Pompidou Centre, Paris, the Vitra Chair Museum, Basel and the Brooklyn Museum, New York. Clients include NIGEL COATES, Ben Kelly, Jean Paul Gaultier and Terence Conran. Today he has his own studio, Space, in London. 1.89, 90

Jiří Dokoupil, a painter, was born in Krnov, Czechoslovakia, in 1954, and now lives and works in Cologne, Tenerife, Madrid and New York. He belongs to the generation of artists who, under the name of the "Neue Wilde", radically changed the international art scene in the late 1970s. 4.9

Marie-Christine Dorner was born in Strasbourg in 1960 and graduated from the École Camondo in 1984. She lived for a year in Japan before returning to Paris in 1987 and setting up her own company which is active in the fields of architecture, interior design, furniture and product design. She has produced many furniture prototypes for Cassina and Artelano, and her major interior design projects include the hotel La Villa in St Germain de Prés, for which she also designed all the furniture. Besides personal exhibitions in galleries in Tokyo, Paris, New York, Geneva and Los Angeles, she has taken part in a number of group exhibitions, including "Design Français 1960–1990" at the Georges Pompidou Centre, "Avant-Première" at the Victoria and Albert Museum in London and "Women in Design" at the Design Centre in Stuttgart. 3.10

Nathalie du Pasquier was born in Bordeaux in 1957 and is self-taught, her work being inspired by her extensive trips to Africa, Australia and India. In 1980 she set up a studio with GEORGE SOWDEN and in 1981 became a founder member of the Memphis Group, working with ETTORE SOTTSASS. Today she has her own studio with a more intensive orientation towards painting. 4.41

Mark Dziersk, the Design Manager of Group Four Design, trained at the University of Michigan where he was awarded a Fine Arts Degree in industrial design. Prior to joining Group Four, he worked as a senior consultant industrial designer for several leading design firms, most notably as Senior Industrial Designer with Gregory Fossella Associates and as a corporate designer for the Genrad Corporation. He is adjunct professor at the Rhode Island School of Design and the New England School of Art and Design. 5.9

Fumio Enomoto was born in Tokyo where he graduated from the University in 1979. He worked with Shiro Kuramata for six years, then in 1986 founded his own studio, Fumio Enomoto Atelier. In 1988 he held a one-man furniture exhibition at AXIS. 1.40, 53

Siggi Fischer was born in Cologne in 1954 and studied industrial design at Wuppertal University. Since 1990 he has worked freelance with clients including Thomas Schulte Design. He has exhibited in both Germany and Japan. 1.33, 34

Piero Fornasetti trained as an artist and is now recognized world-wide as a designer of objects from buttons to pieces of furniture. His designs are made in his private workshop, recently with his son Barnaba's collaboration. He has received many design awards, including the Neiman Marcus Award, and examples of his work can be found in several Italian and foreign collections, such as the collection of the Victoria and Albert Museum, London and the Bischofberger collection, Zurich. In 1991–92 the Victoria and Albert Museum held a retrospective exhibition of his work which moved to Italy and other European centres. A monograph, *Piero Fornasetti: Designer of Dreams* (Thames and Hudson), is available in English, French and Italian. 1.47

Sam Francis was born in 1923 in San Mateo, California. After initially training in medicine, he turned to the study of painting and art history in 1948. He moved to Paris in 1950 but is now living in California. He has exhibited widely in Europe and the United States, at venues including the Whitney Museum of American Art, New York and the Georges Pompidou Centre, Paris. 4.10

Dan Friedman trained in graphic design at the Carnegie Institute of Technology, later spending periods of time at the Hochschule für Gestaltung in Ulm, Germany, and the Allgemeine Gewerbeschule in Basel, Switzerland. In the 1970s he worked as a corporate graphic designer with clients such as Anspach Grossman Portugal and Pentagram. Since the late 1970s he has worked in furniture and art-based product design, where he has found most support in Europe, establishing ongoing relationships with ALESSANDRO MENDINI and the avant-garde Alchimia group. He has recently been invited to lecture on his investigations into the radicality of Modernism in design. His first limited production furniture with Néotù and Driade is out and he is working with Mendini on a project for Alessi. 1.16, 5.53

Michal Froněk and Jan Němeček were born in 1966 and 1963 respectively. Both studied at the Academy of Applied Art in Prague under BOŘEK ŠÍPEK, and in 1990 they founded their own studio, "Olgoj Chorchoj". 3.21, 5.47

Gerhard Fuchs was born in 1966 and trained initially as a toolmaker. From 1988 he became increasingly interested in art and design, and spent a year at Goldsmiths' School for Design and Decoration in Pfortzheim, Germany. Since 1990 he has worked on the design team of Silhouette International. 5.30

Naoto Fukasawa was educated at Tama Art University, Tokyo, and is now the Senior Industrial Designer for IDEO Product Development. Previously, he was chief designer of the R&D Design Group at Seiko Epson Corporation in Japan. His product designs have often been selected at the ID Annual Design Reviews. 5.28, 35

Jane Fulton has responsibility for human factors at IDEO, researching design requirements for products in international markets. Before joining IDEO in 1987, she was a Senior Research Ergonomist at the Institute of Consumer Ergonomics in Loughborough, England. She has taught ergonomics to designers and engineers, and was a visiting research fellow in Human Factors at the Institute of Transportation Studies, University of California, Berkeley, during 1986–87. She has a Bachelor of Arts, Honours, in psychology. 5.35

Olivier Gagnère was born in 1952 in Paris where he continues to live and work. His furniture designs and his work in glass and terracotta have been widely exhibited, and he has received several awards, most notably from the Centre VIA in 1982. 3.8, 22

Jorge Garcia Garay was born in Buenos Aires, Argentina, and since 1979 has been working in Barcelona where he heads Garcia Garay Design. He now works almost exclusively on lighting. In 1989 his ceiling lamp *Fenix* and floor lamp *Enterprise* were chosen for exhibition in the London Design Museum. He has also exhibited in Spain and the USA. 2.11

Elizabeth Garouste and Mattia Bonetti were born in Paris and Lugano, Switzerland, in 1949 and 1952 respectively, and have worked together since 1980. Their designs have been exhibited in Europe, Japan and New York, and examples can be seen in the permanent collections of the Musées des Arts Décoratifs in Paris and Bordeaux. They have designed sets and costumes for the theatre, and have worked on interior design projects, notably the conversion of the Château de Boisdeloup for the Picasso family. 1.120–2, 125

Frank Gehry is Principal-in-Charge of the firm Frank O. Gehry and Associates Inc. which he established in 1962. He studied architecture at the University of Southern California and city planning at Harvard University's Graduate School of Design. His architectural career spans three decades and has produced public and private buildings in America, Japan and, most recently, Europe. He has received international acclaim for his designs. In 1989 he won the Pritzker Architecture Prize, and he has been named a trustee of the American Academy in Rome. His work has been featured in major professional publications and national and international trade journals, and can be found in permanent museum collections. In 1986 a major retrospective exhibition of his designs entitled "The Architecture of Frank O. Gehry" was organized by the Walker Art Centre which travelled throughout the USA. 1.57, 72

Ginbande Design was formed in 1985 by Klaus-Achim Heine and Uwe Fischer who met at the University of Design in Offenbach. They describe their furniture designs – which include a folding chair that folds out of the floor and the *Tabula Rasa* which accommodates two, four or eighteen people – as "experimental". Today Heine and Fischer are designing for industrial production. Their designs include the *Nexus* table system for Vitra, upholstered furniture for Sawaya & Moroni and the *Contor* office furniture for Anthologie Quartett. 4.38

GK Design Group was founded in 1953 in Japan. The company offers a wide range of design-related services, from industrial, environmental and graphic design to market survey, product planning and community and corporate identity development. 5.26

Elisabetta Gonzo and Alessandro Vicari both graduated from the University of Florence in 1988. Their designs are influenced strongly by the concepts and materials used in architecture and they have worked extensively with architects, for example, with Italo Rota on the Grand Louvre project in Paris. In their design of furniture and lamps they have collaborated with several Italian firms, including Moroso, Up&Up and Progetti Bernini. They have exhibited their work widely within Italy, and in 1992 were invited by ALESSANDRO MENDINI to participate in the design collection for the Museo del Nuovo e Bel Design. In 1991 they were awarded first prize at the Interdisciplinary Awards for Young Artists held by the Italian Consulate General in Paris for their design of a vacuum bottle, *Alfiere*. 1.25

Zaha Hadid was born in Baghdad, Iraq, in 1950. She trained in architecture at the Architectural Association, London, where she won the Diploma Prize in 1977. She has a London-based practice and lectures internationally, as well as being involved with the AA Council. Her projects include Eaton Place, London and the Peak Club, Hong Kong, a folly for the Osaka Garden Festival, Moonsoon restaurant in Sapporo, a music video pavilion in Groningen and a fire station for Vitra in Weil am Rhein. 4.11

Koji Hamai was born in Japan and graduated from the Bunka Fashion College. He joined the Miyashin Corporation in Hachioji to learn about textile design, and in 1986 became a fashion designer for the Issey Miyake Design Studio. He has won many design awards in Japan. 4.19–21

K. David Harris trained at the Carnegie-Mellon University, Pittsburgh, graduating with a BFA in industrial design, and is at present the Senior Designer at Group Four Design. He has worked in a wide range of product types, from lighting to cosmetics, and achieved recognition for his designs for Polaroid. Other clients include AT&T, Singer and Ingersoll-Rand. 5.9

Trix Haussmann studied in Zurich at the Swiss Institute of Technology and graduated in architecture and urban planning in 1963. In 1967 she founded her own design company with **Robert Haussmann** who had been practising design since 1931 in Zurich. She is a teacher at the Swiss Institute of Technology and at the Academy of Art in Stuttgart. 1.23

Leonne Hendriksen was born in San Sebastian, Spain, and educated in The Netherlands at the Academy of Industrial Design in Eindhoven and the Academy of Fine Arts, Maastricht. She is interested in conceptual art which she expresses in a mixture of media, and she is at present working on applied art in textile design. She exhibits her work and lectures widely throughout Europe. 4.35

Jochen Henkels was born in 1956 in Solingen, Germany. He studied at the Solingen Workshop for Wood and Metal, then studied industrial design at Wuppertal University. From 1986–89 he studied under Dieter Rams at the Hochschule für Bildende Künste in Hamburg. He has worked as a freelance designer since 1989. 1.39

Hironen, an architecture, interior and furniture design team, was founded by Ronen Levin and Hiroyuki Okawa. Levin studied architecture at the Architectural Association, London; Okawa is a self-taught sculptor. In 1988 they moved to Tokyo and worked on several interior co-ordination projects, culminating in a commission for the total architectural co-ordination of the Coelacanth restaurant and bar, from its façade to the furniture and *objets d'art* inside it. In 1990 they held their first one-man show at the Face Gallery in Japan and in 1991 represented Japanese design at the "Abitare il tempo" exhibition in Italy. Hironen's designs have been published in major design magazines. 1.124, 2.44, 45

Yoshiki Hishinuma is a fashion and textile designer who was born in Sendai, Japan, in 1958. He has presented collections from 1984 onwards, showing both in Japan and Europe. He designs theatrical costume, and in 1990 created the uniform and monument for the Friendship Pavilion in the International Green and Greenery exhibition in Osaka, Japan. 4.1, 2

David Hockney was born in 1937 in Bradford, England. He studied at Bradford College, then the Royal College of Art, London. He now lives in California. His work includes painting, stage design and photography. He has also held teaching posts in the USA. In 1988 a retrospective of his work was held at the Los Angeles County Museum of Art, the Metropolitan Museum of Art, New York and the Tate Gallery, London. 4.6

Radovan Hora was born in Prague in 1969. He studied furniture design at the Secondary School for Applied Arts, graduating from the University of Applied Art in Prague in 1988. 3.40

Bohuslav Horák was born in Pardubice, Czechoslovakia, in 1954 and attended both the Zizkov Art School in Prague and the College of Applied Arts. In 1987 he became a member of the design group Atika, also in Prague. 1.30

Massimo Iosa Ghini is an Italian designer working in the areas of furniture, textiles, fashion and advertising. Born in 1959 in Borgo Tossignano, he studied in Florence and graduated in architecture from Milan Polytechnic. In 1981 he joined the group Zak-Ark, and from 1984 has collaborated with the firm AGO. Since 1982 he has worked on a number of discothèques, video projects and magazines. In 1986 he took part in the Memphis Group's "12 New" collection. 1.17, 27, 64, 65, 84, 3.7, 9

James Irvine was born in London and graduated from the Royal College of Art in 1984. He moved to Italy and worked as a consultant designer with Olivetti, ETTORE SOTTSASS and MICHELE DE LUCCHI. He participated in the "12 New Memphis 86" and is a member of the group Solid. In 1988 he opened his own studio in Milan, designing interiors, furniture and industrial products, and collaborating with companies including Alessi, Cappellini International and Design Gallery, Milan. In 1990 he became a visiting lecturer at the Domus Academy, Milan. 1.10

Yoshifumi Ishikawa graduated in design from Tamagawa University, Tokyo, and since 1984 has been part of the Canon Inc. Camera Design Centre team. 5.21

Satoko Ito was born in 1961 in Japan, and graduated from the Women's College of Fine Art in 1984. She is at present part of the Toshiba Corporation Design Team in charge of designing visual appliances. 5.24

Nazanin Kamali was born in Iran in 1966 and was educated in England. She holds a Bachelor of Arts in 3D-design from Wolverhampton Polytechnic, and a Master of Arts in furniture design from the Royal College of Art. Now working as a freelance designer, she draws inspiration from both cultural backgrounds, and uses a variety of materials. 1.105

Vivianne Karlsson was educated at the Rönnowska School, Helsingborg and Gothenburg University School of Applied Arts where she studied ceramics and product design respectively. She has exhibited her work widely within Sweden, holding her first one-woman show "Two K" at the Orrefors Gallery in Stockholm in 1991. 3.2, 3

Wolf Karnagel was born in Leipzig in 1940 and studied in Braunschweig under Bodo Kampmann. He has collaborated with, amongst others, Rosenthal, Amboss, Lufthansa and Toro. He is at present Professor of Design in Krefeld. 3.11

Toshiko Kawaguchi was born in Niigata, Japan, in 1956 and obtained a Master's degree in architecture from the Nihon University. She worked for Maki Associates, Tohata and Associates and Hans Hollein in Vienna, before founding her own Tokyo-based design studio, Archistudio OZONE, in 1989. 1.99, 100

Motomi Kawakami graduated in design from the Tokyo National University of Fine Arts and Music in 1966. He gained experience in Italy, winning an award in the MIA competition, and on his return to Japan taught at the University of Tokyo. In 1971 he opened his own design office in Tokyo and has received acclaim for his furniture designs. In 1978 he received first prize in the Open International Chair Competition of the AIA (USA). He has organized exhibitions within Japan and is a member of the Japan Design Committee. 1.22

Kouji Kikuchi was born in 1965. Whilst working for an embroidery company, he studied textile design at The Weaving Design Department of the Ohtauka Textile Design Institute. He worked for the textile division of Towa Textile Co. Ltd for several years, and has now founded his own studio. 4.14

Toshiyuki Kita was born in Osaka in 1942 and graduated in industrial design from the University in 1964. He works in Milan and Japan, and his designs can be seen in the permanent collection of the Museum of Modern Art in New York. He has been the recipient of many international awards. 1.6

Milan Knizak is a Czechoslovakian designer who trained and works in Prague. His work can be seen in the permanent collection of the Austrian Museum of Applied Art, Vienna. 1.61, 123

Tobias Koeppe gained experience as a factory metal-worker before training in technical engineering, and later industrial design, at the University for Applied Science in Hanover. He worked as a freelance designer/consultant for industrial products until 1989 when he became a product designer and manager for the import/export company Heinz Tröber GmbH and Co., Hamburg. 5.45

Makoto Komatsu was born in 1943 in Tokyo. He graduated from art school there, then went to work for the Swedish glass-maker Gustavsberg. After returning to Japan he began work as an independent designer. In 1990 he held a one-man exhibition, "Spin", in Tokyo and in 1991 a one-man exhibition of the *Kaseki* series. His work is in the permanent collections of the Museum of Ceramics, Faenza, the Museum of Modern Art, New York and the Victoria and Albert Museum, London. 3.23

Masayuki Kurokawa was born in Nagoya, Japan, in 1937 and graduated from the Department of Architecture at the Nagoya Institute of Technology in 1961. In 1967, after further study in Tokyo at the Graduate School of Architecture, Waseda University, he established Masayuki Kurokawa Architect and Associates. He has received national and international design awards, and his work is on permanent display at the Metropolitan Museum of Art, New York. 2.10, 5.44

John Lai was born in Hong Kong in 1963 and grew up in Northern California. He studied engineering at U.C. Berkeley and went on to obtain a degree in industrial design from San Jose State University. In 1988 he joined IDEO Product Development (formerly Matrix Product Design), where he has worked on products including high-tech computers and accessories, medical products and sports equipment. In 1991 he received a silver award from I.D.E.A. for the design of CoStar's *Address Writer*. 5.36

Danny Lane was born in Urbana, Illinois, in 1955. Largely self-taught, he moved to England in 1975 to work with the stained-glass artist Patrick Reyntiens, then attended the Central School of Art in London, studying painting with a strong emphasis on the esoteric tradition in art and design. In 1983 he co-founded Glassworks with John Creighton and began a three-year association with RON ARAD. He has extended his designs to include work with metal and wood, and has participated in numerous museum and gallery exhibitions and international furniture shows. In 1988 he held three one-man shows in Milan, London and Paris, and started producing work for Fiam Italia. Since then he has participated in further individual shows and in 1990 received commissions for architectural artworks in Tokyo and Osaka. For the last two years he has been creating unique and humorous sculptural pieces. 1.119, 2.36, 3.56

Roberto Lazzeroni was born in Pisa where he currently lives and works. He studied art and architecture in Florence, and at the same time gained experience in conceptual art and radical design, participating in shows and competitions. After finishing his studies at the end of the 1970s, he began his professional career, working in industrial design and interior architecture. 1.28, 29

Alberto Lievore is studying architecture in Buenos Aires where he works in industrial design. Based originally in Barcelona, since the mid-1970s he has established a reputation in furniture design, collaborating with Perobell, Kron and Andreu World. 1.69

Elliott Littmann holds a Bachelor of Architecture and a Master's in Architecture and Urban Design from the University of Washington. He is a member of many professional organizations, including the Austrian Society of Architects and the Goethe Institute in Germany. He has spent his career lecturing and publishing, major appointments being the Associate Professorship of Architecture and Planning at Columbia University and the Associate Professorship of Architecture and Industrial Design at the Rhode Island School of Design. Recent work includes two major publications: *Margins: The New York Daybooks*, an inquiry into the city of New York as a discovered archaeological landscape; and *An American Archaeology* (also an exhibition) which is a collection of interior spaces of lesser-known abandoned buildings. 1.75

Josep Lluscà was born in Barcelona in 1948. He studied industrial design at the Escola Eina where he is now professor, and at the École des Arts et Métiers, Montreal. He was vice-president of ADI-FAD (Industrial Designers' Association) from 1985 to 1987, and was one of the founder members of the ADP (Association of Professional Designers). He is a member of the Design Council of the Catalonian government. He has been the recipient of several major awards, including the 1990 National Design Award, and frequently attends international exhibitions and conferences, most recently "Catalonia 90's" in New York and "International Design" at the Design Museum, London. 1.7, 68, 5.29

Vittorio Locatelli and William Bertocco were both born in 1962 and studied architecture at the University of Engineering and Architecture in Milan. They collaborated first in the fields of interior design and architecture and, from 1990, in furniture design for Driade. 5.51, 54

Richard Long, a photographer and landscape artist, was born in Bristol, England, in 1945. 4.7

Vít Lukas was born in Prague in 1969. From 1983–87 he studied furniture design at the Secondary School for Applied Arts in Prague, after which he worked in an architectural studio there. In 1990 he undertook a course at the Pentiment in Hamburg. 3.41

Vico Magistretti was born in Milan in 1920. He took a degree in architecture in 1945 and subsequently joined his father's studio. Until 1960 he was mainly concerned with architecture, town planning and interiors. He began designing furniture and household articles for his buildings in the 1960s and now collaborates closely with a number of manufacturers who produce his designs. He has participated in nearly all the Milan Triennale since 1948 and has won numerous awards. Fifteen of his pieces are in the permanent collection of the Museum of Modern Art, New York. 1.20

Kaori Maki studied at the Rhode Island School of Design and with Jack Lenor Larsen in New York. She worked as a freelance, then in 1992 set up Maki Textile Studio in Tokyo. 4.16

Giuliano Malimpensa is a designer-craftsman and a member of ADI, the Italian Association for Industrial Design. 3.5

Roberto Marcatti was born in 1960 in Milan and graduated in architecture from the Polytechnic. From 1985 he was a member of the Zeus Group and for six years worked in collaboration with MAURIZIO PEREGALLI at Studio Noto. Recently, he co-founded Marcatti and Associates in Milan. He often participates in national and international architecture and design competitions. 5.13

Leonardo Marelli is the name which encompasses the work of the Estiluz Design Team. 2.7

Enzo Mari is an Italian designer, born in 1932. He studied at the Brera Academy of Fine Art in Milan and taught design methods at Milan Polytechnic. In 1972 he participated in "Italy: The New Domestic Landscape" at the Museum of Modern Art, New York. Since the 1950s he has worked on the design of glass for Danese, as well as on furniture for Driade and Gabbianelli. He has been awarded the Compasso d'Oro twice: in 1967 for his research, and in 1979 for his *Delfina* chair, manufactured by Driade. 1.9, 19, 36, 37

Javier Mariscal, a Spanish designer, was born in 1950. He trained as an artist and graphic designer and collaborated on the Memphis collection of 1981. He has designed lights with Pepe Cortès, for the Barcelona firm Bd Ediciones de diseño, textiles for Marieta and carpets for Nani Marquina. His most recent projects are a cartoon series on Cobi, the mascot for the Barcelona '92 Olympic Games, which he designed in 1988, and work with ALFREDO ARRIBAS on the interior of the Torres de Avila bar in Barcelona. 4.3

Ingo Maurer was born in Germany in 1932. After training as a typographer and graphic artist, he emigrated to the USA in 1960. He moved back to Europe in 1963 and started his own lighting design firm in 1966. He now designs furniture, and his work has been collected by the Museum of Modern Art, New York and Die Neue Sammlung, Munich. He has also exhibited in Germany, Italy, France and Russia. 2.26, 39, 43

Alessandro Mendini is the publisher of the design magazines *Casabella*, *Modo* and *Domus*. For several years he has been the theorist of avant-garde design, co-establishing the Global Tools Group in 1973 as a countermovement to established Italian design. In 1978 he started his collaboration with Studio Alchimia in Milan and developed the so-called "banal design" which sought to change items in daily use into new and ironical objects. In 1983 he became Professor of Design at the University of Applied Art in Vienna, and from 1983–88 collaborated with designers such as ACHILLE CASTIGLIONI, RICCARDO DALISI and Aldo Rossi in the Casa della Felicità for Alessi. Interior design projects include the Groningen Museum in Holland and – with Yumiko Kobayashi – the Paradise Tower, Hiroshima. 4.39, 5.52

Eiji Miyamoto was born in the textile manufacturing city of Hachioji, Japan, in 1948, graduating from the Hosei University in Tokyo in 1970. He joined his father's textile firm, Miyashin Co. Ltd, and is today the Managing Director. In 1988 he joined the Hachioji Fashion Team. He has exhibited his designs within Japan and lectures at the Bunka Fashion College. 4.24, 25

Marre Moerel was born in Breda in Holland in 1966 and studied fashion design at the St Joost Academy. She moved first to Rotterdam and then to England to study sculpture, then attended the Royal College of Art where she studied furniture design. She is currently sculpting and making furniture in London. 2.42

Giancarlo Montebello was born in Milan in 1941 and started his career as a furniture designer in a collaboration with Dina Gavina. In 1966 he co-founded his own studio, Gem, with Teresa Pomodora which encouraged artists to experiment with metal in the design of jewellery and *objets d'art*. His work is influenced by Man Ray who he met in 1970 and subsequently worked with. 3.16

Francesco Castiglione Morelli is an Italian designer currently working in a collaboration with Artemide, Milan. 2.25

Ulf Moritz graduated in 1960 from Krefeld Textilingenieurschule and worked as a textile designer for Weverij de Ploeg before setting up his own design studio in 1970. His work includes collection co-ordination, corporate identity, art direction, exhibition stands and architectural projects. He has collaborated with Felice Rossi, Montis, Ruckstuhl and Reim Interline. The textile collection *Ulf Moritz* by Sahco Hesslein was established in 1986. His work is represented in the Stedelijk Museum, Amsterdam, the Cooper-Hewitt Museum, New York and the Textielmuseum, Tilburg. Since 1971 he has been a professor at the Academy of Industrial Design in Eindhoven. 4.28–34

Massimo Morozzi, who lives and works in Milan, was, until 1972, a member of the avant-garde design group, Archizoom Associates, and the products he designed during this period can be seen in the communication archives at the University of Parma. From 1972–77, whilst co-ordinating the Montefibre Design Centre for the development of furnishing textile products, he was active in the experiments into "Primary Design". Before opening his own domestic product design studio in 1982, he worked in corporate identity and design for clients including Louis Vuitton of Paris. In 1991 he established a new office, Morozzi and Partners, with Silvia Centeleghe and Giovanni Lauda, and has collaborated with many leading manufacturers, including Alessi, Cassina, Driade and Fiam. He is at present Art Director and Corporate Graphic Designer for Edra and Mazzei. He gives lectures and seminars in Amsterdam, San Paolo, Melbourne and at the Domus Academy and Istituto Europeo di Design in Milan. 1.46

Jasper Morrison is a British furniture designer, educated in New York, Frankfurt and England. He graduated from the Royal College of Art, London, in 1985 and since then has designed and made limited batch production pieces. In 1986 he started in private practice and took part in Zeus' exhibition in Milan. He has also produced a number of projects for Sheridan Coakley (SCP), Idée, and Cappellini. His prototypes have been donated to the Vitra Museum, Germany. 1.70, 71

Paola Navone was born in Turin in 1950. After graduating from the Turin Polytechnic, she spent several years researching in the field of radical architecture and working with designers including ETTORE SOTTSASS and ALESSANDRO MENDINI, and was involved in the founding of Alchimia. In 1976 she became a product development consultant for the company Abet Laminati. She founded Mondo with Giulio Cappellini in 1987. 1.66

Guido Niest was born in 1958 in Venezuela. He came to Europe in 1979 and from 1982 studied industrial design in Munich at the Fachhochschule where he specialized in product design. Since 1986 he has worked for Sabattini Argenteria and has also founded his own design studio, Atelier Canaima, in Como which produces silver jewellery, tableware and household objects. 3.4, 5.32

Ninaber/Peters/Krouwel Industrial Design was established in 1985 by Bruno Ninaber van Eyben, Wolfram Peters and Peter Krouwel with the aim of producing a wide variety of line assembly and mass-produced products for the consumer and professional market. Ninaber graduated from Maastricht Art Academy in 1971, Peters and Krouwel from the Delft Technical University in 1978. Their work is characterized by a strong international orientation and covers all stages from design through development to pre-production management. They have won recognition both within The Netherlands and abroad, and their work can be seen in the permanent collections of the Museum of Modern Art, New York, the Stedelijk Museum, Amsterdam and the Design Museum, London, among others. In 1990 nine of their products received a Gute Industrieform recognition. 5.4, 6–8

Charlotte Packe was educated at Goldsmiths' College, London, graduating in fine art and textile design. She is now active in furniture design and collaborates with architects on retail projects, as well as undertaking private commissions. She has exhibited in Germany, Italy and Japan. 2.17

Mimmo Paladino was born in 1948 in Paduli, Italy. A painter and sculptor, he studied at the Art School in Benevento. He has exhibited widely at locations including the Kunsthalle, Basel, the Stedelijk Museum, Amsterdam and the Royal Academy, London. 4.8

David Palterer was born in Haifa, Israel, in 1949 and was educated at the University of Florence, graduating with a Laurea degree in architecture. He has worked as consultant to leading design manufacturers, including Zanotta, Driade, Alterego and Artemide, and has achieved international recognition for his work, most notably at the Milan Triennal Exhibition in 1981 and the Architectural Review International in 1982. Major projects include the Florence Air Terminal, Bird's Park in Tel Aviv and an Italian restaurant in Mito, Japan. He has been Assistant Professor of Design at the Adolfo Natalini University of Florence and professor at the Bezalel Academy in Jerusalem. He exhibits his work widely both in Israel and throughout Europe. 2.15, 32–4, 3.32–5

Marcello Panza was born in Naples in 1956 and studied there. In 1983 he founded Studio Minimo, working in interior planning and design and as a consultant in the furniture industry. In 1984 he began collaborations with Driade and Anthologie Quartett, and participated in shows in Italy and abroad. In 1990 he founded a design management office, Design . . . Connections Italia, with Claudio Giunnelli. 3.24

Tim Parsey graduated from the Central School of Art, London, with a Bachelor of Arts in industrial design in 1982. Shortly afterwards he moved to the USA, his first project design being a bobsled for the US Olympic team. He has experience in designing and managing a broad range of project types and in 1987 was awarded a Recognition of Design Achievement award from the Industrial Designers Society of America for a child's corrective footbrace for Langer Biomechanics Group. He joined ID Two in 1988 but left in 1991 before it became IDEO Product Development. He is at present with Apple Computer Inc. 5.35

Paolo Pedrizzetti was born in 1947. He studied science and architecture at the Milan Polytechnic, then started a product design collaboration with Davide Mercatali, founding an associated studio in 1982. His work can be seen in the permanent collections of museums in Chicago, San Diego, Munich and in Prato and he has been the recipient of major design awards, including the Compasso d'Oro. In 1988 he became Chief Editor of the trade magazines *Blu & Rosso* and *Bagni & Bagni* which deal with technical and aesthetical problems in bathroom design. 5.31

Jiří Pelcl was born in 1950 in Sumperk, Czechoslovakia, and trained at the Art School in Brno, the Academy of Applied Art in Prague and the Royal College of Art in London. He now works as a freelance interior and furniture designer, and in 1990 was responsible for giving a new look to President Václav Havel's study and meeting room in Prague Castle. He has exhibited in Czechoslovakia, Germany, Austria and France. 1.118, 2.41

Jorge Pensi is a Spanish architect and industrial designer, born in 1946 in Buenos Aires, Argentina. In 1977 he formed Grupo Berenguer, Design, Form and Communication with ALBERTO LIEVORE, Norberto Chaves and Oriol Pibernat. Since 1979 he has been associated with Perobell, the SIDI group and the magazine *On Diseño*. His products have been shown in exhibitions in Barcelona, Valencia and Cataluna, and he has been featured in many Spanish and international publications. 1.5, 44, 2.16, 23

Christophe Pillet graduated from the Arts Décoratifs in Nice and undertook a Master's degree at the Domus Academy in Milan in 1986. Since 1989 he has been working with PHILIPPE STARCK and has produced work for Memphis and Algorithme. He has exhibited in France, Italy and Japan, and his work has been published in various design magazines. 1.62, 2.21

Alessio Pozzoli and Sam Ribet, born in Milan and London respectively, have been collaborating since 1990, before which they both worked for Isao Hosoe. Sam Ribet graduated in industrial design and Alessio Pozzoli in car styling. 3.20

Wolf Prix and Helmut Swiczinsky see **Coop Himmelblau**

Puls Design was created in 1984 by Dieter Fornoff, Eberhard Klett and Andreas Ries who all graduated from the Darmstadt School of Design. Their services range from the development of innovative products to consumer goods, as well as 2-D design, logotypes and corporate identity. Their products range from medical implements to injection-moulding machines for plastics, and they were responsible for the first electrically-operated chair for climbing stairs. They have been the recipients of many prizes at international competitions and exhibitions. 5.10

Daniela Puppa, an architect and designer, was born in 1947 and graduated from Milan Polytechnic in 1970. A former co-editor of *Casabella* and *Modo*, she took part in the Venice Biennale of 1980, and the Milan Triennale of 1981 and 1983. She has worked in theatre design and fashion, and since 1983 has been an assistant on the fashion design course at the Domus Academy. 2.19, 20

Prospero Rasulo was born in 1953 in Stigliano, Matera, Italy. He studied at the Milan Academy of Fine Arts, then in 1980 set up a studio where he paints, sculpts and designs stage sets. He collaborated with Alchimia and ALESSANDRO MENDINI, and during the same period worked with the Occhiomagico studio, designing scenery for videos, photographs and exhibitions. In 1979 he took part in the Milan Triennale. He first began to design furniture and objects for his own personal use, then for manufacturers such as Poltronova and Foscarini. 2.8

Bernd Reibl was born in Vaihingen/Enz, Germany, and studied industrial design at the Academy of Fine Art in Stuttgart. From 1990–92 he worked for Kodak AG and is at present self-employed. 5.23

André Ricard has his own design practice in Barcelona and lectures widely both nationally and internationally. He has been the recipient of many major design awards, including the Premio Nacional de Diseño 1987, and is a member of various design juries. He organized the exhibition "Diseño España" at the Design Centre in Brussels within the Europalia in 1985, and designed the Barcelona 1992 dossier for the Olympic Games. Examples of his work can be found in the permanent collection of the Stedelijk Museum, Amsterdam. 5.48

Lino Sabattini is an Italian silversmith, born in 1925. His metalwork first attracted international attention in 1956 when it was exhibited in Paris at a show organized by the architect Giò Ponti. Since then Sabattini has continued to be closely associated with a simple, sculptural approach to metal and glassware, working for companies such as Rosenthal and Zani. He exhibits at the Milan Triennale and other major venues. In 1979 he was awarded the Compasso d'Oro. His work is in the permanent collections of the Museum of Modern Art and the Cooper-Hewitt Museum, New York, as well as the British Museum, London. 3.14, 15

Massimo Sacconi graduated in architecture in 1981 from Florence University. At present he works in lighting design and has collaborated with firms such as Osram, Nordlight and Unione Plastiche (Targetti Group). 2.6

Robin Sarre is a Senior Industrial Designer at IDEO Product Development, on exchange from the firm's London office, Moggridge Associates. Initially involved with a development programme for kitchenware, he is currently working on a wearable medical device. He was educated at the Royal College of Art in London and at the West Sussex College of Design in Worthing. He was on the jury of the 1990 RSA Design Bursaries and is a part-time lecturer at various colleges, including the Royal College of Art, London, EIVE, Eindhoven and, currently, CCAC in San Francisco. Other project clients have included Boots Co., Concord Lighting, Electrolux, HP Foods, Parker Pens and Renault. 5.35

William Sawaya was born in Beirut in 1948 and graduated from the National Academy of Fine Arts, Beirut, in 1973. An architect, he is particularly interested in the definition of internal spaces. He began his career in the Lebanon, subsequently working in the USA, France and Italy. He moved to Italy in 1978 and in 1984 established Sawaya & Moroni with Paolo Moroni. His work has been published in various magazines and newspapers throughout Europe and the USA. 3.19

Allan Scharff is one of Denmark's leading silversmiths. He trained at Georg Jensen Silversmiths during the 1960s and has now returned to Georg Jensen/Royal Copenhagen. He has recently begun to work in glass and porcelain. 3.18

Winfried Scheuer was born in Germany and graduated from the Royal College of Art, London, in 1981. He has been employed as a designer by various leading consultancies in Munich, San Francisco and London, where he has been working as a freelance since 1985. He is a visiting lecturer at the Royal College of Art. 5.11

Andreas Schulze is an artist who lives and works in Cologne. He was born in 1955 in Hanover and studied under Professor Krieg at the Academy of Art, Düsseldorf. He has exhibited in countries including Germany, Spain, Italy and the United States. 4.5

Luigi Serafini was born in Rome in 1949 and is involved in various aspects of the artistic, architectural, cinematographic and literary worlds of Rome and Milan. He designs mainly for Sawaya & Moroni. 1.85, 110, 117, 2.24

Christoph Seyferth was born in Cologne in 1966. After spending a year at art school, he served several apprenticeships in different professions, eventually becoming a furniture designer. From 1989–1991 he was an assistant at Studio Šípek in Amsterdam, after which he founded his own company. At present he is working mainly in industrial and interior design and is the technical co-ordinator of a large modern art exhibition in Gorinchem, The Netherlands, called "Brain – Internal Affairs". In 1992 he was awarded the Ko Liangl Stimulation award. 1.58, 5.15, 17

Lharne Shaw graduated from Stourbridge College of Art in 1987, having studied fine art. He has established his own studio, Tobias Associate Design and specializes in kiln-formed glass, designing and making small-batch work and producing corporate commissions. 3.30

Tadao Shimizu trained at the Cranbrook Academy of Art, Michigan, after which he worked for the Burdock Group. From 1984–87 he taught industrial design at the University of Washington. He is at present Professor of Environmental Product Design at Chiba University in Japan. He has received many national and international awards, including the first prize at the ID Annual Design Review in 1987. 1.60

Dieter Sieger established his own architect's firm in Münster-Albachten, Germany, following his graduation as an architect from the Dortmund School of Arts and Crafts in 1964. From 1965 to 1976 he was occupied with the design and construction of terraced houses and single-family houses in Greece, Spain, France, the USA and Saudi Arabia. An interest in sailing led to his interior design for sailing and motor yachts, which in turn has resulted in a collaboration with Dornbracht, and designs for modern equipment for private bathrooms. In recent years he has also ventured into ceramic design. 3.6, 5.12, 14

Bořek Šípek was born in Prague in 1949. He studied furniture design in Prague, architecture at the University of Fine Art in Hamburg and philosophy at the Technical University in Stuttgart. From 1977 to 1983 he was a lecturer at universities in Hanover and Essen. In 1983 he moved to Amsterdam where he set up his own studio, designing for companies such as Sawaya & Moroni, Vitra, Driade and Cleto Munari, as well as for the Dutch company Alterego. In 1990 he accepted the position of Professor at the Academy of Decorative Arts in Prague. His works are included in the collections of the Museum of Modern Art, New York, the Museum of Decorative Arts, Prague and museums in Düsseldorf and The Hague. 1.63, 95, 96, 107, 3.29, 31, 48–51, 60–62

Finn Sködt was born in Århus, Denmark, and studied at the Jutland Academy of Art and the Graphic College of Denmark in Copenhagen. He has worked in Italy and the USA, as well as in his native country. His collaboration with the Danish textile company Kvadrat began in 1977. 4.26, 27

Vicente Soto was born in 1948 in Almeria, Spain, and graduated as an architect and interior designer in 1960. He worked as a technical manager in various furniture factories between 1971 and 1979, and today is a freelance industrial designer. 1.2

Ettore Sottsass was born in Innsbruck, Austria, in 1917. He graduated as an architect from Turin Polytechnic in 1939, and opened an office in Milan in 1946. Since 1958 he has been a design consultant for Olivetti but is also active in fields as various as ceramics, jewellery, decorations, lithographs and drawing. He has taught and exhibited widely. In 1980 he established SOTTSASS ASSOCIATI with other architects, and in 1981 founded Memphis. He has received the Compasso d'Oro on many occasions. 1.93, 101, 103, 108, 3.52–55, 4.37, 43

Sottsass Associati is an internationally known design company based in Milan and headed by founding partners ETTORE SOTTSASS and Marco Zanini. Sebastiano Mosterts is the general manager, and Johanna Grawunder, Mike Ryan and Marco Susani have recently been named junior partners. The associati are active in the fields of architecture, interior design, industrial design, graphics and corporate image. 2.3

George Sowden was born in Leeds in 1939 and graduated in architecture from the Gloucestershire College of Art. In 1970 he moved to Milan and began his close collaboration with ETTORE SOTTSASS which resulted in a range of calculators and computers for Olivetti. From 1980–87 he had a joint studio with NATHALIE DU PASQUIER, and in 1981 was one of the founding members of Memphis for whom he designed a large number of pieces of furniture and objects with a clear reference to the Arts and Crafts movement. During 1990–91 a travelling exhibition of his works was held in the Musées des Arts Décoratifs in Bordeaux, Marseilles and Lyons. 4.42

Peter Spreenberg graduated from the Institute of Design, Chicago, with a Bachelor of Science and a High Honors in design. He joined IDEO's San Francisco office in 1988 as an interaction designer. He recently completed a one-year exchange to IDEO's London office where he helped to establish an interaction design service, as well as working on the design of various European telephony and consumer products. He teaches at the Royal College of Art, London, the California College of Arts and Crafts, San Francisco and the Sozosha College of Design, Osaka, Japan. 5.28

Philippe Starck was born in Paris in 1949 and works as a product, furniture and interior designer. In Paris he refurbished part of the Elysée Palace, and designed the Café Costes, together with a number of fashion shops. In New York he remodelled the interior of the Royalton Hotel, and in Tokyo he has designed two restaurants. His recent projects include the Teatriz nightclub in Madrid and the Paramount Hotel in New York. His furniture design has been commissioned by companies such as Disform, Driade, Baleri and Idée. Among his industrial design projects are cutlery for Sasaki, clocks for Vittel and kitchen accessories for Alessi. 1.52, 98, 112–14, 2.18, 40, 3.57–9, 5.50

Reiko Sudo was born in 1953 in the Ibaragi Prefecture, Japan. She was educated at the Musashino Art College where, following graduations, she assisted the textile professor until 1977. In 1984, after working as a freelance textile designer, she helped found Nuno Corporation of which she is still director. She has exhibited widely in Japan and abroad, and has work in permanent collections in the Cooper-Hewitt Museum, New York, the Museum of Art, Rhode Island School of Design and the Museum of Applied Arts, Finland. 4.23

Martin Szekely, born in 1957, is a French furniture and interior designer who lives and works in Paris. He has exhibited widely in Europe, the USA, Japan and Israel, and his work can be seen in the permanent collections of the Musée des Arts Décoratifs, Paris, the Cooper-Hewitt Museum, New York and the Kunstgewerbe Museums in Berlin and Cologne. His interior designs include the Musée de Picardie, Amiens, France and the Reading Room for the "Encyclopedia Universalis", Paris. In 1987 he was elected Designer of the Year by the Salon du Meuble, Paris. 1.11, 5.49

Masahito Takasuna was born in 1958 in Japan and graduated from Tokyo University of Art and Design in 1982. Since then he has been working for the Design Centre of Toshiba Corporation on kitchen design and household appliances. 5.38

Chifuyu Tanaka graduated from the industrial design course, Nihon University, Tokyo, and since 1979 has been part of the Canon Inc. Camera Design Centre Team. 5.22

Antonio Tena and Vicenç Mutgé are both architects who graduated from the Superior Technical School of Architecture, Barcelona, in 1986 and 1989 respectively. They set up Av Mutgé i Tena Arquitectes in 1989, then in 1990 founded Av Disseny, a furniture design studio. 5.1

Anthony Theakston was born in Singapore and educated in the UK where he studied ceramic design and art history. Awarded the first prize from the National Association of Graduate and Post Graduate Education in Ceramic Art, he has exhibited his work in group shows within the UK. He is at present visiting lecturer at Goldsmiths' College and at the Faculty of Art and Design at Bristol Polytechnic. 3.1

Matteo Thun was born in Bolzano, Italy, in 1952. He attended the Oscar Kokoschka Academy in Salzburg and graduated in architecture from the University of Florence. He was a partner of SOTTSASS ASSOCIATI and a member of the Memphis Group from 1979 to 1984. At present he deals mainly with industrial design, architecture, furnishings and corporate culture for product design, graphics and packaging. His works appear in the permanent collections of many of the leading art and design museums, including the Cooper-Hewitt Museum, New York and the Victoria and Albert Museum, London. He exhibits and lectures widely both nationally and internationally, and his products have won numerous awards. He is also a member of the jury for various design competitions. 1.79, 80, 2.1, 2

Oscar Tusquets Blanca was born in Barcelona in 1941. He attended the Escuela Técnica Superior de Arquitectura, Barcelona, and in 1964 established Studio Per with Lluís Clotet, collaborating on nearly all their projects until 1984. He has been a guest professor and lecturer at universities in Germany, France and the USA, and his work has been exhibited worldwide. Both his architecture and his design projects have received many awards. 1.12, 3.26, 28

Shigeru Uchida was born in Yokohama, Japan, and graduated from the Kuwasawa Design School in Tokyo. In 1970 he established Uchida Design Studio which expanded into Studio 80, a collaboration with Toru Nishioka, in 1981. Representative projects include the Il Palazzo hotel in Fukuoka, and the armchair *September* which can be seen in the permanent collection of the Metropolitan Museum of Art, New York. He lectures nationally and internationally, currently at the Universities of Columbia and Washington and the Parsons School of Design in the USA and at the Domus Academy in Milan. 1.86, 87, 91

Masahiko Uchiyama is a product planner and designer, born in Shizuoka, Japan, in 1956. Before graduating from the Chiba University, he worked in the design laboratory of Hitachi. In 1987, after working for several years with GK Industrial Design, he established his own studio, Step Design. In 1992 he held his first one-man exhibition at the Seibu Loft in Tokyo. 3.17

Masanori Umeda was born in Kanagawa, Japan, and graduated from the Kuwasawa Design School in Tokyo. He has worked for ACHILLE CASTIGLIONI's studio and for Olivetti in Milan, and from 1981–83 participated in Memphis. In 1986 he set up U-MetaDesign Inc. 5.2

André Vandenbeuck was born in Lille in 1931 and graduated from the École des Beaux Arts, where he studied sculpture and interior design. He has often collaborated with major European companies, such as Strässle in Switzerland and Faram SpA in Italy, and is active in all aspects of interior design, public through to domestic. At present he teaches design at the Institute of Design and Architecture in Paris. 1.13

Lella Vignelli was born in Udine, Italy, receiving a degree from the School of Architecture at the University of Venice, and registering as an architect in Milan in 1953. Before establishing Vignelli Associates with MASSIMO VIGNELLI in 1971, she worked for Skidmore, Owings and Merrill, and as head of the interiors department for Unimark International Corporation in Milan and New York. In 1978 the Vignellis formed Vignelli Designs, a company dedicated to product and furniture designs and of which Lella is President. Her award-winning work can be found in the permanent collections of numerous museums, including the Museum of Modern Art and the Cooper-Hewitt Museum, New York, and she is a frequent speaker and juror for national and international design organizations, as well as belonging to most of the major design societies in America. The Vignellis have been the subject of two feature-length television programmes that have been shown world-wide. 1.92

Massimo Vignelli was born in Milan and studied architecture in Milan and Venice. He went to the USA in 1957 and in 1960 started his collaboration with LELLA VIGNELLI, establishing first the Vignelli Office of Design and Architecture in Milan, then Unimark International Corporation, followed by Vignelli Associates and, finally, Vignelli Designs in 1978. His work includes graphic and corporate identity programmes, architectural graphics and interior, furniture, exhibition and product design for many leading American and European companies and institutions. He has lectured, published and exhibited throughout the world, and his work can be found in the permanent collections of leading design museums, including the Museum of Modern Art and the Cooper-Hewitt Museum, New York. He is vice-president of the American Architectural League and a member of the Industrial Designers Society of America, and his designs have achieved national and international recognition, being awarded the first Presidential Design Award by Ronald Reagan in 1985 and the Interior Product Designers' Fellowship of Excellence in 1992. 1.92

Hannes Wettstein was born in Ascona, Switzerland, in 1958 and, after working in furniture design, decided to specialize in interior design and architecture. He has worked with Baleri Italia since 1985. 2.5

Peter Wheeler was born in Austria in 1947. After graduating from the Royal College of Art, London, in 1977, he established a studio in London working on a wide range of capital goods projects. This work received awards in Britain and the USA, notably two IBD gold medals in 1983 and the Design Council Awards in 1980 and 1986. Since 1986 he has had a continuing collaboration with JANE DILLON and Floris van den Broecke on projects for furniture manufacturers in Europe, Japan and the USA, and in 1992 he began a collaboration with Mary Little. He is a visiting lecturer at colleges and universities in the UK, Ireland and Portugal. 1.14

Theo Williams was born in 1967 and graduated from Manchester Polytechnic, Department of Industrial Design, in 1990. Since 1992 he has been working with MARCO ZANUSO in Milan. His work has been published in *Design* and *Domus* magazines. 5.19

Marco Zanuso was born in 1954 in Milan and studied architecture at the University of Florence. He became assistant to the Professor of Industrial Design at Milan Polytechnic in 1980, and in the same year set up his own practice which specializes in architectural, industrial and exhibition design. In 1981 he was one of the founder members of the lighting trademark Oceano Oltreluce. 2.22

Niek Zwartjes was born in The Netherlands in 1962 and studied design at the Art Academy of Arnhem. He now teaches as an assistant at the Academy of Applied Arts in Prague. He has worked on several solo projects, as well as on collaborations with BOŘEK ŠÍPEK for Alterego. 1.59, 3.36–9, 5.16

SUPPLIERS

Acerbis International SpA. Via Brusaporto 31, 24068 Seriate, Bergamo, Italy. *Outlets* Argentina: Interieur Forma SA, Paraguay 541/555, 1057 Buenos Aires. Belgium: Artiscope-Zaira Mis, 35 Bd St. Michel, 1040 Brussels. Brazil: Forma SA, Rua Alfredo Wolf 150, 06750 Taboao da Serra. France: Francis Helven, 21 Côte des chapeliers, 26000 Valence. Greece: J. Deloudis A.E., Kifisias 217/Parnasou 2, Amaroussion, Athens. Holland: Biermans Kees, Parkstraat 9, 4818 Breda. Hong Kong: William Artists Int. Ltd, Furniture Division, 3F Shing Dao Ind. Bldg, 232A Main Road, Aberdeen. Scandinavia: Interstudio, Ludersvej 4, Frihavnen, 2100 Copenhagen, Denmark. Spain: Axa International SA, carretera Granollers, Sabadel Km, 13,5, 08185 Lica de Vall. Switzerland: Wohn Design Ag-Kaufmann Peter, Rychenbergstrasse 123. UK: Environment, The Studio, 120 High Street, South Milford, Leeds LS25 5AQ. USA: Atelier International Ltd, c/o Int. Design Centre, 30–20 Thomson Avenue, Long Island City, NY 11101.

Airon Srl. 10 Don Sturzo, Triuggio 20050, Milan, Italy. *Outlet* UK: H.N.B., 19–30 Alfred Place, London WC1E 7EA.

Aleph. See *Driade*.

Alessi SpA. Via Privata Alessi 6, 28023 Crusinallo, Novara, Italy. *Outlets* Denmark: Gense AS, 17 Maglebjergvej, 2800 Lyngby. Finland: Casabella OY, 24 Yliopistonakatu, 20100 Turku. France: Société Métallurgique Lagostina, 62 rue Blaise Pascal, 93600 Aulnay-sous-Bois. Germany: Van Der Borg GmbH, 6 Sandbahn, 4240 Emmerich. Japan: Italia Shoji Co. Ltd, 5-4 Kojimachi, 1-chome, Chiyoda-ku, Tokyo 102. The Netherlands: Interhal BV, 8 Zoutverkoperstraat, 3330 CA Zwijndrecht. Sweden: Espresso Import, 10E Furasen, 42177V Frolunda. Switzerland: Guido Mayer SA, 9 rue du Port Franc, 1003 Lausanne. UK: Penhallow Marketing Ltd, 3 Vicarage Road, Sheffield S9 3RH. USA: The Markuse Corporation, 10 Wheeling Avenue, Woburn, MA 01801.

Alias Srl. Via Respighi 2, 20122 Milan, Italy. *Outlets* France: Roger Von Bary, 18 rue Lafitte, 75009 Paris. Germany: Peter Pfeifer, Focus, 87 Leopoldstrasse, 40 Munich 8. Japan: Casatec Ltd, 2-9-6 Higashi,

Shibuya-ku, Tokyo 150. The Netherlands: Kreymborg, 63 Minervaalan, 1077 Amsterdam. Sweden: Design Distribution, 38a/1 Doebelnsgatan, 11352 Stockholm. Switzerland: Renato Stauffacher, 2 Capelli, 6900 Lugano. UK: Artemide GB Ltd, 17–19 Neal Street, London WC2H 9PU. USA: International Contract Furniture, 305 East 63rd Street, New York, NY 10021.

Alterego. 572 Egelantiersgracht, Amsterdam 1015 RR, The Netherlands. *Outlets* France: Néotù, 25 rue du Renard, 75004 Paris. Hong Kong: Le Cadre Gallery, 10th Floor, Bay Tower, 2–4 Sunning Road, Causeway Bay. Italy: Driade SpA, Via Padana Inferiore 12, 29012 Fossadello di Caorso, Piacenza. Japan: Chambres d'Amis, 3-18-20 Minami-Aoyama, Minato-ku, Tokyo 107. UK: The Ikon Corporation, B5L Metropolitan Wharf, Wapping Wall, London E1 9SS.

Amat-3 Internacional, SA. 8 Camino Can Bros, Martorell 08760, Barcelona, Spain. *Outlets* Austria: Design Agentur Rudolf Greinecker, Herbeckstrasse 27, 1183 Vienna. Belgium: Tradix, 90–92 rue du Mail, 1050 Brussels. Canada: Triede Design, 256 King Street East, Toronto, Ontario M5A 1K3. Finland: Inno Interior KY, Merikatu 1, 00140 Helsinki. France: Contrast, 11 rue de Cambrai, 75019 Paris. Italy: Hi Design, Via Marco Polo 9, 20124 Milan. Japan: Cassina Japan, 2-9-6 Higashi, Shibuya-ku, Tokyo 150. The Netherlands: Contract Design Molenaar, Rijksweg 79, Showroom Palladium, 1411 GE Naarden. Portugal: Paragrama Gestao E Servicios Ltd, Rua da Cerca 88–94, 4100 Porto. Singapore: Business World Services, 4 Shenton Way, 11–10 Shing Kwan House. Sweden: Miranda Stockholm AB, Box 3158, 10363 Stockholm. Switzerland: Dieter Haldimann, CEHA Design, Uferstrasse 90, 4057 Basel. UK: HNB Systems Ltd, 19–30 Alfred Place, London WC1E 7EA. USA: Knoll International, 655 Madison Avenue, New York, NY 10021.

Emilio Ambasz. 636 Broadway, New York, NY 10012, USA.

Ambiente Electronica. Philips Consumer Electronics, Alexander Strasse 1, 2000 Hamburg, Germany.

Andreu World SA. Cno de los Mojones, KM 2.5, 46970 Alaquas, Valencia, Spain. *Outlet* UK: Kesterport Ltd, Kestrel House, 111 Heath Road, Twickenham, Middx TW1 4AH.

Anthologie Quartett. Schloss Huennefeld, Haus Sorgenfrei, 4515 Bad Essen, Germany. *Outlets* Belgium: Surplus, 9 Zwarte Zusterstraat, 9000 Ghent. France: Altras, 24 rue Lafitte, 75009 Paris. Hong Kong: Le Cadre Gallery, 8 Sunning Road G/F, Causeway Bay. Italy: Design . . . Connections, Via R. Drengot 36, 81031 Aversa. Lebanon: Intermeuble Sarl, Boite Postale 316, Beirut. The Netherlands: Binnen, 82 Keizersgracht, 1015 Amsterdam. Switzerland: Andome Engros, 76 Dorfstrasse, 8302 Kloten.

K.K. Arai Creation System. No. 503, 5-16-8 Roppongi, Minato-ku, Tokyo 106, Japan. *Outlet* Nuno Corporation, Axis Bldg B1, 5-17-1 Roppongi, Minato-ku, Tokyo 106.

Arflex. 27 Monterosa, Cimbiate 20051, Milan, Italy. *Outlets* Austria: Ing. Manfred Prunnbauer, Selzergasse 10, 1050 Vienna. Belgium: Tradix SA, 90–92 rue du Mail, 1050 Brussels. Denmark: Lysign, Horseager 1, 2670 Greve. Finland: Stanza OY, Annankatu 24, 100 Helsinki. France: Maison Altras, 24 rue Lafitte, 75009 Paris. Germany (postal codes 1–3): H.E. Heining, Bergstrasse 24–26, 4803 Steinhagen; (postal codes 4–6): Holger Werner, Nachtigallenweg 1c, 6240 Königstein TS; (postal codes 7–8): Gotthilf Riexinger, Vorstadt 7, 7034 Gärtringen. Holland: Andrea Kok Agenturen, Pilatus 4, 1186 EK Amstelveen. Switzerland: Handelsagentur Karl Kasper, Löwengraben 24, 6000 Lucerne 5. UK: Neil Rogers Int., Unit 23, Abbeville Mews, 88 Clapham Park Road, London SW4 7BX. USA: Jerome M. Nocerino, 205 Vanderbilt Street, Brooklyn, New York, NY 11218.

Arredaesse Srl. Via S. M. Maddalena 37, 22060 Arosio, Como, Italy.

Artifort/Wagemans Maastricht BV. St. Annalaan 23, 6214 AA Maastricht, The Netherlands. *Outlets* France: Artifort/Wagemans Maastricht BV, Route de Pont Veyle, Replonges 01750. Germany: Artifort/Wagemans Möbel GmbH, 7 Siegesstrasse, Ludwigsburg.

Arteluce (Division of Gruppo Flos SpA). Via Angelo Faini 2, Bovezzo, Brescia 25073, Italy. *Outlets* Belgium: Flos SA, Gossetlaan 50, 1720 Groot Bijgaarden. France: Flos Sarl, 23 rue de Bourgogne, 75007 Paris. Germany: Flos GmbH, Am Probsthof 94, 5300 Bonn 1. Japan: Flos Co. Ltd, Dowa Bldg 4F, 18-18 Roppongi, 5-chome, Minato-ku, Tokyo. Spain: Flos SA, c/Bovedillas 16, San Just Desvern, 08960 Barcelona. Switzerland: Flos SA, 36 Place du Bourg de Four, 1204 Geneva. UK: Flos Ltd, The Studio, 120 High Street, South Milford, Leeds, Yorks. LS25 5AQ. USA: Flos Inc., 200 McKay Road, Huntington Station, New York, NY 11746.

Artemide SpA. Via Bergamo 18, 20010 Pregnana Milanese, Milan, Italy. *Outlets* Australia: ECC Lighting Ltd, 18–20 Allen Street, Pyrmont, NSW 2009. Austria: Vertreter Design Agentur R. Greinecker, Herbeckstrasse 27, 1183 Vienna. Canada: Artemide Ltd, 2150 Hymus Blvd, Dorval, Quebec H9P 1J7. France: Artemide E.u.r.l., 6–8 rue Basfroi, 75011 Paris. Germany: Artemide GmbH, Itterpark 5, D-4010 Hilden. Hong Kong: Artemide Ltd, 102–103 Ruttonjiee Centre, Duddel Street. Japan: Artemide Inc., 2nd Floor Axis Bldg, 5-17-1 Roppongi, Minato-ku, Tokyo 106. Spain: Artemide SA, C/Ripolles 5 y 7 08820 Prat de Llobregat, Barcelona. Switzerland: Artemide Illuminazione AG, Via Trevano 72, 6900 Lugano. UK: Artemide GB Ltd, 17–19 Neal Street, London WC2H 9PU. USA: Artemide Inc., National Sales and Customer Service Center, 1980 New Highway, Farmingdale, NY 11735.

Asahi Optical Company (Pentax Industrial Design). 2-36-9, Maeno-cho, Itabashi-ku, Tokyo 174, Japan. *Outlets* Belgium: Pentax Europe NV, Weiveldlaan 3–5, 1930 Zaventem. France: Pentax France, Z.I. Argenteuil, 12 rue Ambroise Croizat, 95106 Argenteuil. Germany: Pentax Handelsgesellschaft mbH, Julius-Vosseler-Strasse 104, 2000 Hamburg 54. Japan: Pentax Japan, 1-11-1 Nagata-cho, Chiyoda-ku, Tokyo. The Netherlands: Pentax Nederland, Spinveld 25, 4815 HR Breda. Scandinavia: Pentax Scandinavia AB, Falhagsleden 57, 75127 Uppsala, Sweden. UK: Pentax UK Ltd, Pentax House, South Hill Avenue, South Harrow, Middx HA2 0LT. USA: Pentax Corporation, 35 Inverness Drive East, Englewood, Colorado 80112.

Au Bain Marie. 12 rue Boissy D'Anglas, Paris 75008, France.

Audiovox. 150 Marcus Blvd, Happaugh, New York, NY 11788, USA.

Avocet International. 171 University Avenue, Palo Alto, California 94301, USA.

Baleri Srl. Via San Bernardino 39, Lallio 24040, Bergamo, Italy. *Outlets* France: Francis Helven, 21 Côte des Chapeliers, Valence 2000. Germany: Walter Schiedermeier, Marienbergerweg 12, Cologne 5000. Japan: Casatec Ltd, 9-6 Higashi, 2-chome Shibuya-ku, Tokyo 150. The Netherlands: Kreymborg, 66 Avenue Molière, Brussels 1180, Belgium. Scandinavia: Lysign, 1 Horseager, Greve 2670, Denmark. Spain: Josep Cunill Bonmati, San Juan Batista de la Salle, Esc.A, Premia de Mar 8330. UK: Liberty Public Ltd

Co., Regent Street, London W1R 6AH. USA: I.C.F. Inc. International, 305 East 63rd Street, New York, NY 10021.

Bañó & Asociados. Gran via Germanias 36, 46006 Valencia, Spain.

Bar Metals. G.F.R. Srl, Via Lanza 4, Milan, Italy.

Baxter Healthcare Corporation, Novacor Division. 7799 Pardee Lane, Oakland, California 94621, USA.

B & B Italia SpA. Strada Provinciale, Novedrate 22060, Como, Italy. *Outlets* France: Jean Bernard Negre, 9 rue Raspail, Toulouse 31500. Germany: Berndt Schmidt, 25 Tannenweg, 8000 Munich 50. Italy: Castelletti Marco, Via Bisceglie 35, Milan 20152. Japan: B&B Japan, Higashi 2-9-8, Shibuya-ku, Tokyo 150. The Netherlands: Johan Spek, Postbus 637, CC Uithoorn 1420, Holland. Scandinavia: Renzo d'Este, H. E. Teglersvej 5, Charlottenlund 2920, Denmark. Spain: Federico Alvarez de Arcaya, 3 C/LA Platxa, Ametzaga de Zuya Alava 01139, Spain. UK: Keith de la Plain, Milroy House, 5 Sayers Lane, Tenterden, Kent TN30 6BW. USA: B&B Italia Inc., Idncy, Center Two, Space 401, 30–20 Thomson Avenue, Long Island City, NY 11101.

Bd. Ediciones de Diseño. 291 Mallorca, 08037 Barcelona, Spain. *Outlets* Belgium: Quattro, Centre Le Bosquet, Jodoigne-Geldenaken 5900. Canada: Triedei, 460 McGill, Montreal, Quebec H2Y 2H2. France: Nestor Perkal, 8 rue des Quatre Fils, 75003 Paris. Germany: IMD Inter-Marketing Distribution AG, Flothbruchstrasse 11, 4156 Willich 2, Anrath. Hong Kong: Le Cadre Gallery, 8 Sunning Road G/F, Causeway Bay. Italy: Bd Italia, Piazza San Marco 1, 20100 Milan. Japan: Gendai Kikakushitsu, Koshin Bldg, 302 2-2-5, Sarugaku-cho, Chiyoda-ku, Tokyo. Switzerland: IMD Inter-Marketing Distribution AG, Eerburnestrasse 26, Hausen (AG) 5212. UK: The Ikon Corporation, B5L Metropolitan Wharf, Wapping Wall, London E1 9SS. USA: Manifesto, 200 West Superior Street, Chicago, Illinois; Lymnn, 457 Pacific Avenue, San Francisco 94133.

Beargrip Tool. Ruinerweg 12, 7932 PD Echten, The Netherlands.

Bieffeplast. 78 Via Pelosa, Caselle di Selvazzano 35030, Padua, Italy. *Outlets* France: Protis, 135 Avenue Louis Roche, Gennevilliers 92230. Germany: Schmitz Werner, 151 Düsseldorfer Strasse, Düsseldorf 11 4000. Japan: Nova Oshima Co. Ltd, Sakakura Bldg, 9-6-14 Akasaka, Tokyo. The Netherlands: Horas International, 25 Beemdstraat, Ruisbroek, Brussels 1601, Belgium. Spain: Kaes Internacional, B. de Ventas Casa Errota, Zahar, Bajos, Zarauz 20800. UK: OMK Design Ltd, Stephen Bldg, 30 Stephen Street, London W1P 1PN. USA: Gullans International Inc., 67 Poland Street, Bridgeport, CT 06605.

B.Lux. Poligono Eitu, s/no, Berriz 48240, Vizcaya, Spain.

Bosse Telekomsysteme GmbH. 80 Reichenberger Strasse, 1000 Berlin 36, Germany.

BRF. Via Cassina Nord 45, 50021 Barderino Val d'Elsa, Florence, Italy. *Outlet* France: Jean-Louis Lambert, 22 Allée du Plateau, Le Raincy, 93340.

Bros's Srl. Via Sotto Rive 1, S. Giovanni al Matisone 33048, Udine, Italy. *Outlets* Austria: Otto Silhavicek, Nussdorgerstrasse 36, 1060 Vienna. Belgium: Horas International, 22 rue Copernic, Brussels 1180. France: Horas International, 136–50 rue Championet, 75918 Paris. Germany: Sedia GmbH, Zoppenbroich 1, 4050 Mönchengladbach 2. Greece: J. Deloudis AE, Kifisias 217 ET, Parnasou 2, Amaroussion, 15124 Athens. The Netherlands: Horas International, Zonnebos 29, NN Vught 5263. Sweden: Sedia, PO Box 138, Lammhult 376030. Switzerland: O Daehnel, Zollierstrasse 28, Zollikon, Zurich. UK: Interior Marketing, 36 Stansted Road, Hockerill, Bishop's Stortford, Hertfordshire CM23 2DY. USA: Cy Man Design Ltd, 150 Fulcron Avenue, Garden City Park, New York, NY 11140.

Canon Inc. PO Box 5050, Shinjuku Dai-ichi Seimei Bldg, Tokyo 163, Japan. *Outlets* Austria: Canon, Modecenterstrasse 22 A-2, 1030 Vienna. Belgium: Canon Copiers Belgium, NVISA, Luidlaam 33-Bus 6, 100 Brussels. Canada: Canon Canada Inc., 3245 American Drive, Mississauga, Ontario L4V 1N4. Denmark: Christian Bruhn AS, Vasekaer 12, 2729 Herlev. France: Canon France SA, PO Box 40, 93151 Le Blanc Mesnil. Germany: Canon Copylux GmbH, Leurriper Strasse 1–13, 4050 Mönchengladbach. Italy: Canon Italia SpA, Centro Direzionale, Palazzo Verocchio, 20090 Milan 2-Segrate MI. The Netherlands: Canon Verkooporganisatie Nederland BV, Cruquiusweg 29, 2102 LS Heemstede, Amsterdam. Norway: Noiseless AS, Tventenveien 30B, Oslo 6. Spain: Canon Copiardoras de España SA, Avd. Menendez Pelayo, 57 Torre del Retiro, Madrid. Sweden: Canon Svenska AB, Box 2084, Stensatrava gen 13, 12702 Stockholm. Switzerland: Canon SA, 1 rue de Hesse, 1204 Geneva. UK: Canon (UK) Ltd, Canon House, Manor Road, Wallington, Surrey SM6 0AJ. USA: Canon USA Inc., One Canon Plaza, Lake Success, New York, NY 11042-9979.

Cappellini Arte. Via Marconi 35, 22060 Arosio, Italy. *Outlets* Austria: Wolfgang Bischof OHG, Judenplatz 6, 1010 Vienna. Belgium: Rika Andries, Turnhoutsebaan 144b, 2200 Borgerhout. France: Cerutti Giuseppe, Loc. Grand Chemin 1, 11020 Saint Christophe. Germany: Novus (Sig. Pfeiffer), Gartenstrasse 26, 7959 Achstetten Bronnen 3. The Netherlands: Hansje Kalff Meubelagenturen, Puttensestraat 8, 1181 Je Amstelveen, Holland. Sweden: Mobile Box AB, Nybrogatan 11, 11439 Stockholm. Switzerland: Yves Humbrecht Diffusion, Mon Repos 3, 1066 Epalinges. UK: SCP Ltd, 135–139 Curtain Road, London EC2. USA and Canada: Ivan Luini, 453 West 19th Street, App. 6A, New York, NY 10011.

Carlos Jané Camacho SA. S/no Pol. Industrial "Els Xops", Granollers 08400, Barcelona, Spain. *Outlets* France: Philippe Siraud, 32 rue Hamelin, 75116 Paris. Japan: Mohly Shop Co. Ltd, 1-15-9 Minami Horie, Nishiku, Osaka 550. The Netherlands: Amda BV, Oosterhootlaan 37, 1181 Al Amstelveen, Holland.

Casas. Polignono Santa Rita, Calle 2, Manzana 4, Castellbisbal 08755, Barcelona, Spain.

Cassina SpA. Via Luigi Busnelli 1, Meda 20036, Milan, Italy. *Outlets* France: Sanda, 168 rue du Faubourg Saint Honoré, Paris 75008. Germany: Pesch GmbH & Co. KG, Kaiser Wilhelm Ring 22, 5000 Cologne 1. Japan: Cassina Japan Inc., 2-9-6 Higashi, Shibuya-ku, Tokyo 150. The Netherlands: Mobica, 31 Middenweg, 3401 Ijsselstein. Spain: Mobilplast, 40 calle Milagro, 08028 Barcelona. UK: Marcatré, 179 Shaftesbury Avenue, London WC2H 8AR. USA: Atelier International Inc., The International Design Center, 30–20 Thomson Avenue, Long Island City, NY 11101.

Castelli SpA. Via Torreggiani 1, Bologna 40128, Italy.

Chairs. Axis Bldg 4F, 5-17-1 Roppongi, Minato-ku, Tokyo, Japan.

Ciatti Spa. Via del Botteghino, loc, Borgo ai Fossi, 50010 Badia a Settimo, Scandicci, Florence, Italy.

Cidue SpA. Via S Lorenzo 32, 36010 Carre, VI, Italy. *Outlets* France: Jacques Dollard, 32 Bis rue des Jardiniers, Nancy 54000. Germany: Cidue ServiceBuro, Fliegenstrasse 8, 8000 Munich 2. Hong Kong: Executive Design, 53 Wong Nei Chong. Japan: Italcomm Ltd, Likura Comfy Bldg B 101, 4-4 Azabudai 3-chome, Minato-ku, Tokyo. The Netherlands: Espaces et Lignes, P.O. Box 406, 2040 Zandvoort. Spain: Xarma SI, C/San Martin 57–3, San Sebastian 20007. Sweden: Inside AB, P.O. Box 7689, Stockholm 10395. UK: Atrium, 113 St Peter, St Albans, Herts. AL1 3ET. USA: Niels Olehansen Inc., 1129 Magnolia Avenue, Larkspur 94939.

Michael Clapper Design. 18 Dig Road, Lansing, New York 14882, USA.

Nick Crowe Design. 90–92 Highgate Road, Kentish Town, London NW5 1PB. *Outlets* France: Turbulence, 4 Allée du Clos Fleury, Clamart 92140. The Netherlands: Intermezzo, Voorstraat 178, 3311 ES Dordrecht. Turkey: Atelye Derin, Abdi Ipekci Cad 1411, 80220 Nistanasi, Istanbul. UK: The Study, 55 Endell Street, Covent Garden, London WC2H 9AJ.

Cuisinarts. 1 Cummings Point Road, Stamford, Connecticut, CT 06902, USA.

Daisalux SA. Ibarredi 4, Pol. Industrial de Júndiz, Vitoria 01195, Alava, Spain. *Outlets* Belgium: Lichtplanning Erik Huysmans, 1A Dijkstraat, Lokeren B.9100. Italy: I Guzzini, SS 77 km 102, Recanati 62019.

Greg Daly. Raintree-Marra, Cowra 2794, NSW, Australia.

Design 134. Stradvejen 134, 2900 Hellerup, Denmark.

Design Gallery Milano. Via Manzoni 46, 20121 Milan 46, Italy.

Design House AWA. 1-21-1 Jingumae, Shibuya-ku, Tokyo 150, Japan.

Design Studio TAD. 3-8-16-608 Nishiogi-Minami, Suginami-ku, Tokyo 167, Japan.

Divano SA. En Proyecto 2, 46470 Albal, Valencia, Spain.

Dobro. See *Alterego*.

Driade SpA. Via Padana Inferiore 12, Fossadello di Caorso 29012, Piacenza, Italy. *Outlets* Austria and Bavaria: Die Kommode, Lerchenfelderstrasse 12, A-1080 Vienna. France: Arturo Del Punta, 7 rue Simon Le Franc, 75004 Paris. Germany: Stefan Müller, Hildegardstrasse 5, 8000 Munich 22. Japan: Ambiente International Inc., Sumitomo Semei Bldg 3-1-30, Minami-Aoyama, Minato-ku, Tokyo. The Netherlands: Espaces et Lignes, Nassaulaan 2A, 2514 JS'S Gravenhague. Scandinavia: Design Distribution, Doebelnsgatan 38a/1, 11352 Stockholm, Sweden. Spain: Sellex Po D. de Mandas, Torre Atocha, 1o Pianta, No. 53A, 20012 San Sebastian. UK: Viaduct Furniture, Spring House, 10 Spring Place, London NW5 3BH. USA: Tonia Pozzoli, 14 Silver Pine Terrace, 94903 San Rafael, CA.

Duravit AG. Werderstrasse 36, Postfach 240, Hornberg 7746, Germany.

e De Padova. 14 Corso Venezia, Milan 20121, Italy. *Outlets* Belgium: Andries P.V.B.A., Turnhoutsebaan 144b, Antwerp 02140. Germany: Pesch GmbH & Co. KG, Kaiser Wilhelm-Ring 22, 5000 Cologne 1. Japan: Interdecor/Casatec Ltd, 2-9-6 Higashi, Shibuya-ku, Tokyo 150. The Netherlands: Hansje Kalff, Puttensestraat 8, Je Amstelveen, Holland. Scandinavia: Inside AB, 76 Sveavaegen, Box 3310, 103 66 Stockholm, Sweden. Spain: IDEA Mueble SA, 185 Via Augusta, Barcelona 21. USA: Limn Studio, 290 Towsend Street, 94107 San Francisco, CA.

Edra SpA. Via Toscana 11, 56030 Perignano, Pisa, Italy.

Epiag – Porcelan Dalovice. 20 Hlavni, Karlovy Vary 360 13, Czechoslovakia.

Estiluz SA. S/n Ctra de Ogassa, S. Juan Abadesses 17860, Gerona, Spain.

Edward Fields Carpet Makers. 232 East 59th Street, New York, NY 10022, USA.

Flight (Division of Flos SpA). Via Angelo Faini 2, Bovezzo, Brescia 25073, Italy.

Flos SpA. Via Angelo Faini 2, Bovezzo, Brescia 25073, Italy. *Outlets* Belgium: Flos Sarl, Gossetlaan 50, 1720 Groot Bijgaarden. France: Flos Sarl, 23 rue de Bourgogne, 75007 Paris. Germany: Flos GmbH, Am Probsthof 94, 5300 Bonn 1. Japan: Flos Co. Ltd, Dowa Bldg 4F, 18-18 Roppongi 5-chome, Minato-ku, Tokyo. Spain: Flos SA, c/Bovedillas 16, San Just Desvern, 08960 Barcelona. Switzerland: Flos SA, 36 Place du Bourg de Four, 1204 Geneva. UK: Flos Ltd, The Studio, 120 High Street, South Milford, Leeds, Yorks. LS25 5AQ. USA: Flos Inc., 200 McKay Road, Huntington Station, New York, NY 11746.

FontanaArte. Alzaia Trieste 49, 20094 Corsico, Italy. *Outlets* Austria: Einrichtungs-Verkaufs GmbH Co. KG, 27 Hagenstrasse, 4020 Linz. Belgium: M. Frank PVBA, 25 Wijngaardstraat, 2000 Antwerp. Canada: Angle International, 296 St Paul West, Montreal, Quebec. France: Giuseppe Cerutti, 1 Loc Grand Chemin, 11020 Aosta, Italy. Germany: Fr. Van der Beck, 52 Bahnhofstrasse, 3472 Beverungen 1. The Netherlands: Silvera BV, Postbus 163, 1250 AD Laren. Switzerland: Formatera AG, 54 Stockerstrasse, 8022 Zürich. USA: Interna Design Ltd, The Merchandising Mart, Space 6-168, Chicago, Illinois 60654.

Foscarini Murano SpA. 1 Fondamenta Manin, Murano, Venice 30141, Italy. *Outlets* France: Horas International, 150 rue Championnet, Paris. Germany: Alta Linea GmbH, 6 Sandhof, 4040 Neuss 21 Norff. The Netherlands: Horas International, Beemdstraat 25, Ruisbroek 1610. UK: Liaison, 917–919 Fulham Road, London SW6 5HU.

Fujie Textile Co. Ltd. 4-7-12 Sendagaya, Shibuya-ku, Tokyo 151, Japan.

Galerie Maeght. 12 rue Saint Mervie, Paris 75004, France.

Garcia Garay SA. 13 San Antonio, Santa Coloma de Gramanet 08923, Barcelona, Spain. *Outlets* Austria: Plan Light, 25 Fiecht Au, Schwaz A-6130. France: Inedit, 5 rue Charenne, Paris 75011. Germany: Mega Light, 4 Tilsiter Strasse, Frankfurt 6000. The Netherlands: Gaga Design, 31 Sandbergstraat, NL 1391 Ek Abcoude. UK: Into Lighting, 49 High Street, Wimbledon Village, London SW19.

Glass Design. Via Rivolta 6, 20050 Macheno, Milan 30, Italy.

Koji Hamai. Daisanishigen-Haim B33, 1-5-10 Kamitakaido, Suginami-ku, Tokyo, Japan.

Jochen Henkels Büro für Produktgestaltung. Gausstrasse 15, 2000 Hamburg 50, Germany.

Hip Shing Fat Co. Ltd. Rooms 1829–1832, Star House, 3 Salisbury Road, Tsim Sha Tsui, Kowloon, Hong Kong. *Outlet* Germany: Heinz Tröber GmbH & Co., Saseler Bogen 5+6, 2000 Hamburg 65.

Hironen. 502 Seiho Residence, 2-7-18 Osaki, Shinagawa-ku, Tokyo 141, Japan.

Hishinuma Associates. 5-41-2 Jingumae, Shibuya-ku, Tokyo 150, Japan.

Hop-Là. Via Manzoni 11, Milan, Italy.

Bohuslav Horák. 270 Bri Capku, Holice v Cechach 53401, Czechoslovakia.

Hour-Lavigne. 1 rue Rataud, 78005 Paris, France.

Interflex SpA. Via Indipendenza 161–3, 20036 Meda, Milan, Italy. *Outlets* Denmark: Interstudio, Luedersvej 4, Frihavnen, 2100 Copenhagen. Switzerland: Inter-Marketing Distribution, Eerburnestrasse 26, 5212 Hausen. UK: Neil Rogers Interiors, Unit 23, Abbeville Mews, 88 Clapham Park Road, London SW4 7BX.

Interform MFG Inc. 1-4-9 Kyomachibori, Nishi-ku, Osaka 550, Japan. *Outlet* Italy: Nito Arredamenti Srl, Via E. Mattei 19, 53041 Asciano, Siena.

Kouji Kikuchi. 621-1 Minami-Ishikicho, Ougakishi Gifu, Japan.

Kingirikōgei. 1-8-7 Shinmei-cho, Kamo-shi, Niigata-ken 959-13, Japan. *Outlet* Archistudio Ozone, 6-1-6-301 Minami-Aoyama, Minato-ku, Tokyo 107.

The Knoll Group. 655 Madison Avenue, New York, NY 10021, USA. *Outlets* France: Knoll-France, 268 Boulevard St. Germaine, Paris 75007. Germany: Knoll-Germany, Mecklenburgische Strasse 20, Berlin W-1000 31. Italy: Knoll-Italy, Via dei Tornabuoni 8–10, Florence 50100. Japan: Knoll-Japan, Kokusai Bldg, 3-1-1 Marunouchi, Chiyoda-ku, Tokyo 100. The Netherlands: Knoll-Netherlands, Vreeswijksestraatweg 22, Nieuwegein 3424. Spain: Knoll-Spain, Idea Madrid, Paseo de la Habana 24, Madrid 28036. UK: Knoll-England, 20 Savile Row, London W1X 1AE.

Makoto Komatsu. 500-2 No., Gyoda-shi 361, Saitama-Ken, Japan.

Kron SA. S/n Camino Ancho, 28814 Daganzo, Madrid, Spain. *Outlet* UK: Co-Existence Ltd, 288 Upper Street, London N1 2TZ.

Masayuki Kurokawa. Flat Aoyama 101, 5-15-9 Minami-Aoyama, Minato-ku, Tokyo 107, Japan.

Kvadrat Boligtextiler A/S. 10 Lundbergsvej, Ebeltoft 8400, Denmark. *Outlets* Italy: Rapsel SpA, Via Alessandro Volta 13, I-20019 Settimo Milanese, Milan. Japan: Euro Design Ltd, 6F Matsuki Bldg, 3-8 Shiba Park 1-chome, Minato-ku, Tokyo 105. The Netherlands: Danskina, Postbus 22620, Hettenheuvelweg 14, NL-1101 BN Amsterdam ZO. Switzerland: Kvadrat AG, Postfach 87, CH-8370 Sirnach. UK: Kvadrat Ltd, 62 Princedale Road, London W11 4NL.

Kyushu Matsushita Electric Co., Ltd. Business Equipment Division, 4-1-62 Minoshima, Hakata-ku, Fukuoka City, Fukuoka 812, Japan.

Danny Lane. 19 Hythe Road, London NW10 6RT, UK.

Lorenz SpA. Via Marina 3, Milan 20121, Italy. *Outlet* UK: John Lewis Partnership, 171 Victoria Street, London SW1E 5NN.

Magis Srl. 15 Via Magnadola, Motta di Livenza 31045, Treviso, Italy. *Outlets* Germany: Elmar Floetotto Haudelsi, 28 Am Öl Bach, Gütersloh 4830. Korea: Genoa Corporation, 55-5 Nou Hyon Dong Kangne, Seoul. The Netherlands: Quattro Benelux SA, 25 rue de la Regence, Brussels 01000, Belgium. Scandinavia: Swedia Mobel AB, Box 138, Lammhult 36030, Sweden.

Maki Textile Studio. Chiaki Maki, 899-7 Tothara, Itsukaichi-machi, Nishitamagun, Tokyo 109-01, Japan.

Manufactura Toro Ceramica Valencia. 9 de Octubre 41, E-46113 Moncada, Valencia, Spain.

Marsberger Glaswerke Ritzenhoff GmbH. 84 Paulienenstrasse, 3538 Marsberg 1, Germany. *Outlets* Belgium: Interhal Select BV, Zoutverkoopersstraat 8, NL 3334 KJ Zwijndrecht. Germany: Van der Borg GmbH, Postfach 100264, Ossenbruch 5, D-4240 Emmerich. Italy: Carlo Gianolini SpA, Via Caporalino 9, 25060 Cellatica, Brescia. Mexico: Nacional Imporradora NISA de CV, Av. Sonora 103, Col Roma, 06700 Mexico DF. Switzerland: Guido Mayer SA, 1312 Eclepens-Gare VD, Case Postale. USA and Canada: Oggetti, 48 Northwest 25th Street, Miami, Florida 33127.

Matsushita Electric Works Ltd. 1048 Kodama, Osaka 571, Japan. *Outlets* Australia: Panasonic (Australia) Pty Ltd, PO Box 319, 95–99 Epping Road, North Ryde, NSW 2113. Germany: Panasonic Deutschland GmbH, Winsbergring 15, D-2000 Hamburg 54. Italy: Fratelli Milani Srl, Via Valsolda 20143, Milan 13. The Netherlands: Haagtechno BV, Rietveldenweg 60, Postbus 236, Den Bosch. Scandinavia: Panasonic Svenska AB, Instrumentagen 29–31, PO Box 47327, 10074 Stockholm, Sweden. UK: Panasonic Business Systems UK, Panasonic House, Willoughby Road, Bracknell, Berks. RG12 4FP. USA: Panasonic Communication & Systems Company, Communication Systems Division, 2 Panasonic Way, Secaucus, New Jersey 07094.

Matsushita Seiko Co. Ltd. 62-2-6 Chome, Imafuku Nishi, Joto-ku, Osaka 536, Japan.

Ingo Maurer. 47 Kaiserstrasse, 8000 Munich 40, Germany. *Outlets* France: Altras Sarl, 24 rue Lafitte, Paris, 75009. Italy: Pierre Daverio & C. SAS, Via del Colle 3, Casciago 21020. The Netherlands: Peter A. Hesselmans, 284 P. J. Oudstraat, Papendrecht 3354 VJ. Scandinavia (except Sweden): Finn Sloth, 2 Heilsmindevej, Charlottenlund, Denmark 2920. Switzerland: Domani AG, 231 Seefeldstrasse, Zurich 8008. USA: Ivan Luini, 453 West 19th Street, Apt. 6a, New York, NY 10011.

Eva-Maria Melchers. 3 Domsheide, Bremen 2800, Germany.

Memphis Milano Srl. Via Olivetti 9, Pregnana Milanese 20010, Italy. *Outlets* Australia: Artemide Pty Ltd, 69 Edward Street, Pyrmont, NSW 2009. Austria: Prodomo, 35–7 Flachgasse, 1150 Vienna. Belgium: Horas SA, 25 Beemstraat, 1610 Ruisbroek. Canada: Artemide Ltd, 354 Davenport Road, Designers Walk, 3rd Floor, Toronto M15 RK5. Denmark: D'Este Renzo, H.E. Teglersvej 5, Charlottenlund 2920. France: Roger Von Bary, 18 rue Lafitte, 75009 Paris. Germany: Artemide GmbH, Itterpark 5, Hilden 4010. Hong Kong: Le Cadre Gallery, 8 Sunning Road G/F, Causeway Bay. The Netherlands: Copi, 90A Prinsestraat, 2513 OG, The Hague. Switzerland: Bell'Arte C. Arquint, 13 Loostrasse, 6430 Schwyz. UK: Artemide GB Ltd, 17–19 Neal Street, London WC2H 9PU. USA: Urban Architecture Inc., 15 East Kirby Street, Detroit, Michigan 48202.

Merkur Solingen. Friedrich Wilhelm Strasse 18, 5650 Solingen, Germany. *Outlets* Germany: Fierus Design, Am Gierlichshof 10, D-5090 Leverkusen 3. UK: Winfried Scheuer, 53 Leicester Square, London W2.

Mesa Snc. Via Marinotti 3, Cadorago 22071, Como, Italy.

Miyashin Co. Ltd. 582-11 Kitanomachi, Hachiioji-Shi, Tokyo 192, Japan.

Mondo Srl. Via Vittorio 25, 22060 Carugo, Italy. *Outlets* Austria: Wolfgang Bischoff, Judenplatz 6, 1010 Vienna. Belgium: Rika Andries, 144b Turnhoutsebaan, Borgerhout 2200. France: Giuseppe Cerutti, Loc Grand Chemin 1, 11020 Saint Christophe. Germany: Novus, 26 Gartenstrasse, 7959 Achstetten 3. The Netherlands: Koos Rijkse Agency, P.R. Christinalaan 1, 7437 XZ Bathmen. Spain: Jose Martinez Medina SA, Camino del Bony S/N, Catarroja Valencia. Sweden: Mobile Box AB, Hargs Saeteri, 19490 Upplands Vasby. Switzerland: Yves Humbrecht Diffusion, Saleve 10, 1004 Lausanne. UK: Essential Business Contacts, Lawnfield House, Westmorland Road, Maidenhead, Berks. SL6 4HB.

Moormann Möbel-Produktions-und-Handels GmbH. Kirchplatz, Aschau/Chiemgau 8213, Germany. *Outlets* The Netherlands: Richard Klees, 431 Tarthorst, 48 Wageningen 6708. Switzerland: Andome Engros, Pfungener Strasse 77, Oberembrach 8425.

Moroso. Via Nazionale 60, Cavalicco di Tavagnacco, 33010 Udine, Italy. *Outlets* Australia: Canberra Flair Pty Ltd, 8 Ipswick Street, Fyshwick Act. 2609. Austria: Michel Pilte, Via dei Colli 24, 33019 Tricesimo, Udine, Italy. Belgium: Interdiff SPRL, rue de la Sablonnière 21, 1000 Brussels. Denmark and Sweden: Swedia Moebel AB, PO Box 138, 36030 Lammhult. Finland: Stanza OY, Annankatu 24, 00100, Helsinki. France (Paris): Signature's, avenue de l'Observatoire 34, 75015 Paris; (regions): François Carlier, avenue Jean Jaurès 113, 92120, Montrouge. Germany (postal codes 1–3): Thomas Graeper, Enzianstrasse 8, 4902 Bad Salzuflen; (postal codes 4–5): Walter J. Schiedermeier, Marienbergerweg 12, 5000 Cologne 71; (postal codes 6–8): Hubert Essenko, Maxim-Wetzgerstrasse 6, 8000 Munich 19. Hong Kong: Le Cadre Gallery Ltd, 4B Sunning Road G/F, Causeway Bay. Japan: Corrente Corporation, 3-2-chome, Kanda-Isukasa-cho, Chiyoda-ku, Tokyo. The Netherlands: Ivo Verbeek Meubelimport, Johan Huizinhgalaan 288, 1065 JN Amsterdam. Singapore: Abraxas Design Pte Ltd, 4 Shenton Way, 01–01 Shing Kwan House, Singapore 0106. Spain: Roger Sin Roca, Ronda Gral. Mitre 174–176, 08006 Barcelona. Switzerland: Oliver Ike, Kroenleinstrasse 31/a, 8044 Zurich. UK: Orchard Associates, 2 Davenport Close, Teddington, Middx TW11 9EF.

Néotù. 25 rue du Renard, 75004 Paris, France. *Outlet* USA: 133 Greene Street, New York, NY 10012.

Christopher Nevile Design Partnership. 55 Endell Street, London WC2, UK.

Guido Niest (Atelier Canaima). Via Resistenza 16, Bregnano 22070, Como, Italy.

Noto. Via Vigevano 8, 20144 Milan, Italy. *Outlets* France: Jean Gabriel Robin, Chemin des Sables, F 69970 Chaponnay. Japan: Ambiente Int. Inc., Sumitomo Seimei Bldg, 3-1-30 Minami-Aoyama, Minato-ku, Tokyo 107. The Netherlands: Andrea KOK Agenturen, Pilatus 4, 1186 EK Amstelveen, Holland. Scandinavia: Casalab, Mosebakken 19, DK 6 2830 Virum, Copenhagen, Denmark. UK: Viaduct Furniture Ltd, Spring House, 10 Spring Place, London NW5 3BH. USA: Luminaire, 7300 SW 45th Street, Miami, Florida 33155.

Nuno Corporation. Axis B1, 5-17-1 Roppongi, Minato-ku, Tokyo 106, Japan.

Oceano Oltreluce Snc. Via Tortona 14, 20144 Milan, Italy. *Outlets* Austria: Die Kommode, 12 Lerchenfelderstrasse, Vienna 1080. France: Gilles Chennouf, 15 rue du Petit Musc, Paris 75004. Germany: Armin Preiss, 33 Hasenstrasse, Stuttgart. Mexico: Design Primario, 235 Temistocoles Col. Polanco, Mexico City. The Netherlands: Carla Doesburg, 172 Mechelsesteenweg, Antwerp B-2018.

Ocsa (Cultural Olympics). Diputacion, 250, Barcelona, Spain.

Oken. Narváez, s/no Pol. Industrial "Can Jardí", Rubi 08191, Barcelona, Spain. *Outlets* Australia: Executive Office Interiors, 260 City Road, South Melbourne 3205. Germany: Andreas Jaek Agentur, Neue Strasse 3, Oldenburg 2900. The Netherlands: Bax, Hakgriend 46, Hardinxveld-Giessendam 3371 KA. Scandinavia: OY Olisystems AB, Mannerheimintie 108, Helsinki 00250, Finland. UK: Psychology, 6 Bow Street, Birmingham B1 1DW.

Olgoj Chorchoj. Atelier Libensky Ostrov, Prague 8, Czechoslovakia 18000.

OLuce. Via Cavour 52, San Giuliano Milanese, Milan 20098, Italy. *Outlets* Belgium: Kreymborg, 66 avenue Molière, Brussels 1180. Finland: Funkiio, 7 Loennrotinkatu, Helsinki 12. France: Devoto, 11 rue Azais Barthes, Beziers 34500. Germany: Floetotto Handelsagentur, 38–40 Ringstrasse, 4835 Rietberg 2. Greece: Deloudis, 3–5 Spefsippou, Kolonaki, Athens. Japan: Flos Japan Co. Ltd, 1-23-5 Higashi-Azabu J., Minato-ku, Tokyo 106. The Netherlands: Carlo Wanna, PO Box 1035, Zwijndrecht 3330. Scandinavia: Inside, PO Box 3310, Stockholm, Sweden. Spain: Idea International, 12–18 Vico, Barcelona 21. UK: Flos Ltd, The Studio, 120 High Street, South Milford, Leeds, Yorks. LS25 5AQ.

Orrefors AB. S-38040 Orrefors, Sweden. *Outlets* France: AG Distribution, 8 rue Martel, 75010 Paris. Germany: Mercantile Edgar Lindenau GmbH, Robert-Koch-Strasse 4, D-8033 Planegg/Munich. Italy: Messulam SpA, Via Rovigno 13, I-20125 Milan. Japan: J. Osawa & Co. Ltd, 2-8 Shibaura 4-chome, Minato-ku, Tokyo 108. The Netherlands: Postava-Continent BV, Burg van Baaklaan 21, NL-3648 XS, Wilnis. Spain: Riera, Vilamari 72, Barcelona 08015. UK: Dexam International Ltd, Haslemere, Surrey GU27 32QP. USA: Orrefors Crystal Group, 140 Bradford Drive, Berlin, New Jersey 08009.

Parker Pen UK Ltd. Parker House, New Haven, East Sussex BN9 0AU, UK. *Outlets* France: Parker Pen France, 16 rue Chauveau Lagarde, Paris 75008. Germany: Parker Pen GmbH, Postfach 2160, Baden-Baden 7570. Japan: Parker Pen Japan Ltd, 42F Shinjuku Mitsui Bldg, 2-1-1 Nishi Shinjuku, Shinjuku-ku, Tokyo 163. The Netherlands: Parker Pen Benelux BV, PO Box 2037, 4800 CA, Breda. Spain: Parker Pen Española SA, 6 Vicente Muzas, Madrid 28043. USA: Parker Pen USA Ltd, Janesville, Wisconsin 53545.

Atelier Pelcl. 3 Melnicka, Prague 150 00, Czechoslovakia.

Philips International BV. PO Box 218, 5600 MD Eindhoven, The Netherlands. *Outlets* Austria: Österreichische Philips Industrie GmbH, 64 Triester Strasse, 1100 Vienna. Belgium: NV Philips, 2 De Brouckereplein, PO Box 218, 1000 Brussels. Denmark: Philips Elapparat AS, 80 Pragsboulevard, 2300 Copenhagen. Finland: OY Philips AB, 8 Kaivokatu, Helsinki. France: SA Philips Industriale et Commerciale, 50 avenue Montaigne, 75380 Paris. Germany: Philips GmbH, Unternehmensbereich Haustechnik, 19 Kilanstrasse, 8500 Nuremberg; Allgemeine Deutsche Philips Ind. GmbH, 94 Steindamm, 2000 Hamburg. Italy: Philips Italia SA, Piazza IV Novembre 3, 20100 Milan. Japan: Philips Industrial Development and Consultants Co. Ltd, Shuwa, Shinagawa Bldg, 26-33 Takanawa 3-chome, Minato-ku, Tokyo 108. Norway: Norsk AS Philips, PO Box 5040, 6 Soerkedaksveien, Oslo 3. Spain: Philips Iberica SAE, 2 Martinez Villergas, Apartado 2065, 28027 Madrid. Sweden: Philips Norden AB, 11584 Stockholm. UK: Philips Electrical and Associated Industries Ltd, Arundel Great Court, 8 Arundel Street, London WC2 3DT. USA: North American Philips Corporation, 100 East 42nd Street, New York, NY 10017.

Playline. SCEP Industria per L'Arredamento Srl, Via Melitiello, 80017 Melito, Italy. *Outlets* France: Arredamento, 18 Quai des Celestins, Paris 75004. Germany: Wohn Design GmbH, 66 Heinrichsallee, Aachen 51100; George Seyfarth, 64 Plock, Heidelberg 6900. Greece: Silvestridis C., 95 Via Patission, Athens 10434.

Poltronova Design Srl. Via Prov. Pratese 23, Montale, 51037 Pistoia, Italy. *Outlets* Belgium: C.V. Novalis G., Gallery "Bourdon Arcade", Emile Braunplein 45, 9000 Ghent. France: Paul-Patrice Vischel, 43 Bd. Alfred Wallach, F-68100 Mulhouse. Japan: Ambech Co. Ltd, Sumimoto Seimei Bldg 3-1-30, Minami-Aoyama, Minato-ku, Tokyo 107. Spain: Via Agents Asociados scp, Av. del Enlace 2, 08190 Sant Cuga T Del Vallès, Barcelona. Switzerland: Guido Mayer SA, Z.I. Portettes, CH-1312 Eclepens Gare VA.

Randstad Uitzendbureau. Postbus 12600, 1100 AP, Amsterdam, Holland. *Outlets* Germany: Teunen and Teunen, Postfach 36, 6227 Geisenheim 2. The Netherlands: Kreymborg BV, 63 Minervalaan, 1077 Amsterdam.

Bernd Reibl. 14 Schoneberger Weg, 7032 Sindelfingen, Germany.

Royal College of Art. Kensington Gore, London SW7 2EU, UK.

Royal Copenhagen Ltd. 45 Smallegade, DK-2000 Frederiksberg, Denmark. *Outlets* France: Georg Jensen Sarl, 239 rue Saint-Honoré, F-75001 Paris. Germany: Royal Copenhagen GmbH, Musterhaus am Messekreisel, Deutz-Mulheimer Strasse 30, D-5000 Cologne 21. Hong Kong: Royal Copenhagen Ltd, 122–123 Prince's Bldg, Charter Road. Italy: Messulam SpA, Via Rovigno 13, I-20125 Milan. Japan: Royal Copenhagen Japan Ltd, 10th Floor Mita Kokusai Bldg, 1-4-28 Mita, Minato-ku, Tokyo 108. Scandinavia: Royal Copenhagen Svenska AB, Västra Hamngatan 12, S-411 17 Göteborg, Sweden. UK: Royal Copenhagen Ltd, 70 St John Street, London EC1M 4DT. USA: Royal Copenhagen Ltd, 27 Holland Avenue, White Plains, NY 10603.

Sabattini Argenteria SpA. Via Don Capiaghi 2, Bregnano 22070, Como, Italy. *Outlets* Germany: Gräfin V. Bethusy-Huc Handelsvertretung, 24 Lärchenstrasse, Krailling 8033, Bavaria. Japan: Studio De. Co. Inc., 604-2-14-7 Mita, Minato-ku, Tokyo 108. The Netherlands: Mobica NV, 50 Gossetlaan, Groot-Bijgaarden 1720, Belgium. Scandinavia: Linea Domani, 159 Smakkegardsvej, Gentofte 2820, Denmark.

Sahco-Hesslein. Prinsengracht 770, 1017 LE Amsterdam, The Netherlands. *Outlets* Belgium: Louizalaan, 262 Avenue Louise, Brussels. France: 17 rue du Mail, F-75002, Paris. Germany: Kreuzburger Strasse 19, W-8500 Nuremberg 51. Italy: Via Durini 7, I-20122 Milan. Japan: Manas Trading Inc., 5F Nissan Bldg, 4-21 Himon-ya, Meguro-ku, Tokyo 152. UK: 101 Cleveland Street, London W1P 5PN. USA: 979 Third Avenue, D & D Bldg, 17th Floor, New York, NY 10022.

Saniplast. Via Kennedy 10, Passirano 25050, Italy.

Santa-Cole Ediciones de Diseño. 10 Stma. Trinidad del monte, Barcelona 08017, Spain. *Outlet* Several in the UK, including Liberty, Regent Street, London W1.

Sawaya & Moroni SpA. Via Manzoni 11, 20121 Milan, Italy. *Outlet* UK: The Ikon Corporation, B5L Metropolitan Wharf, Wapping Wall, London E1 9SS.

Franz Schatzl Design Werkstätte. A-4801, Traunkirchen, Austria. *Outlets* Belgium: Creadis Design Distribution, Obterrestraat 67–69, B-8994 Proven. Japan: Alphax Inc., Canal Tower 9–3, Nihonbashi, Koami-cho, Chuo-ku, Tokyo 103. The Netherlands: Binnen, Keizersgracht 82, NL-1015 CT Amsterdam.

Thomas Schulte Designmanufaktur. Brückenstrasse 2, 5090 Leverkusen 3, Germany. *Outlets* The Netherlands: C. M. van Egdom BV, 146 Bronebrocksestraat, NL 7601 BJ Almelo. Switzerland: Trend Design, 44 Moosstrasse, CH-8630, Rüti ZH.

F. Schumacher & Co. 939 3rd Avenue, New York, NY 10022, USA.

Sharp Corporation. 22-22 Nagaike-cho, Abeno-ku, Osaka 545, Japan.

Silhouette International GmbH. 24 Ellbognerstrasse, Linz 4020, Austria. *Outlets* France: New Charmes, 2 rue des Quatre Fils, Paris 75003. Germany: ADM Silhouette/Dünnwald-Metzler GmbH & Co., 30 Ringstrasse, Fellbach 7012. Italy: Silhouette Srl, Via Rovelli 40, Como 22100. Japan: Silhouette Kabushiki Kaisha, 45-9 Yushima 3-chome, Bunkyo-ku, Tokyo 113. Scandinavia: Silhouette Norge A/S, Haavard Martinsens Vei 19, 0978 Oslo 9; Kaukomarkkinat OY, Optical Department, Martin-Kyläntie 54, 01720 Vantaa, Finland; Nilax Optik AB, Rattgatan 6, 65002 Karlstad, Sweden. Spain: Silhouette Optical España SA, 74 Entlo. Ausias March, Barcelona 08013. UK: Silhouette Fashion Frames Ltd, 333 High Road, Wood Green, London J22 4LE. USA: Silhouette Optical Ltd, 266 Union Street, Northvale 07647, NJ.

Smith Sport Optics. PO Box 74, Sun Valley, Idaho 83353, USA. *Outlet* USA: Paul Bradley, 660 High Street, Palo Alto, California 94301, CA.

Space. 12 Dolland Street, London SE11 5LN. *Outlet* Gladys Mougin, 30 rue de Lille, Paris 75007.

Steltman Editions. 330 Spulstraat, Amsterdam 1012 VX, Holland.

Step Design. 5-18-19-503, Roppongi, Minato-ku, Tokyo, Japan.

Stiebel Eltron GmbH & Co. KG. Dr. Stiebel Strasse, Holzminden 3450, Germany.

Strässle Söhne AG. PO Box 261, Kirchberg, St Gallen, Switzerland. *Outlets* Australia: Diethelm Office Furniture Pty Ltd, PO Box 2794, North Parramatta 2152. Belgium: BEST Technology of Design, 4 rue Morel, 7500 Tounai; P.V.B.A. a Venir Sprl, rue Cinquant 31B, 7890 Ellezelles. France: ARIA-Industrie, Philippe Morel-Lab, 31 rue Eugene-Dubois, 0100 Bourg-en-Bresse; Aire Industrie, Selection Pierre Cardin, Division Strässle, 138 Bd Haussmann, 75008 Paris. Germany (postal codes 2–3): Hans-Peter Sauter, Strässle Söhne AG, CH-9533 Kirchberg; (postal codes 4–5): Manfred Stader, Postfach 180169, 5600 Wuppertal 1; (postal codes 6–7): Wilhelm Schilcher, Goethestrasse 22, 7031 Motzingen; (postal codes 1 & 8): Marco Steinlin, Wolfsbohlstrasse 4, 9050 Appenzell. Hong Kong: Fitzroy Engineering Co., Fitzroy International Trading Co., PO Box 96709, Rm 1202 Lee Wai Comi Centre 1–3, 12/F Hart Avenue, TST Kowloon. Italy: Costi CSpA, Via Trebbia 22, 20135 Mailand. Japan: XTRA Inc., 5-2-3 Minami-Azabu, Minato-ku, Tokyo 106. The Netherlands: AHVA, Amsterdamse Handelsvertegen-woordigingen & Agenturen, Postbus 85169, ED Amsterdam. Scandinavia: Don Batchelor ApS, Vidaesdal 25, 2840 Holte. Singapore: Diethelm Industries Pte. Ltd, Furniture Division, 34 Boon Leat Terrace; Texmet Trading, Collection of Fashion Textile, Tanglin, PO Box 432. USA: MONEL Contract Furniture Inc., PO Box 291, Oakland Gardens, NY 11364.

Tapetenfabrik Gebr. Rasch GmbH & Co. D-4550 Bramsche, Germany.

Technische Industrie Tacx. Rijksstraatweg 52, 2241 BW Wassenaar, The Netherlands. *Outlets* Australia: Hanley, 16 McCauley, St Matraville, 2036 Sydney, NSW. Austria: Thalinger GmbH, Postfach 182, 4600 Wels. Belgium: ICC, Postbus 73, 4527 ZH Aardenburg. Canada: OGC, 2708 Diab, St-Laurent, Quebec H4S 1E8. Denmark: Frits Sorensen, Kanalholmen 14–18, 2650 Huidovre. France: Alvarez, 21 Route d'Agen R.N., 32002 Auch Cedex. Germany: Van Bokhoven, Mühlenreute 63, 7981 Schlier. Italy: G & G, Via Pacinotti 16, 36040 Brendola, VI. Japan: FET, 30–11 Chitosedai 4-chome, Setagaya-ku, Tokyo. Norway: DBS Stasjonsveien 51, 0385 Oslo 3. South Africa: Coolheat, PO Box 740, Johannesburg 2000. Spain: Comet, Apartado de correos 125, 20140 Andoain. Sweden: Monark, Bicycle Department, 43201 Varberg. Switzerland: Intercycle, Haldematte, 6210 Sursee. USA: Veltec, 1793 Catalina Sand City SA, California 93955.

Theakston Ceramics. Orchard Cottage, Greystoke, Cumbria, UK.

Tobias Associate Design. No. 7, Mettham Street, Lenton, Notts. NG7 1SH, UK. *Outlet* Iceland: Ms A. I. Siguroardóttir, Stigahlio 43, 105 Reykjavik.

Toshiba Corporation. 1-1 Shibaura 1-chome, Minato-ku, Tokyo 105-01, Japan.

Uchino. 1-7-15 Nihonbashi-horidome, Chuo-ku, Tokyo 103, Japan.

Ultima Edizione Srl. Via Olivetti 74, Massa (PT) 54100, Italy. *Outlets* Germany: Walter Schiedermeier, 12 Marienberger Weg, Cologne 5000. Switzerland: Guido Mayer SA, 1312 Eclepens Gare.

UMS-Pastoe BV. Rotsoord 3, 3523 GL Utrecht, Postbus 2152, Holland. *Outlets* Germany: Andreas Franoschek, 11 Wiedesbaches Strasse, Nuremberg 8500 60. Italy: Dix Italia, Via Provinciale 92, Albino BG, 24021. Spain: Side Group, 4 Bajo Pro Srolar, Lasarte 20160. UK: John Summerhill, Lancaster Road, London W11 1UG.

Unione Plastiche. Via Meucci 32, Calenzano 50132, Florence, Italy. *Outlets* Australia: Targetti Australia Pty Ltd, George Patterson House, 107 Mount Street, North Sydney 2060. Belgium: s.a. Hugo Neumann nv, rue de l'Eclipse, 2–6 Eclipsstraat, Brussels 1000. France: Targetti Sankey SA, 15–16 rue des Marronniers, entrée: 61 rue de Bicêtre, 94240 L'Hay-Les-Roses. Germany: Targetti Licht, Vertriebs GmbH, Zum Eisenhammer 7/a, 4200 Oberhausen 1. The Netherlands: Targetti BV, Postbus 2649, 3500 GP Utrecht. New Zealand: Targetti N.Z. Ltd, PO Box 37–044, Parnell, Auckland 1. Portugal: Sociedade de Representacoes Marques Neto LDA, Av. Infante D. Henrique, Lote 4-E-1800, Lisbon. Scandinavia: Targetti Scandinavia AB, Snapphanevägen 24, 34322 Almhult, PO Box 95, Sweden. Spain: Targetti Iluminacion SA, Calle Cromo 120, 08907 Hospitalet de Llobregat, Barcelona. Switzerland: Intercolux Leuchten, Gstaadmattstrasse 41, 4452 Itingen/BL. UK: Crompton Targetti Ltd, PO Box 74, Doncaster, Yorks. DN2 4ND.

Unitalia Domestic Design. Via Livornese Est 39, Perignano, Pisa 56030, Italy.

Up & Up Srl. Via Acquale 3, 54100 Massa, Italy. *Outlets* Austria and Germany: Giovanni Marelli, Casella Postale 148, 20036 Meda, Milan. Belgium: Trueno, 78 OL Vrouwstraat, 2800 Mechelen. Canada: Marble Trend, Unit 3, 2050 Steeles Avenue West, Dowsview, Ontario. France: Roger Von Bary, 18 rue Lafitte, 75009 Paris; Studio Enea, 2 Place St Sulpice, 75009 Paris. Japan: Everfast Ltd, Iwoki Bldg 9-6-12 Akasaka, Minato-ku, Tokyo; Joint Inc., Daikanyama-Parkside-Vill., 207-9-8 Sarugakucho, Shibuya-ku, Tokyo 150. USA: Inside, 715 5th Street, San Diego, CA 92101; Italdesign Center Inc., 8687 Melrose Avenue, Suite 547, Los Angeles, CA 90069; Design Studio Inter Inc., 908 Linden Avenue, Winnekta, Illinois 60007; Frederich Williams, 200 Lexington Avenue, New York, NY 10016; Modern Living, 4063 Relwood Avenue, Los Angeles, CA 90066.

VeArt (Division of Artemide SpA). Via Bergamo 18, 20010 Pregnana Milanese, Milan, Italy. *Outlets* Australia: ECC Lighting Ltd, 18–20 Allen Street, Pyrmont NSW 2009. Austria: Vertreter Design Agentur R. Greinecker, Herbeckstrasse 27, 1183 Vienna. Canada: Artemide Ltd, 2150 Hymus Blvd, Dorval, Quebec H9P 1J7. France: Artemide E.u.r.l., 6–8 rue Basfori, 75011 Paris. Germany: Alleinvertrieb Artemide GmbH, Itterpark 5, D-4010 Hilden. Hong Kong: Artemide Ltd, 102-103 Ruttonjiee Centre, Duddel Street. Japan: Artemide Inc., 2nd Floor Axis Bldg, 5-17-1 Roppongi, Minato-ku, Tokyo 106. Spain: Artemide SA, C/Ripolles 5 y 7 08820 Prat de Llobregat, Barcelona. Switzerland: Artemide Illuminazione AG, Via Trevano 72, 6900 Lugano. UK: Artemide GB Ltd, 17–19 Neal Street, London WC2H 9PU. USA: Artemide Inc., National Sales and Customer Service Centre, 1980 New Highway, Farmingdale, NY 11735.

Brion Vega. Via Fratelli Gabba No. 9, Milan, Italy.

Vitra (International) AG. Klünenfeldstrasse 20, CH-4127 Birsfelden, Switzerland. *Outlets* Austria: Vitra Ges.m.b.H., Pfeilgasse 35, A-1080 Vienna. Belgium: N.V. Vitra Belgium S.A., Woluwelaan 140A, B-1831 Diegem. France: Vitra Sarl, 40 rue Violet, F-75015 Paris. Germany: Vitra GmbH, Charles-Eames-Strasse 2, D-7858 Weil am Rhein. Italy: Vitra Italia Srl, Corso di Porta Romana 6, I-20122, Milan. Japan: Haller Japan Ltd, Canal Tower, 9-3 Koamicho Nihonbashi, Chuo-ku, Tokyo 103. The Netherlands: Vitra Nederland BV, Assumburg 73, NL-1081 GB, Amsterdam. Saudi Arabia: Vitra Middle East Ltd, P.O. Box 64 80, Dammam 31442. Spain: Vitra Hispania SA, Serrano No. 5, 4o, 4a, E-28001, Madrid. UK: Vitra Ltd, 13 Grosvenor Street, London W1X 9FB. USA: Vitra Seating Inc., 30–20 Thomson Avenue, Long Island City, New York, NY 11101.

Friedrich Vorlaufer GmbH. Dieselstrasse 1, A-3362 Amstetten, Germany.

Vorwerk and Co. Teppichwerke GmbH & Co. KG. Ruhlmannstrasse 11, 3250 Hameln, Germany.

Theo Williams. Via Bergognone 45, Milan 20144, Italy.

XO. Cide 4 Servon, 77170 Brie Comte Robert, France. *Outlets* Australia: Mobili Pty Ltd, 38 Queen Street, Woollahra, NSW 2025. Austria: Die Kommode, Lirchenfelderstrasse 12, 1080 Vienna. Belgium: Espaces et Lignes, rue Ulens Straat 55, Brussels 1210. Canada: Angle International, 286 Ouest St-Paul, Montreal, Quebec H2Y 2A3. Greece: Avepe SA, Varangis, 40m Botsari, Peeki Attica. Hong Kong: Le Cadre Gallery, 8 Sunning Road, Causeway Bay. Ireland: O'Hagan Design Ltd, 99 Capel Street, Dublin 1. Japan: IDEE, 5-4-44 Minami-Aoyama, Minato-ku, Tokyo. The Netherlands; Espaces et Lignes, Nassaulaan 2A, 2514 JS'S Gravenhague. Portugal: Paragrama, 1 argo Eng. Antonio de Almeida 70, 4100 Porto. Scandinavia: Design Distribution, Doebelnsgatan 36d, 11352 Stockholm, Sweden. UK: Viaduct Furniture Ltd, Spring House, 10 Spring Place, London NW5 3BH.

Yamada Shomei Lighting Co. Inc. 3-16-12 Sotokanda, Chiyoda-ku, Tokyo 101, Japan. *Outlet* Italy: I Guzzini Illuminazione Srl, 62019 Recanati, P.O. Box 39–59.

Yamaha Corporation. 1-7-1, Yuraku-cho, Chiyoda-ku, Tokyo 100, Japan. *Outlet* Japan: Yamaha Corporation, 10-1 Nakazawa-cho, Hamamatsu 430.

Zanotta SpA. Via Vittorio Veneto 57, 20054 Nova Milanese, Italy. *Outlets* Australia: Arredorama International Pty Ltd, 1 Ross Street, Glebe, NSW No. 2037. Austria: Prodomo, 35–37 Flachgasse, 1060 Vienna. Belgium: Zaira Mis, 35 Boulevard Saint Michel, 1040 Brussels. Denmark: Paustian, 2 Kalkbraendrilbskaj, 2100 Copenhagen. Germany: Fulvio Folci, 14 Dahlienweg, 4000 Düsseldorf 30. Japan: Nova Oshima Co. Ltd, Sakakura Bldg, Akasaka, Minato-ku, Tokyo. The Netherlands: Hansje Kalff, 8 Puttensestraat, 1181 Je Amstelveen, Holland. Norway: Bente Holm, 64 Parkveien, Oslo 2. Spain: Bd Ediciones de Diseño, 291 Mallorca, 08037 Barcelona. Sweden: Inside, 37 Hamngatan, 11147 Stockholm. Switzerland: Peter Kaufmann, 123 Rychenbergstrasse, 8400 Winterhur. UK: The Architectural Trading Co. Ltd, 219–29 Shaftesbury Avenue, London WC2H 8AR. USA: International Contract Furnishings, 305 East 63rd Street, New York, NY 10021.

Zerodisegno (Division of Quattrocchio). Via Isonzo 51, Alessandria 15100, Italy. *Outlets* Germany:

Present Perfect, 95 Frauenlobstrasse, Mainz 6500. The Netherlands: Evato-Thea Verhoeven Design, 5/a Lambertusstraat, TB Hedikhuizen 5256. Spain: Jose Cunill Bonmam, San Juan B./La Salle 1, Esca 3o, 29, Premia de Mar 08330, Barcelona. Switzerland: Pur Sitzmobel, 33 Gaswerkstrasse, Langenthal 4900. USA: Zero US Corporation, Industrial Circle, Lincoln, RI 02865.

Zumtobel Lighting. 30 Schweizerstrasse, Dornbirn A-6850, Italy. *Outlets* Belgium: N.V. Zumtobel Benelux SA, 47 Rijksweg, Paars Kmo-Zone 2670. France: Zumtobel France Sarl, 2 Avenue de la Cristallerie, Sèvres 92310. Germany: Zumtobel GmbH & Co., 2–4 Achtzehn-Morgen-Weg, Usingen 6390. Italy: Zumtobel Italiana, Viale Berrera 49, Milan 20162. Japan: Zumtobel-Koizumi, 3-12 Kanada-Sakumacho, Chiyoda-ku, Tokyo 101. Scandinavia: Zumtobel Belysning AB, 140A Ulvsundavägen, Bromma, Stockholm 16130. Spain: Zumtobel Ibérica SA, 9y11 Ausias March, Barcelona 08010. Switzerland: Zumtobel Licht AG, 7 Riedackerstrasse, Rumlang, Zurich 8153. UK: Zumtobel Lighting Systems Ltd, Unit 5, The Argent Centre, Hayes, Middx UB 3BL. USA: Zumtobel Lighting Inc., 141 Lanza Avenue, Bldg 160, Garfield, New Jersey 07026.

PUBLICATIONS

AUSTRALIA

Australian Design Series (14 issues a year, ten titles). Australia's leading niche-market publication on domestic and commercial design, each title looking at a specific subject.

Belle (bi-monthly). Showcase for contemporary Australian architecture and interior design, with a round-up that includes many imported influences.

Interior Design (bi-monthly). Dedicated to decoration, with a mixture of articles on avant-garde designs and traditional interiors.

Interior Designers' and Decorators' Handbook (twice a year). A handbook aimed at the professional market, covering all aspects of design and home decorating.

Interiors (bi-monthly). Comprehensive analysis of latest upmarket trends in fabrics, textiles and designs.

CANADA

Canadian Interiors (eight issues a year). Quality magazine targeted at professionals with an interest in architecture and their environment. English text.

Contract Magazine (bi-monthly). Geared towards qualified designers, it deals with the planning and management of interiors for commercial establishments and public institutions. English text.

Décormag (monthly). Deals with interior decoration, offering articles on different styles and editorials on specific rooms. French text.

Designs (quarterly). With a text in French and English, this is the first and only bilingual trade magazine in Quebec. It deals with residential and commercial furniture, lighting, materials and interior decoration.

DENMARK

Arkitekten (23 issues a year) and **Arkitektur** (eight issues a year). Edited by the Danish Architectural Press for the professional federations of architects and building contractors.

Bo Bedre (monthly). Translates into English as "Live Better", precisely the editorial policy behind this consumer home-interest magazine.

Design Danmark (four issues a year). Magazine which presents news about Danish and international design, as well as comprehensive articles focusing on case stories and a variety of design-related subjects.

Design from Scandinavia (annual). A useful index of designers and manufacturers, set against a background of illustrated stories of architectural interest.

Fair Facts (quarterly). Published in Danish and English, the magazine deals with the major European furniture fairs and exhibitions.

Living Architecture (twice a year). Scandinavia's best-looking glossy magazine on buildings and their interiors, by the celebrated photographer and architect Per Nagel. English text.

Rum og Form (annual). "Space and Form", edited by the Danish Association of Furniture Designers and Interior Designers.

FINLAND

Design in Finland (annual). Published by the Finnish Foreign Trade Association to promote the year's products abroad, with good quality illustrations and an index of manufacturers and designers.

Form Function, Finland (quarterly). A magazine concerned with mass production and functional design in Finland, aimed at the export market, published by the Finnish Society of Craft and Design.

Muoto (monthly). Magazine on interior and industrial design, with articles on individual designers.

Space & Place (annual). Contract furniture collections presented by the Furniture Exporters' Association.

FRANCE

Architecture Intérieure Créé (bi-monthly). Leading professional design magazine with an architectural background.

Art et Décoration (eight issues a year). Concerned primarily with the plastic arts and interior decoration.

L'Atelier (ten issues a year). Specializes in objects, gadgets and the more individual design.

Beaux Arts (monthly). This celebrated art and architectural magazine includes contemporary design articles.

Décoration Internationale (monthly, but erratic). Eclectic publication, covering houses, objects and painters in exotic locations.

Elle-Décoration (eight issues a year). Fashion-based design magazine aimed at the younger market.

Intramuros (monthly). Large-format design and interiors magazine featuring in-depth interviews with people ahead of the pack. Technical information, freshly presented, is aimed at professionals, but the layout makes it generally appealing.

La Maison de Marie Claire (monthly). "Le style français" in a glossy magazine in which everything from plates to pastries is chic.

Maison et Jardin (monthly). High-life review of famous interiors and gardens, with specific design articles included in most issues.

Maison Française (monthly). Covers furniture, interiors and architecture with special regional bias and promotional features.

Vogue Décoration (quarterly). Weighty and opulent interiors magazine with beautiful presentation and in-depth interviews.

GERMANY

Ambiente (bi-monthly). A consumer magazine on interior design.

Architektur und Wohnen (monthly). Interviews with the architects and owners of remarkable homes. It links professional and consumer interests, and contains exhaustively researched product reports.

Art Aurea (quarterly). Theme-related articles on art, design and fashion, with text in German and English.

Design Report (bi-monthly). Factual magazine on the state of design in Germany, with reports, interviews and commentaries.

Form (quarterly). Articles discussing international design and the market-place.

Häuser (monthly). House case-histories, architectural portraits, design product round-ups and extensive floor plans. There is an English-language supplement.

MD Möbel Interior Design (monthly). Modest (black-and-white), interesting publication on furniture, with bold graphic covers.

Schöner Wohnen (monthly). The world of architecture and design in Germany, with reports from correspondents in all other major countries. Popular, informative and technical.

Wolkenkratzer Art Journal (bi-monthly). Art, design, image, architecture and music.

ISRAEL

Architecture in Israel (quarterly). Published by the Architects' Association, it is aimed at the professional market.

Architecture of Israel (quarterly). Publicizes the interiors and exteriors of many of Israel's new and more interesting buildings.

Binyan Diur (three issues a year). Hebrew language magazine featuring articles on design and interior architecture, together with interviews and special projects. Aimed at the domestic market.

ITALY

Abitare (ten issues a year). English text published alongside the Italian in a heavily merchandized, up-to-the-minute round-up of new designs. Architects and interior designers look to its photographic stories for an international perspective. Some issues are devoted to a single country.

L'Arca (ten issues a year). Dedicated to architecture, design and visual communication, with technical monographs.

AReA (bi-monthly). Design-as-art magazine concentrating on objects and decoration for the interior. Interviews with designers, artists, architects and students.

Casa Vogue (11 issues a year). Definitive listing of new trends-in-the-making around the world in interiors, decoration, houses and furniture. An invaluable talent-spotters' magazine, famous for the inspired art direction of its merchandizing stories.

Disegno (quarterly). Technical, covering the tools, instruments and software needed for graphic and industrial design.

Domus (monthly). Giò Ponti founded this authoritative magazine on architecture, interiors, furniture and art; now Mario Bellini is its outspoken, informed editor. More textual than visual, it is consulted by architects and designers who submit schemes.

Gap Casa (monthly). Trade figures and commercial marketing strategies sit alongside the product lines in this stylish magazine aimed at retailers.

In Design (bi-monthly). Bilingual (English/Italian) review of architectural projects, designs and interior design, aimed at a specialist market.

Interni (monthly). More than its name suggests, a round-up of products relating to external, as well as interior, design. Has interesting supplements, catalogues of addresses and international editions.

Modo (monthly). Articles and opinions on design in depth, with a directory of products and producers, created by the omnipresent Alessandro Mendini. Regarded as the magazine of the avant-garde in Italian design.

Ottagono (quarterly). A review of architecture, interior design, furniture and industrial design world-wide, published in Italian and English editions by eight Italian manufacturers – Arflex, Artemide, Bernini, Boffi, Cassina, Flos, ICF and Tecno. Leading writers contribute to this small-format publication.

JAPAN

AXIS (bi-monthly). First-rate international publication with coverage of a wide variety of furniture, product and interior design projects, with a special interest in Italy. Some English summaries.

Design News (eight issues a year). Aimed at professionals and sold on subscription, this has a good coverage of Japanese design projects with an emphasis on industrial and product design.

FP: Fusion Planning (bi-monthly). With an emphasis on architecture and interior design, this is a well-produced and edited magazine featuring a good selection of international design projects.

GA: Global Architecture (irregular). Editor Yukio Futagawa established this as the première photo-essay magazine of architecture world-wide.

Japan Architect (monthly). Architectural and interior design magazine aimed at the professional market, featuring exclusively Japanese designs.

Portfolio (bi-monthly). A less glossy, slightly down-market version of *AXIS* with more emphasis on quirky urban interiors and architecture.

SD: Space Design (monthly). Interior space – a thoroughly Japanese magazine concept – with a broad international coverage of projects which fits into theme-edited issues.

W.IN.D (quarterly). International coverage of interior design – shops, restaurants and commercial space – with frequent special issues on non-superstar designers. Japanese only.

MEXICO

Magenta (quarterly). Produced by a private foundation to promote design, this is proof of the need for private initiative.

THE NETHERLANDS

Avenue (monthly). Stylish photo-reportage of design products (including lighting and furniture), travel, interviews, avant-garde fashion and art festivals.

Industrieel Ontwerpen (bi-monthly). Eminently technical and professional publication covering industrial design and product development.

Textiel-Visie (14 issues a year). Predominantly fabrics for home furnishing with styling forecasts and articles on lifestyles and consumer psychology.

NEW ZEALAND

New Zealand Home & Building (bi-monthly). A magazine aimed at the general reader with features on interior design and architecture.

New Zealand Home Journal (monthly). A home-interest magazine with interior design coverage.

NORWAY

Byggekunst (eight issues a year). Covers building, landscape architecture and interior design.

Hjem & Fritid/Bonytt (monthly). A consumer magazine on interior design, aimed at the wealthy connoisseur rather than the professional.

Hus og Hem (quarterly). Glossy magazine on decoration and interiors.

Skala (monthly). Architecture and design from around the world.

POLAND

Design – Wiadomości Instytutu Wzornictwa Przemysłowego (bi-monthly). Aimed at the professional market, this magazine, produced by the Institute of Industrial Design in Poland, covers national and international history and theory of design, plus new design solutions and events.

SPAIN

Ardi (bi-monthly). Brilliantly art-directed publication introduces the best Spanish designers, architects, cartoonists and graphic artists to the world, alongside special reports on the international avant-garde.

La Casa 16 de Marie Claire (monthly). Spanish edition of the French magazine, edited by Group 16.

Diseño Interior (eleven issues a year). Professional magazine dealing with architecture and interior design world-wide; intended to act as a forum between architects and designers and manufacturers.

Futura (twice a year). Covers art and design and is excellently printed in northern Spain.

Hogares (monthly). "Homes" is published in colour with photographic spreads on Spanish houses and interviews with Spanish designers.

Nuevo Estilo (monthly). Major publication on design and furniture, aimed at a wide public; not avant-garde, but the editing is exemplary.

ON Diseño (monthly). Pioneer in design, with articles on home-grown talent, and an international round-up of graphics and architecture.

SWEDEN

Arkitekten (monthly). A small, in-house official publication for the Federation of Architects and allied building trades in Sweden.

Arkitektur (ten issues a year). A round-up of architects' projects in Sweden, with plans and pictures.

Form (eight issues a year). The professional magazine for interior, graphic and industrial designers. Text in Swedish and English.

Möbler and Miljö (ten issues a year). This specialist magazine, "Furniture and Environment", is read by the decision-makers who buy and make furnishings for interior designers.

Sköna Hem (monthly). Up-market home-orientated magazine with photographic coverage of architecture and interior design.

SWITZERLAND

Innendekorateur (monthly). Professional, black-and-white magazine dealing with interior design. (German/French).

Schöner Wohnen Schweiz (monthly). Swiss supplement of the German magazine *Schöner Wohnen*; gives information solely on the Swiss architectural and interior design scene. (German).

Textile Suisse (quarterly). Published by the Swiss Office for the Development of Trade, a review of the state of the textile business.

Werk, Bauen und Wohnen (monthly). Austere, sober publication on architecture and industrial design. (German/French/English).

UK

Architects' Journal (weekly). The professional, opinionated and sometimes controversial magazine for British architects.

Architectural Review (monthly). A well-written and informed magazine which examines projects, with plans, world-wide.

Art and Design (bi-monthly). Art, architecture, design, fashion, music, photography, news.

Blueprint (ten issues a year). Fast-forward into what is being planned, built, assembled, launched or revived. Racy layouts in a large format, mostly black and white, with informed, hard-hitting comment.

Creative Review (monthly). Well-presented review of mainly graphic design, whether applied to computers, textiles or advertising.

Design (monthly). The official publication of the British Design Council, parochial and sometimes carping.

Design Week (weekly). Energetic design publication, highly agile in image and content, with news and views on the industry.

Designers' Journal (monthly). The enlightened companion to the *Architects' Journal*, aimed at a predominantly contract market, with interviews covering all aspects of design from theatre to products.

Homes & Gardens (monthly). The home-interest magazine equivalent to the high-street design shop, seen as inspirational by those who buy it.

House & Garden (monthly). Condé Nast's biggest-selling design and decoration magazine in the UK. Although the emphasis of the editorial is on interior decoration, the design and architectural information is strongly merchandized, and the magazine sponsors the annual competition "The New Designers".

World of Interiors (11 issues a year). The interiors magazine to be seen in, offering a voyeuristic tour around some of the world's most lavishly decorated homes, with international gallery listings that are wide-ranging and talent-spotting.

USA

Architectural Digest (six issues a year). An authoritative celebrity round-up of the lavish homes of the rich and famous, presented in a highly successful coffee-table format.

Architectural Record (monthly). A professional and trade-orientated architectural magazine.

Assemblage (three issues a year). Explores contemporary issues in architecture and design culture.

Design News (bi-weekly). Ideas for solving design problems, and reports on technological trends in the mechanical, electrical/electronic and material fields.

ID (bi-monthly). The industrial designer's product guide, with some coverage of the design industry, graphics and fashion.

Interiors (monthly). Rigorous and professional coverage of decoration for interior designers.

Metropolis (ten issues a year). The only magazine that covers all facets of design, architecture, interiors, furniture, preservation, urban design, graphics, crafts and more besides.

Metropolitan Home (monthly). An energetic trend-spotting magazine for the upwardly mobile, with fashions in furnishings and furniture presented by a young editorial team with a strong sense of direction. Plenty of consumer information.

Progressive Architecture (monthly). One of America's two heavyweight architectural journals, it addresses design and the latest technology.

Terrazzo (twice a year). Magazine dealing with architecture and design. Interviews and in-depth articles.

ACQUISITIONS

Acquisitions by design collections in 1992. Dates given in parentheses refer to the dates of the designs (from 1960 to the present day).

AUSTRIA

Austrian Museum of Applied Arts, Vienna. The Design Collection is to reopen next year after extensive refurbishment.

DENMARK

Museum of Decorative Art, Copenhagen.
S. Bernadotte and A. Bjørn: calculating machine (1960s)
Riccardo Dalisi: espresso coffee-pot (1987), manufactured by Alessi
Norman Forster: desk (1986), manufactured by Tecno
Ursula Munch-Petersen: service (1991), manufactured by Royal Copenhagen
Sony Headphones, Model *8MDR-R10* (1990)
My First Sony portable radio-cassette recorder (1989)
Sony Compact Hi-Fi, Model *CDP-M48* (1990)
Hans J. Wegner: chair, *Ring* (1986), manufactured by P & P Furniture, Copenhagen

FRANCE

Musée des Arts Décoratifs, Paris.
François Arnal: table and stool, *Elice* (1970), manufactured by Atelier A.
Bang and Olufsen: television set
Arlon Bayliss: carafe, manufactured by Rosenthal
Mario Bellini: table service, manufactured by Rosenthal
Cini Boeri: armchair, *Ghost* (1987), manufactured by Fiam
Achille Castiglioni: place setting, manufactured by Alessi
César: desk (1966), manufactured by Marcel Lefranc
Joe Colombo: armchair, *Elda* (1964), manufactured by Marcel Lefranc
Joe Colombo: plastic chair, manufactured by Kartell
Mattia Garouste and Elizabeth Bonetti: salad bowl, manufactured by Faienceries de Gien
Mattia Garouste and Elizabeth Bonetti: cafetière, manufactured by Faienceries de Gien

Mattia Garouste and Elizabeth Bonetti: various items of tableware, manufactured by Faienceries de Gien
Paolo and Teodoro Gatti: chair, manufactured by Zanotta
Michael Graves: whistling kettle, manufactured by Alessi
Baldwin and Guggisberg: carafe, manufactured by Rosenthal
Toshiyuki Kita: armchair, manufactured by Cassina
Danny Lane: table, *Atlas* (1988), manufactured by Fiam
Yonel Lebovici: lamp, *Satellite* (1969)
Enzo Mari: ashtray, manufactured by Danese
Alberto Meda and Paolo Rizzatto: lamp, *Lola* (1988), manufactured by Luceplan
Alberto Meda and Paolo Rizzatto: lamp, *Titania* (1990), manufactured by Luceplan
Pascal Mourgue: armchair, *Piccolo* (1990), manufactured by Fermob
Verner Panton: screen (1969)
Gaetano Pesce: armchair, manufactured by Cassina
Ferdinand-Alexander Porsche: table lamp, manufactured by Edition PAF
Pol Quadens: paper knife (1991)
Aldo Rossi: cafetière, manufactured by Alessi
Zofia Rostad: rug, *City* (1990), manufactured by Louis de Poortere
Zofia Rostad: rug, *Fidji* (1990), manufactured by Louis de Poortere
Lino Sabattini: cutlery set, manufactured by Rosenthal
Richard Sapper: table lamp, manufactured by Artemide
Richard Sapper: whistling kettle, manufactured by Alessi
Afra and Tobia Scarpa: chair, *Liberta* (1989), manufactured by Meritalia
Philippe Starck: toothbrush and holder (1992), manufactured by Fluocaril
Philippe Starck: lemon squeezer, manufactured by Alessi
Philippe Starck: kettle, manufactured by Alessi
Martin Szekely: various items of tableware, manufactured by Faienceries de Gien
Toulemonde Bochart: series of rugs by Andrée Putman (*Les Galets*, *Erie Vert* and *Camille et Sophie*);
Pascal Mourgue (*Mémoire de Terre Vert*); Hilton McConnico (*Mildred et Maurice* and *Arizona Sunset*);

France Grand (*Patmos Négatif*); J.J. Baune (*Okapi*) and A. and A. Chazotte (*Plume Taupe*)

GERMANY

Kunstmuseum, Düsseldorf.
Walter Zeischegg: pencil holder (1970), manufactured by Helit

Vitra Design Museum, Weil am Rhein. The collection is devoted primarily to the development of the chair over the last 140 years. It was opened in November 1989 and is intended to serve as an exhibition space as well as a permanent collection. Some major acquisitions of last year include:
M. Breuer: Isokon dining group (table and chairs)
Frank O. Gehry: several pieces, including the experimental edges table *Imperial*
Frank O. Gehry: lamp, *Snake*
Ginbande Design: most important prototypes
Eileen Gray: two table prototypes
Alessandro Mendini: chair, *Lassù*
Carlo Mollino: table, *Arabesque*
J. Morrison: complete installation of his exhibition "Some New Items for the House"
Serge Mouille: several lamp designs, including the famous *Signal*
Jean Prouvé: several rare pieces, among them the *Bibliothèque Tunisie* made in collaboration with Charlotte Perriand
Gerrit T. Rietveld: aluminium chair
Otto Wagner: *Post* saving bank stool

JAPAN

There is no permanent design collection in Japan at the present time, although there are a few private collections. Several museums of modern art do have good examples of contemporary international design, but these almost always have a practical purpose and are not part of their displays. Temporary design exhibitions have been increasing dramatically, however, and there is a strong possibility of a permanent design collection being founded.

THE NETHERLANDS

Museum Boymans-van Beuningen, Rotterdam.
Gerry Baptist: cupboard, *Metafour* (1991)
Friso Kramer: table, *Facet* (1964), manufactured by Cirkel/Oda
Floris Meydam: wine carafe, *Partymix* (1969)
Dietrich Rams in collaboration with Dietrich Lubs: alarm clock, *AB22*, manufactured by Braun AG
Theo Remy: cupboard (1991)
Roberto Sambonet: set of cooking pans (1964), manufactured by Sambonet
Bořek Šipek: coat stand (1989), manufactured by Vitra
Bořek Šipek: vases, 407, 212, *Isotta* (1990–1991), manufactured by Alterego and Driade

SWEDEN

Nationalmuseum, Stockholm.
Tom Ahlström and Hans Ehrich of A & E Design: floor lamp, *Stella Polaris* (1982–83), manufactured by Yamagiwa Corporation
Tomas Anagrius: ceramic dish (1991)
Rut Beskow: tapestry, *Hylla* (1989)
Anne-Beth Borselius: earthenware bowl (1990)
Gunnar Cyrén: cutlery, tableware and kitchen items designed for Dansk International Designs Ltd and Dansk Gourmet Designs (1967–1983)
Gutte Eriksen: stoneware jar (1990)
Jonas Fredlund: printed fabric, *No. 5* (1990)
Susanne Grundell: furniture upholstery, *Kapu* (1990)
Torbjørn Kvasbø: stoneware object (1990)
Ralf Lindberg: stackable chair, *Elle* (1989), manufactured by Gärsnäs AB
Bodil Manz: porcelain bowl (1990)
Signe Persson-Melin: parts of stoneware service (1990), manufactured by Nya Höganäs-Keramik
Thomas Sandell: wall cupboards, *Bröllopsskåp*, manufactured by Källemo AB
Oiva Toikka: object, *Trädt* (1990–91), manufactured by Notsjö Glassworks

Röhsska Konstslöjdmuseet, Göteborg.
Ron Arad: chair, *Rover* (1981)
Love Arbén: cabinet, *Ono* (1991), manufactured by Lammhults Möbel AB
Elsa Pärs Berglund: damask linen, *I vassen* (1991)
Torun Bülow-Hübe: cutlery (1986), manufactured by Dansk International Designs Ltd
Dale Chihuly: glass object, *Cobalt, violet venetian with yellow prunts* (1989)
A. Copier: wine glasses, *Neckar* (1980), manufactured by Schott-Zwiesel
Karen Disen: stainless steel container (1991)
Darryle Hinz and Anja Kjaer: glass plate (1991)
Anders Högberg: silver box with cover (1989)
John Kandell: cupboard (1960)
Johanna Lagercrantz: cabinet, *Parad* (1990), manufactured by Lammhults Möbel AB
Gillis Lundgren: chair, *Ögla* (1984), manufactured by IKEA
Annika Malmström: a collection of printed cotton fabrics (1960–1990)
Kerttu Nurminen: examples from the set of glasses, *Mondo* (1988), manufactured by Nuutajärvi
Ritva Puotila: *From sea to forest* and *Rya* (1991)

Markku Salo: examples from the set of glasses, *Olivii* (1989), manufactured by Nuutajärvi
Thomas Sandell: table, *Låda* (1990), manufactured by Element Design AB
Jin Sook So: wall-hanging, *Transparent Black* (1991)
Kerstin Åsling Sundberg: carpet, *Snow fall* (1991)
Leo Tafvelin: chair, *Emma T* (1989)
Mats Theselius: cupboard (1991)
Kati Tuominen: bowl, *Vekki* (1991)

The Nobel service 1991 as a whole: chinaware design **Karin Björquist**, glasses and cutlery design **Gunnar Cyrén**, tablecloth design **Ingrid Dessau**; manufactured by Hackman-Rörstrand; Orreforsglasbruk AB; Älghults AB and Klässbols Linneväveri AB

SWITZERLAND

Kornhaus, Berne.
Carla Baumann: lace needlepoint
Heidi Gassner: textile object, *Tagebuchblätter*
Elsi Giauque: textile object, *Les Féministes*
Susanne Klups: textile object, *Lucy in the Sky*
Anneliese Konrat: textile object, *Das klassische Paar*
Verena Lafargue: textile object, *Heidenweg*

Museum für Gestaltung, Zurich.
At present the Design Collection is not accessible to the public, although a permanent exhibition space is being planned.
Les ateliers du Nord: mixing desk (1984), manufactured by Sonosax
Rosmarie and Rico Baltensweiler: three lamps (1976–1988), manufactured by Baltensweiler AG
Mario Botta: two chairs (1991), manufactured by Alias Srl
Philip Anton Bruckner: salt and pepper containers, *Shake* (1991)
Andreas Christen: aluminium cupboard (1986), manufactured by Lehni
Création Baumann (Langenthal): different fabrics (1985–1991)
Fabric Frontline (Zurich): different fabrics (1985–1991)
Cornelia Hesse-Honegger: rucksack and bag (1992), manufactured for Globus
Fridolin Naef: two lamps (1983), manufactured by Regent
Ludwig Roner: folding table (1986), manufactured by Wogg AG
Benjamin Thut: lamp, *Lifto* (1989), manufactured by Belux AG

UK

The Design Museum, London.
The Design Museum continues to make a major contribution to the preservation of contemporary design. Recent acquisitions include:
Ron Arad: chair, *Soft Little Heavy* (1991), manufactured by Moroso SpA
Belling Cookers: series No. 325 (1990)
Braun: coffee mill (1965); heater, *H6* (1965); kettle, *HE1* (1961); quartz clock, *AB4* (c. 1980)
Canon: laptop computer, *A1 Note IN 300* (1990)
Kai Franck: range of tableware, *Teema*, manufactured by Arabia
GEC: floor polisher (c. 1960)

IBM: *Selectric Composer* (c. 1970)
IKEA: children's tables, *Panter*
Sillis Lundren: children's stools, manufactured by IKEA
Maws: knife and fork set (1990); *Dri Tot* one-way nappy liners (1990s)
Several items from the *Mothercare* range of products
Olivetti: *Logus 270* (c. 1970)
Olympus Optical Company: camera, *Olympus Ecru IS-1000* (1990)
Playtex: feeding bottle, *Nurser* (c. 1980)
Praktica: camera, *BMS* (1991)
Ulla Procope: range of tableware, *Ruska*, manufactured by Arabia
Ernest Race: dining chairs, *BA* (reproductions of 1945 originals), manufactured by Race Furniture
Ernest Race: chair, *Antelope* (1991, reproduction of 1951 original), manufactured by Race Furniture
Mark Robson: chair, *GRP* (1991)
Eero Saarinen: dining chair, *Tulip* (1990s), manufactured by Knoll International
Eero Saarinen: chair, *Tulip* (1990s), manufactured by Knoll International
George Sowden: fruit bowl (1990), manufactured by Bodum (Schweiz) AG
Philippe Starck: toothbrush and holder (1991), manufactured by Fluocaril
Tommy Tippee: spoon and fork (1990)
Several items from the *Tupperware* range of products
Mies van der Rohe: chair, *Barcelona* (1990, reproduction of 1929 original), manufactured by Knoll International
Louis Vuitton: wristwatches *LV-1* and *LV-2* (1990)
Yamaha: compact stereo, *Astarte-Tiffany System AST-C30* (1989)
Zeiss: camera and case, *Ikon Derval*

Victoria and Albert Museum, London.
No acquisitions were made by the furniture department during the last year. The ceramic and glass department acquired a large number of internationally designed tableware items dating from 1960 to the present day, too extensive to list here, and the textile department acquired the following:
Neil Bottle: two hand-printed and painted silk wall hangings (1990–1991)
Howard Hodgkin in collaboration with Dilys Stinson: tapestry, *Moonlight* (1983)
William Jefferies: tapestry, *March Diver* (1983)
Underfoot Rugs: rug, *San Marco 5* (1990)
Warner Fabrics: range of fabrics, *Fresh Flowers* (1990)

USA

Art Institute of Chicago.
Sam Herman: vase (1982)
Dick Huss: bowl (1986)
Michael Lacktman: coffee-pot (1965)
Steven McCarroll: vase (1985)
Clifton Monteith: armchair (1991)
Thomas Muir: liqueur cups (1984)
Valerie Surjan in collaboration with Michael Nourot: vase (1985)
Brent Young: bottle (1980)

Cooper-Hewitt Museum, New York.

Sergio Asti: light, *Profiterole* (1970), manufactured by Martinelli Luce

Constantin Boym: clock, *Laborious* (1989), manufactured by Elika

Constantin Boym: clock, *Mona Lisa* (1990), manufactured by Elika

Chunghi Choo: teapot (1988)

Jonathan de Pas, Donato d'Urbino and Paolo Lomazzi: settee, *Joe* (1970), manufactured by Poltronova

Andre DeBreuil: side chair, *Spine* (1986)

Guido Drocco and Franco Mello: coat stand, *Cactus*, manufactured by Gufram

Vittori Gregotti: light, *Amalussanta* (1972), manufactured by Bilumen

Thomas Hucker: pair of chairs (1991)

Dakota Jackson: side chair, *Vik-ter* (1991)

Arne Jacobsen: corkscrew and bottle opener (1960s), manufactured by A/S Stelton

Pascal Luthy: light, *Dinosaur* (1988)

Dan Mack: armchair, *Rugbeater* (1991)

Enzo Mari: set of four bowls, *Tongareva* (1969), manufactured by Danese Milano

Enzo Mari: set of three vases (1969), manufactured by Danese Milano

Enzo Mari: vase, *Trifoglio* (1969), manufactured by Danese Milano

Bruno Munari: light, *Falkland* (1964), manufactured by Danese Milano

Bruno Munari: bowl, *Maldive* (1960), manufactured by Danese Milano

Bruno Munari: vase, *Pago-Pago* (1964), manufactured by Danese Milano

Marco Pasanella: rocking chair (1991)

Signe Persson-Melin: tableware, *Primeur* (1978), manufactured by Rorstrand

Gaetano Pesce: chair, *UP 3* (1969), manufactured by Cassina and Busnelli

Gaetano Pesce: chair, *UP 1* (1969), manufactured by Cassina and Busnelli

Gaetano Pesce: chair, *UP 5 Donna* (1969), manufactured by Cassina and Busnelli

Claudio Salocchi: chair, *Palla* and footstool (1969), manufactured by Sormani

Timo Sarpaneva: decanter, *Jurmo* (1980), manufactured by Iittala Glassworks

Mario Scheichenbauer: rocking chair, *Yeti*, manufactured by Elam

Bořek Šípek: set of cutlery (1991), manufactured by Néotù

Smart Design: set of kitchen utensils, *Good Grips* (1990), manufactured by Oxo International

Studio Tetrarch: light, *Frine* (1969), manufactured by Artemide

Paolo Tilche: light, *6P2* (1960), manufactured by Sirrah

Massimo Vignelli: side chair, *Handkerchief* (1982–87), manufactured by The Knoll Group

Robert Wilhite: set of cutlery (1982)

Denver Art Museum. The museum is in the process of forming a comprehensive contemporary design collection. Major acquisitions include:

Mario Bellini in collaboration with Dieter Thiel: office chair, *Figura* (1979–1984), manufactured by Vitra International AG

Mario Bellini in collaboration with A. De Gregori, D.J. De Vries, A. Macchi Cassia, G. Pasini, S. Pasqui and De Diana: calculator, *Divisumma 18* (1972), manufactured by Ing. C. Olivetti & C. SpA

Mario Bellini in collaboration with D. J. De Vries, A. Macchi Cassia, G. Pasini and S. Pasqui: calculator, *Logus 59* (1972), manufactured by Ing. C. Olivetti & C. SpA

Mario Botta: armchair, *Seconda* (1982), manufactured by Alias

Mario Botta: table, *Tesi* (1986), manufactured by Alias

Achille Castiglioni: lamp, *Parentesi* (1970), manufactured by Flos Inc.

Achille Castiglioni and Pier Giacomo Castiglioni: floor lamp, *Toio* (1962), manufactured by Flos Inc.

Achille Castiglioni: lamp, *Gibigiana/52 Red Lamp* (1981), manufactured by Flos Inc.

Eric P. Chan: phone, *EC II* (1991), manufactured by ECCO Design Inc.

Stephan Copeland: lamp, *Tango* (1989), manufactured by Flos Inc.

Marcello Fantoni: vase (1960s), manufactured by Raymor

Suzanne Geismar: armchair, *Chiquita* (1976), manufactured by Vermillion

Edward Gottesman: dining table, two armchairs and four side chairs (1986)

Michael Graves: *White Vase* (1989), manufactured by Swid Powell

Michael Graves: table (1991), manufactured by Swid Powell

Wayne Higby: bowl, *Snow at Red Mesa* (1977)

Wayne Higby: covered jar (1969)

Takenobu Igarashi: *Platter with Dots* (1989), manufactured by YMD

Toshiyuki Kita: armchair, *Future* (1988), manufactured by Casas

Toshiyuki Kita: armchair, *Present* (1988), manufactured by Casas

Toshiyuki Kita: side chair, *Past* (1988), manufactured by Casas

Masayuki Kurokawa: tray set from the *Metal Waves* series (1984), manufactured by Time Studio Co. Ltd

Carl Magnusson and Emanuela Frattini Magnusson: umbrella stand, *Ivy* (1990)

Jorge Pensi: armchair, *Toledo* (1988), manufactured by Knoll International

Gio Ponti: four plates (1967)

Gino Sarfatti: lamp, *600G* (1966), manufactured by Flos Inc.

Gino Sarfatti: lamp, *600P* (1966), manufactured by Flos Inc.

Ettore Sottsass: candlestick, *Silvershade* (1986), manufactured by Swid Powell

Ettore Sottsass: portable typewriter, *Valentine I-47* (1969), manufactured by Ing. C. Olivetti & C., SpA

Philippe Starck: toothbrush with holder (1989), manufactured by Fluocaril

Philippe Starck: book stand, *MacGee* (1978), manufactured by Baleri

Robert A. M. Stern: dinner service, *Moderne* (1988), manufactured by Swid Powell

Robert A. M. Stern: lounge chair, *Savoy* (1991), manufactured by Hickory Business Furniture

Ikko Tanaka: pen stands (1991)

Jacques Toussaint: Toussaint table (1987)

Robert Turner: vases (1970)

Robert Venturi: side chair, *Chippendale* (1979–1984), manufactured by Knoll International

Robert Venturi: side chair, *Queen Anne* (1979–1984), manufactured by Knoll International

Robert Venturi: luncheon plate, *Grandmother* (1984), manufactured by Swid Powell

Robert Venturi: four mugs, *Grandmother* (1984), manufactured by Swid Powell

Los Angeles County Museum of Art.

Tessa Clegg: vessel (1986)

Nanna and Jorgen Ditzel: chair (early 1960s)

Ruth Duckworth: bowl (1970s)

Steven Holt and Michael Pinkus: musical chair (1990)

Jorge Pensi: table and two chairs (1986–88), manufactured by the Knoll Group

Richard Shaw: whiteware, *With an Ocean View* (1979)

Metropolitan Museum of Art, New York.

Ron Arad: armchair, *Big Easy* (1989), manufactured by One-Off

James Cole: armchair, *Susquehanna* (1991)

Kyonghee Hong: centrepiece (1984)

Michael Lacktman: punch bowl and ladle (1963)

Main and Main: chair, *Ribbon* (1981)

Terence Main: side chair, *Fourth Frond* (1991)

Howard Meister: side chair, *Nothing Continues to Happen* (1980)

Scott Rothstein: untitled silk textiles (1988, 1989)

Ettore Sottsass: fruit bowl, *Murmansk* (1982), manufactured by Memphis

Bob Stocksdale: bowl

Brother Thomas: two vases (1986, 1988)

William T. Wiley: scatter pins, *Who is Not a Hostage?*

Museum of Modern Art, New York.

Stephen Armellino: bullet-resistant mask (1983), manufactured by U.S. Armor Corporation

Les Broersma: bicycle helmet (1985), manufactured by Bell Sports, Inc.

William Hudson: facial sponge and body sponge (1988–89), manufactured by Bilange, Inc.

Gaetano Pesce: lounge chair, *Up 5* with ottoman, *Up 6* (1969), manufactured by C&B

Ben Winter: football, *Zwirl* (1985), manufactured by Zwirl Sales Inc.

Philadelphia Museum of Art.

Junichi Arai: length of fabric (1990), manufactured by Nuno Corporation

Michael Lax: table lamp, *Lytegem* (1965), manufactured by Lightolier Inc.

Jens Risom: armchair (1961), manufactured by Risom Manufacturing

Scott Rothstein: stitched construction in silk

Reiko Sudo: stainless steel embossed fabric (1991), manufactured by Nuno Corporation